Logic Programming

Expanding the Horizons

Logic Programming

Expanding the Horizons

Edited by

Tony Dodd
Expert Systems Ltd

Richard Owens
Imperial College

Steve Torrance
Shell UK

Oxford, England

First published in Great Britain in 1991 by
Intellect Books
Suite 2, 108/110 London Road, Oxford OX3 9AW

First published in the US in 1991 by
Ablex Publishing Corporation
355 Chestnut Street
Norwood, New Jersey 07648

Consulting editor: Masoud Yazdani
Copy editor: Jonathan Lewis
Cover design: Steven Fleming

British Library Cataloguing in Publication Data
Logic programming: expanding the horizons.
   1. Computer systems. Programming
   I. Dodd, Tony *1952-* II. Owens, Richard II. Torrance,
Steve
005.1

   ISBN 1-871516-15-03

Library of Congress Cataloging-in-Publication Data available

Printed and bound in Great Britain by Billings & Sons Ltd,
Worcester

Contents

The Authors

Edward Babb
Strategic System Technology, ICL, Lovelace Road, Bracknell, Berks RG12
4SN
babb@sst.icl.stc.co.uk

Tony Dodd
Expert Systems Ltd, Unit 12, 7 West Way, Oxford OX2 0JB
tdo@cs.exeter.ac.uk

Tim Flanagan
Machine Intelligence Ltd, Nine Greens Road, Cambridge CB4 3EF

Dov Gabbay
Department of Computing, Imperial College, London SW7 2BZ
dg@doc.ic.ac.uk

Qinzheng Kong
Centre for IT Research, University of Queensland

Fukimi Kozato
Department of Computing, Imperial College, London SW7 2BZ
fk@doc.ic.ac.uk

Peter McBrien
Department of Computing, Imperial College, London SW7 2BZ
pjm@doc.ic.ac.uk

Richard Owens
Department of Computing, Imperial College, London SW7 2BZ
rpo@doc.ic.ac.uk

Graem Ringwood
Department of Computer Science, Queen Mary and Westfield College, London
gar@cs.qmw.ac.uk

Hamish Taylor
Department of Computer Science, Heriot-Watt University, Edinburgh EH1
2HJ
hamish@cs.hw.ac.uk

Steve Torrance
AI Group, Middlesex Polytechnic, Enfield EN3 4SF
steve5@cluster.middlesex.ac.uk

Howard Williams
Department of Computer Science, Heriot-Watt University, Edinburgh EH1
2HJ
howard@cs.hw.ac.uk

Preface

This volume contains eight of the papers given at the Expanding the Horizons workshop held at Imperial College on 13th-14th February 1989, and retrospectively numbered as the first UK Logic Programming Conference, a subsequent conference having been held in Bristol in 1990 and a third planned for Edinburgh in 1991. The second and third editors organised the workshop together with Chris Moss and John Smith, while the first organised the publication of this volume. The summary programme distributed to delegates appears on the following page.

The editors wish to record their thanks to Intellect Ltd for helping overcome the various problems that arose while the volume was in preparation, and to the authors for their patience and co-operation.

Readers may be interested to know of the existence of the U.K. branch of the Association for Logic Programming, which is ultimately responsible for the UK Logic Programming Conference and offers a number of other services to members. Further details may be obtained from

A.L.P. U.K.
P.O. Box 469
Oxford OX2 0RR

or email alpuk@uk.ac.ic.doc.

Tony Dodd
Richard Owens
Steve Torrance

ALVEY / IED LOGIC PROGRAMMING CLUB
ASSOCIATION FOR LOGIC PROGRAMMING - UK BRANCH
SERC LOGIC FOR IT INITIATIVE

LOGIC PROGRAMMING — EXPANDING THE HORIZONS

TWO DAY WORKSHOP
Monday 13th-Tuesday 14th February 1989
South Side Suite, Imperial College, London SW7

INVITED SPEAKERS	Alan Bundy, University of Edinburgh
	Keith Clark, Imperial College
	Dov Gabbay, Imperial College
	Hervé Gallaire, ECRC, Munich
	Robert Kowalski, Imperial College
	John Lloyd, University of Bristol
	David Morgan, IED
	David Warren, University of Bristol
SESSION SPEAKERS	Ed Babb, ICL
	Mike Brayshaw, Open University
	John Derrick, Leeds University
	Jaap van der Does, University of Edinburgh
	Tim Duncan, AIAI
	Tim Flannagan, Machine Intelligence Limited
	Peter Gray, University of Aberdeen
	Peter McBrien, Imperial College
	Frank McCabe, Imperial College
	Bernard Marsh, Yard Limited
	Graem Ringwood, Imperial College
	Hamish Taylor, Heriot-Watt University
	Imad Torsun, Bradford University
	John Tucker, Leeds University
	Paul Wilk, AIAI
	H. Williams, Heriot-Watt University
SERC LOGIC FOR IT	Harold Simmons, SERC Logic for IT
ALVEY/SERC	Adrian Wheldon, Rutherford Appleton Laboratory
ORGANISERS	Chris Moss, Imperial College
	Richard Owens, Imperial College
	John Smith - Rutherford Appleton Laboratory
	Steve Torrance, Middlesex Polytechnic

Introduction: Alvey and Logic Programming

Tony Dodd   Steve Torrance

On October 31st 1984 Bill Sharpe, Assistant Director IKBS in the Alvey Directorate, wrote to a number of academic and industrial logic programmers, under the heading "A UK Plan for Logic Programming". He began:

> The IKBS directorate would like to put together a number of substantial projects to drive forward R&D in logic programming. It is hoped that a number of projects can be fostered that will establish a critical mass of activity in all areas from fundamental research through to industrial applications. Without an increased level of coordinated activity it appears likely that the significant UK strengths in this area will be under-utilised, or exploited elsewhere.

The plan was to be produced by a number of working groups and then discussed at a workshop at Cosener's House in Abingdon on 11th and 12th January 1985. The titles of the working groups, suggested by Bob Kowalski, were:

1. Applications (Peter Hammond)

2. Rational Reconstruction (renamed Logical Analysis) (Alan Bundy)

3. Parallel Inference Machines (George Pollard)

4. Logic Language (Bob Kowalski)

5. Logic Databases (Howard Williams)

6. Environments (Frank McCabe)

The names are those of the group leaders; in all, thirty three people were involved in the study and invited to Cosener's House. It appears that five of these groups actually met.

The proposed research plan had been announced at the 1984 Alvey conference on Fifth Generation Computer Architectures, the general title being "Declarative Systems Architectures", embracing Parallel Architectures and Large Knowledge Bases as well as Logic Programming. Control of the program was in the hands of the IKBS directorate. The budget for the initiative was to be £3M plus a share of the £5M in the architecture budget for large knowledge bases.

The meeting at Cosener's House was duly held. Bill Sharpe's report states that 'an edited collection of the working papers will be made available soon' but we can find no trace of such a document. However, the major work of the meeting was the formulation of projects under the various headings, and by this criterion it was successful, no fewer than 13 projects being volunteered on the spot, the total cost adding conveniently to £4.44M, to which 10% was to be added for administration. Details of these projects are not given here, because we shall list all the projects later on; suffice it to say that the projects as eventually carried out were surprisingly close to the list written on the overhead projector slides by Bill Sharpe in Abingdon.

In March 1985 Bill Sharpe left the directorate to return to Hewlett Packard Labs and his position as coordinator of the initiative was taken over by Richard Ennals of Imperial College. On 20th March he wrote to those involved urging them to write their proposals down, and suggesting that delay beyond May would lead to reduction of resources available. Those of us who have since participated in the closing day rush to Kingsgate House encumbered with ten copies of every piece of paper within reach might reflect on the more informal style of 1985 with nostalgia; noticeable also in retrospect is the openness with which the plan was drawn up, the contents being volunteered by would-be researchers rather than fired at the industry by a committee in DTI for a few days consultation. Richard's informal pressure must have been effective for in May 1985 there was a presentation of potential projects to the IKBS Advisory Group.

Richard's report to that group makes interesting reading. He concludes that 'in one sense the Logic Programming Initiative has already succeeded, in that there is an unprecedented degree of collaboration within the active community of researchers, both in industry and academia'. It is interesting that this point should be observed so early on; it is difficult now to remember the years before the Logic Programming Initiative, and the damaging divisions in UK logic programming of those days. To those of us participating in the early meetings the sense of change and the feeling of working towards a common program was very striking; that it has survived the ending of Alvey, the years of indecision and the limited IEATP follow-up program is, perhaps, a sign of the growing strength and maturity of logic programming.

In some of his judgements, alas, Richard was unduly optimistic. He looked forward to the agreement on standards for BSI Prolog, in which many of the collaborators were then involved: five years later the collaborators have discovered that they have better uses for their time and the state of the standard is such that it could be best completed by selecting a new name for the language it defines and starting again on standardising Prolog. There was to be a state-of-the-art UK Prolog environment; although much good work was done in this area under Alvey, the essential aims of the original proposal, integration and portability, have not been achieved. Richard's document contains yet another revised list of proposals and a budget.

Then silence. For some reason, the enthusiasm and readiness to get down to work expressed in Richard's May report did not extend to the higher reaches of Alvey, and to all intents and purposes, the project appeared to die until December 1985. An internal progress report reveals what was going on in grisly detail. On July 10th the IKBS advisory group considered 13 projects, threw two of them out and referred back another. On July 21st it presented the surviving 10 projects to the Alvey Board, who liked them, but decided not to pay for them as there was not enough industrial involvement. After this display of energy nothing at all happened, though ICL, and especially Ed Babb, were pressing for a revised plan with more industrial involvement. Suitable amendments were made, and on November 29th ICL, System Designers, Logica and Expert Systems International presented their involvement in the program to the Alvey directorate, who were sufficiently impressed to approve the whole portfolio of grants at one fell swoop three days later.

In December 1985 Richard Ennals resigned as coordinator. His energy in forming and advocating the program had been the major factor behind its eventual approval; ironically, just as approval was agreed he reached the conclusion that the direction in which support for research in the UK was developing was wrong, in particular in its increasing involvement of military interests. If SDI seems less of a danger to researchers (and indeed the rest of the human race) than it seemed in those days, this should be attributed not to failure of foresight on the part of those who campaigned to keep UK research free of this pestilence, but rather to the success of that and other campaigns in making SDI unacceptable to public opinion.

Now we pause to enumerate the Logic Programming Initiative projects. As far as possible we quote from documents by the participants in those projects. If in our comments we have misrepresented any of the projects we apologise; presenting a bare list without detail seems the greater evil.

In the list that follows, the index number is the Alvey project reference. Some of the projects listed here are related projects that were under way when the logic programming initiative grants were approved, but were included within the logic programming initiative and its associated club. It should be explained that as well as ordinary industrial-academic collaborations Alvey set up some projects where the collaborators in the work were all academic, but an industrial "uncle" agreed to participate in project reviews and discussions.

024 Tools for development of logic programs. (Imperial College; Uncle:ICL) £44,000.
   Low-level tools for managing, browsing and editing predicates were produced for IBM PC and SUN Prologs. An interpreter that could give qualified answers to queries was also developed.

043 Implementation and application of Parlog. (Imperial College; Uncle: ICL) £94,130.
   Applications of Parlog to systems programming, rapid specification and prototyping of concurrent systems and distributed knowledge bases were investigated.

045 Logic for representing legislation. (Imperial College; Uncle: ICL) £155,770.
   The project, led by Bob Kowalski, involved fundamental research into representation in logic of time, of rules and exceptions, of meta-level descriptions of rules, of counterfactuals and conditionals. A significant portion of legislation relating to supplementary benefit was represented in Prolog.

   This was perhaps the project that attracted most attention outside logic programming circles, the question of the logical nature of legislation being discussed in *The Guardian* (April 16th 1987) on one occasion.

058 Business applications of expert systems. (Telecomputing; Loughborough University; Brunel University; Dowty Rotol) £1,307,000.
   This IKBS demonstrator was not classified as a logic programming project, but the project participants took an active part in the Logic Programming Club, to its substantial benefit.

   This was the only project in which integration with existing software played a major part. Nor was the software chosen for integration a small and tractable PC package; instead a COBOL/4GL transaction processing system was selected, and integrated with a knowledge based system containing the knowledge of business experts.

079 Evaluating Prolog environments. (Edinburgh; Uncle: ESI) £81,285.
The aim was to evaluate current Prolog environments and produce

1. an analysis of bug types
2. identification of debugging strategies
3. identification of relevant tools
4. a critique of those tools
5. better designs.

In contrast to the projects that set out to design environments from scratch, we have here design by improvement of existing facilities. In fact the work on this project contributed significantly to design-from-scratch projects, and some results from the latter were available in time for assessment in this project.

080 Proving properties of Prolog programs. (Edinburgh; Uncle: Logica) £107,112.
A theorem prover was constructed with the ability to prove that Prolog programs had particular desired properties, or even to construct a program with such properties. In practical terms this makes available a software engineering tool for developing, verifying and transforming programs, and to make the system more useful in practical contexts a module system was added.

081 An advanced graphical tracing/debugging environment for Prolog. (Open University; ESI) £176,082.
The Transparent Prolog Machine is a debugger developed by Marc Eisenstadt and Mike Brayshaw that shows the state of Prolog execution using AORTA diagrams; the authors have described these in detail in their paper in the Journal of Logic Programming. The debugger was developed on Apollo workstations but is now available on SUN 3 and 4 systems.

082 A UNIX implementation of Parlog. (Imperial College; Uncle: SD) £104,000.
A fast portable C implementation of Parlog operating on both single- and multi-processor machines was produced. It incorporated a parallel garbage collector.

083 A deductive environment for logic programming. (Imperial College; Uncle: SSL) £90,550.
An environment was developed with special emphasis on the development of a program through time, with the aim both of effecting changes correctly and of analysing the effects of an arbitrary change.

084 A pure logical language — foundations and theoretical aspects. (ICL; Imperial College; Edinburgh) £658,000.

PLL differs from Prolog in handling negation as in classical predicate logic rather than through negation as failure. A high speed version of the language has been implemented (loop termination is an issue of particular concern) and the use of the language to represent temporal, hypothetical and non-monotonic reasoning has been investigated.

085 Logic databases and their relation to novel hardware and languages. (Heriott-Watt; Uncle: ICL) £119,050.

The aim of the project was to produce a database system that could represent rules as well as facts, together with a query language ('Squirrel') and a mechanism for updating the database. Some of the ideas will be carried forward to the ESPRIT European Declarative Systems project.

090 Parlog on DACTL. (Imperial College; Heriott-Watt; ICL) £260,000.

The Alvey Flagship project set out to produce a highly parallel computer architecture, Alice; this project aimed to implement Parlog by compiling it to Alice DACTL, and to develop appropriate programming tools and environments.

092 Logic database demonstrator. (ICL; Turing Institute; Bradford University) £875,000.

A major component of the project was the PAYE demonstrator. This project was closely associated with the development of PLL (see 084), and therefore, as one might expect, applies full predicate logic.

093 A parallel Prolog machine. (Essex; Uncle: ICL) £125,000.

This project was part of the Systems Architecture Club, but its participants attended the activities of the Logic Programming Club. The aim was to develop a packet-rewrite scheme for parallel execution of logic programs and use it to implement a prototype parallel architecture. The language developed, a Prolog derivative called Brave, incorporates both AND and OR parallelism.

094 Knowledge-based engineering training. (Logica; Engineering Industry Training Board; Imperial College; Kingston CFE; Exeter University) £531,013.

A knowledge base of operating, maintaining and programming techniques for a Numerically Controlled Milling Machine was developed, together with a man-machine interface. The results are applicable to many other areas of engineering training. A video interface was considered.

099 A logic programming environment. (Imperial College; LPA; SD; Sussex; Edinburgh) £849,000.
One of the most ambitious projects in the logic programming initiative, this suffered from very severe delays in getting started. Initially the aim was to develop an environment around the meta-database ideas that had been developed in Edinburgh. As time passed integration of Prolog with objects became an important component of the research.

103 A new logic language. (Logica; Cambridge; Lancaster; Leeds; Open University) £380,000.
The major output of the project has been the Diamond language, but a whole range of other languages have appeared as part of the same research. The claims made for Diamond are similar to those made for PLL, and it has always been a bit of a puzzle to outsiders why two projects were needed in this area.

110 Logic databases. (Imperial College; Uncle: ICL) £152,000.
Closely related to the project for representing legislation in logic, this project has developed a general framework for reasoning about time and events called the event calculus.

It is not really for us, as active participants in some of these projects, to sing their praises; in our view the range and topicality of the research, the large number of collaborating organisations and the balance between theory and applications are evident even in the very abridged descriptions given above.

A rough classification of the above projects with an indication of how funding was shared out between each group within the initiative is given below. This is based by a report in *Alvey News* by Steve Torrance (February 1988).

- Logic databases 085. Logic databases and their relation to novel hardware and languages.
  092. Logic database demonstrator.
  110. Logic databases.
  Total: £1,146,050 (24%)

- Logic programming language design and theory 084. A pure logical language — foundations and theoretical aspects.
  103. A new logic language.
  080. Proving properties of Prolog programs.
  Total: £1,145,112 (24%)

- Parallel logic programming 024. Tools for development of logic programs

> 043. Implementation and application of Parlog.
> 082. A UNIX implementation of Parlog.
> 090. Parlog on DACTL.
> 093. A parallel Prolog machine.
> Total: £627,130 (13%)

- Logic programming tools and environments 083. A deductive environment for logic programming.
  079. Evaluating Prolog environments.
  081. An advanced graphical tracing/debugging environment for Prolog.
  099. A logic programming environment.
  Total: £1,196,917 (25%)

- Logic programming applications 094. Knowledge based engineering training.
  045. Logic for representing legislation.
  058. Business applications of expert systems.
  Total: £686,783 (excluding 058) (14%)

- Grand total: £4,801,992

Those who were involved may well be sceptical both about our classification and about the significance of the cash total for each project; we can find no better way of measuring the size of the project and its division between research areas.

The reader will recall that in our chronological account we have reached the end of 1985. Much of the rest of the narrative will describe the activities of the Logic Programming Club, a part of the Alvey infrastructure designed to make the program more than the sum of its projects.

The Alvey program involved the setting up of quite a number of 'theme clubs' to 'provide focal points for the interchange of ideas and information within the enabling technologies'. Each Alvey project had to be assigned to at least one club. A summary circulated in the IKBS directorate in May 1986 shows that KBS had a club and 3 SIGs, MMI was (as usual) not functioning because Speech could not be persuaded to talk to Natural Language, Vision was very successful (there being no Semaphore and Aldis Lamps group to spoil things) and System Architecture was fairly cohesive. The IKBS directorate set up a Logic Programming Club by the simple expedient of appointing a steering group: the initial members were Robert Worden, who was appointed to the chair, Aaron Sloman, Alan Bundy, Keith Clark, Alan Montgomery and Cliff Pavelin (secretary). This group met in May 1986, just before the Alvey directorate agreed what seem today very generous rules for funding participation in club activities. The terms of reference may be worth recalling:

1. To promote the development of common tools, techniques and infrastructure and to identify further items of research required to complement the activities of the Club projects;

2. To promote the industrial exploitation of the results of Logic Programming research;

3. To exchange research experience and results to the mutual benefit of its members;

4. To reduce, as far as possible, the duplication of research effort among the consortia, and stimulate new research ideas and directions;

5. To present and discuss, within the club, the aims and achievements of research within the projects;

6. To exchange information concerning research and development external to Alvey (having due regard for IPR);

7. To coordinate visits to companies and institutions and organise reports and presentations for the benefit of Club members;

8. To promote liaison with other Alvey clubs and with ESPRIT and other relevant European bodies;

9. To promote the smooth running of LP activities in the Alvey program;

10. To act as a focus for gathering and expressing the views of the UK LP community.

Though plainly it has been ground through the D.T.I. mill, the sense of a common U.K. effort on behalf of logic programming can still be detected in the breadth of this document. For those of us who had two years previously still felt that we were living on tiny isolated islands in the ocean of I.T., it still seemed too good to be true.

A business meeting of the club was held on 16th July at Imperial College during the 1986 International Logic Programming Conference; it took the form of a brains trust with the conscripted committee acting as the panel. Alas, the first item in the notes of the meeting refers to 'input to the "After Alvey" activities, assuming that input was still worthwhile'. No sooner had the initiative gained momentum than we were looking nervously to the future, assuming that there would be general agreement that Alvey was only the first step in collaborative I.T. research funding.

Otherwise the enthusiasm for logic programming perhaps to be expected at the height of an international conference was in evidence: 'The Club should promote use of Logic Programming in the community at large'; 'Current projects making serious use of Prolog...should present their experiences to the Club in order to inform potential designers of new logic languages'; 'a SIG in new logic languages/logic machines...might be possible'. More significant, as it turned out, was the establishment of the international Association for Logic Programming, announced the next day.

It was agreed that the first technical workshop of the Alvey Logic Programming Club should be held at Imperial College on 26th September 1986. There were in all three such workshops, at which the projects presented the work that they were doing to the other projects. The three technical meetings were:

26th September 1986   Imperial College
5th June 1987   Manchester University
27th May 1988   D.T.I. London

The format of these meetings followed a general pattern: the bulk of the morning and afternoon sessions was occupied by technical presentations, and extra sessions were fitted in for discussion of other issues. For example, in September 1986 the last session was entitled 'After Alvey'.

The meetings combined the virtues and the vices of a conference with those of an informal workshop. It was extremely useful to find out what other researchers were doing, and informal contacts over lunch were valuable too; but there was never time or opportunity for discussion. At most a couple of questions to each speaker could be fitted in; while the general consideration of a U.K. program for logic programming, so clearly in evidence at Cosenor's House, began to move into the background. This is not to say that the interests of logic programming on a day-to-day basis were not ably defended by the steering group; merely that positive consideration of steps to be taken next, with the emphasis on what logic programming should be doing rather than on the technicalities of funding, ceased to be a function of the technical meetings.

During 1986, following Richard Ennals' resignation, the Club was managed by Cliff Pavelin, its steering group secretary. In January 1987 Steve Torrance became coordinator of the club and Brian Bainbridge its secretary— later Brian was replaced by John Smith. For the June 1987 technical meeting a list of points for discussion was circulated:

Is Logic Programming's future in the U.K. as a thriving and

well-funded research area assured?

How might the LP Club enhance its links with other parts of the IKBS directorate, and with Alvey in general (Hardware architectures, software engineering, etc.)

Are there specific issues that are worth discussing at a fuller session at the Alvey Conference involving other such groups?

Should there be a corporate response from the LP Club to IT-86? If so, what form should it take?

Can future LP research be geared more to commercial and product-oriented needs? How far is this desirable?

Should the LP community develop a policy for defending the need for long-term theoretical research to complement the need for commercial exploitation?

How can needs for standardization, benchmarking, cataloguing or user experiences, etc., within the LP community be better met?

Should there be more information exchange within the LP community nationally (and internationally)? How might this be effected?

Should there be more international contact?

Should there be more education and training initiatives? Directed to what kinds of groups?

Would it be worthwhile to have a survey of Prolog users in the UK?

Should there be a Prolog Users' club?

There is no written record of the answers to these questions; but perhaps it is the questions that are significant, showing the increasingly defensive attitude adopted in the closing stages of the Alvey Programme, a period when uncertainties over follow-on government funding began to grow.

It was decided that a meeting on the future of logic programming in the U.K. should be held at Imperial College on 21st September 1987. This was not to be a technical meeting but rather a planning exercise. Position papers were invited, with an optimistic and unenforced restriction to one page. In the event, between 20 and 25 members of the community showed up, and there was a lively discussion. The position papers of the various participants contained the makings of a first-rate manifesto for logic programming, and although they are too long to be reproduced in this volume it is worth recalling some of the arguments.

Alan Bundy presented a summary of strengths and weaknesses of logic programming: its strengths

1. Inherent reliability

2. Suitability for parallel processing

3. Suitability for formal methods

4. A basis for understanding other techniques

and weaknesses

1. Impure features of Prolog

2. Lack of a good environment

Dov Gabbay, Ed Babb, Barry Richards and Imad Torsun concluded that

> There have been two fundamental criticisms of logic pro-
> gramming — first that the theoretical foundations claimed for
> it are not as secure as they might be, and second that it is not
> sufficiently practical for *real* applications. If we are not sensi-
> tive to these criticisms there is a danger of logic programming
> being ignored by the rest of the computing community, and the
> much-needed logical features being added in an *ad hoc* manner
> to existing and future imperative languages.

David Warren argued for

> a national research centre similar to SICS. It should aim to
> bring together a critical mass of logic programming researchers,
> as well as researchers from other backgrounds with a common
> interest in advanced computing. It should be separate from, but
> have links with, one or more universities. Industrial involvement
> of the kind seen in SICS is essential, both to achieve technology
> transfer and to stimulate research directions.

Bob Kowalski spelled out the most significant argument: that the U.K. had
led the world in logic programming before the Alvey programme, but that
during that programme, which came to logic programming long choosing,
and beginning late, other research centres with better funding had been
established and other industrial suppliers had been established overseas; so
that now special provisions were needed to bolster UK logic programming.

Two significant decisions were taken: firstly that a coordinated presentation
of the U.K. logic programming community should be made to ESPRIT,

and secondly that a U.K. branch of the Association for Logic Programming (A.L.P.) should be established.

The final technical meeting of the logic programming club was held in May 1988; as usual the meeting finished with a discussion of future funding and the future of the club. By this time the Information Engineering Directorate (IED) had replaced Alvey, and it was inviting inputs from different research communities to its plans for future funding. A letter was sent by the Club Coordinator and Chairman, following discussions at the meeting. This urged IED to pursue support for better Prolog with a better environment, logic programming that went beyond Horn clauses, parallel implementation and convergence of declarative approaches. Members of the logic programming community were subsequently dismayed at how little of what they had recommended was actually taken up by the IED.

In August 1988 the UK branch of the A.L.P. was established, and its first conference, the 1989 Expanding the Horizons conference, whose proceedings are contained in this volume, was also the last activity of the Alvey logic programming club. Not only were there scarcely any logic programming projects left, but it was decided that clubs would no longer be supported, money being directed instead to private bodies that could tender to DTI for the opportunity to supply services to projects in exchange for a grant.

It has seemed worth adding to this largely technical volume some of the bureaucratic and political details of the Alvey project because it seems to us that the development of the U.K. logic programming community is still an important topic. If today it seems to us natural that researchers and Prolog vendors will sit down amicably together and discuss their common interests, we should not forget that it was not always so, and that in large measure the Alvey initiative brought about the excellent spirit of cooperation that exists today. Nor should we forget that the logic programming initiative was not an invention of some D.T.I. technical committee but was put together by the logic programming community after broad and very valuable discussion. Subsequent developments are beyond the scope of this note.

An Incremental Pure Logic Language with Constraints and Classical Negation

Edward Babb[*]

Abstract

The major concern of the Pure Logic Language - PLL - was to improve the match between an application builder's problem and the language used to describe his problem. To this end, PLL is based on classical logic including classical negation. It uses rewrites in the sense that a logic expression Q is always rewritten to a simpler expression Q'. This is done, such that Q and Q' are logically equivalent under a set of rewrites Π - in other words $(\Pi \vdash Q \Leftrightarrow Q')$. It follows that a further query that contained Q can save unnecessary recomputation by containing Q' instead - giving the language an incremental capability. In addition, the language contains a clean metalevel, where the manipulation of expressions is clearly separated from the execution of these expressions. Constraint Technology algorithms based on earlier work at ICL and ECRC [1] are included to give automatic high performance.

1 Introduction

ICL together with Edinburgh University and Imperial College were funded by Alvey [2] to make a fundamental reassessment of logic languages in computer science. The result of this study has been many important results

---

[*]Research carried out at Future Systems Technology, ICL, Lovelace Road, Bracknell, Berks with the support of ICL and Alvey under grants IKBS 084 & 092

[1]European Computer-Industry Research Centre GmbH, jointly owned by ICL, BULL and SIEMENS

[2]Professor B. Richards and Professor D. Gabbay under contract number IKBS 084 - Pure Logic Language: Foundations

in the areas of program termination and temporal logic. However, in particular it has led to the specification and implementation of a Pure Logic programming Language PLL [9] based on Predicate Calculus.

We now present a logical rewrite language, PLL, which rewrites queries written in predicate calculus into simpler queries. The rewrite rules are classical logic valid. Historically this new language derives from early work on improving negation in Logic programming languages and providing more expressive unification [4]. This led to an initial prototype language in LISP [4] [16] leading to the current C implementation described in this paper.

1.1 The essence of PLL

PLL offers incremental execution based on classical predicate calculus and constraint technology.

> *Incremental execution* means we can iteratively approach the answer to a problem by re-entering the answer to one query as part of a new query.
>
> *Constraint Technology* is concerned with reducing the search space by general reasoning before attempting detailed execution of the logic.

1.1.1 Incremental Execution and Classical Negation

The following examples try to illustrate PLL operation in normal mathematical notation plus Predicate Calculus[3].

> Suppose we define male as:
> $$male(x) =_{df} person(x) \land \neg female(x)$$
> This can be interpreted to mean rewrite any occurrence *male* in a query to RHS making appropriate substitutions for parameters. Thus the query:
> $$query: \ male(w)?$$
> gives an answer which is the exact RHS but with x replaced by w:
> $$Answer: \ person(w) \land \neg female(w)$$

---

[3] For those readers not familiar with predicate calculus $\in$ means *element of*, $\neg$ means *not* or $\sim$, $\land$ means *and* or &, and $\lor$ means *or*

Notice how this behaviour is quite different from PROLOG [23] where *person* would be considered unprovable and so the answer *fail* or *unprovable* would be given. However, PLL allows us to continue after defining *person*:

$$person(x) =_{df} x \in \{\text{"Jo"}, \text{"Ja"}, \text{"Ro"}\}$$

We can now issue the answer to the previous query again with this rewrite in place:

query: $person(w) \land \neg female(w)$?

and obtain:

Answer:
$w = \text{"Jo"} \land \neg female(\text{"Jo"}) \lor$
$w = \text{"Ja"} \land \neg female(\text{"Ja"}) \lor$
$w = \text{"Ro"} \land \neg female(\text{"Ro"})$

Now also define *female*:

$$female(x) =_{df} x \in \{\text{"Ja"}, \text{"Ro"}\}$$

The computation so far is retained since we can now issue the previous answer as a further new query:

query:
$w = \text{"Jo"} \land \neg female(\text{"Jo"}) \lor$
$w = \text{"Ja"} \land \neg female(\text{"Ja"}) \lor$
$w = \text{"Ro"} \land \neg female(\text{"Ro"})$?

and we obtain the final answer:

Answer: $w = \text{"Jo"}$

The classical nature of PLL negation can be further illustrated.

PLL will even give the same answer if we had defined something called *notmale* as the negative of our earlier definition:

$$notmale(x) =_{df} \neg person(x) \lor female(x)$$

and then we ask the negative of the earlier query:

query: $\neg notmale(w)$?

the same answer is obtained as before:

Answer: $w = \text{"Jo"}$

Because our answers are logically equivalent to the corresponding query Q, we can use the answer Q' instead of Q in a sub expression of a new query Q''. This can save repeating a computation but equally important Q' also gives an *explanation* of what information might be missing in a program. Therefore, undefined predicates can also be considered as requests for information about these predicates - a kind of read statement.

1.1.2 Constraint Technology

Constraint technology aims to use traditional optimisation methods to obtain massive reductions in the search space of certain Logic programs.

Finite Domains In high performance database systems, bitmaps [3] [7] are used to represent the hits in a file and communicate intermediate results so that the massive process of joining files can be delayed as much as possible to involve only essential records. In the same way bitmaps can be used to assist in the computation on Finite Domains in a logic language.

Suppose we have two predicates:
$$f(x) =_{df} x \in \{1, 3, 6, 9, 15\}$$
$$g(x) =_{df} x \in \{2, 8, 9, 13\}$$
and we have the query $f(x) \wedge g(x)$?. To answer this query we could just generate each value of f in turn and then test g for each of these values. If both f and g are stored as list structures then this takes a time of the order of the product of their lengths to compute.

However, suppose we had stored the set $\{1, 3, 6, 9, 15\}$ as the bitmap:
`[1,0,1,0,0,1,0,0,1,0,0,0,0,0,1]`
and the set $\{2, 8, 9, 13\}$ as the bitmap:
`[0,1,0,0,0,0,0,1,1,0,0,0,1,0,0]`
The answer to the above query in this new representation would be the intersection of these two bitmaps:
`[0,0,0,0,0,0,0,0,1,0,0,0,0,0,0]`
This gives the answer $\{9\}$ when transformed back into set representation. Such a process, if the bits are stored in a computer word takes one machine instruction.

This technique gives immense performance improvements when large numbers of joins are involved. The actual techniques used in PLL is an adaptation of the ECRC techniques [12] and ICL techniques for fast file joining.

Intervals In addition, if we know the upper and lower bounds on a variable, we can propagate [12] these limits through a succession of linear equations.

For example from $1 \leq x \leq 20 \wedge y = x + 30$, we can obtain the lower limit on y by substituting $x = 1$ and the upper limit on y by substituting $x = 20$ in $y = x + 30$ giving the limits on y as 31 to 50. In addition, if we already know the limits on y are between 3 and 34, then we can combine these with the original limit of 31 to 50 to give the more compact limit on y of $31 \le y \le 34$.

These limits on y can be used to produce improved limits on x in the same manner. Thus using the improved limits on y of 31 to 34 in $y = x + 30$ gives limits on x of $1 \le x \le 4$.

Thus, if we specify these limits on x and y in a single query:

Query: $x \ge 1 \wedge x \le 20 \wedge y = x + 30 \wedge y \ge 3 \wedge y \le 34$?

we obtain a simplified query with the limits reduced:

Answer: $x \ge 1 \wedge x \le 4 \wedge y = x + 30 \wedge y \ge 31 \wedge y \le 34$

However, because PLL is incremental, the heavy work that might have produced this answer is not wasted. We can now re-enter this answer as a new query with x and y now ranging over finite integer domains:

Query: $integer(x) \wedge integer(y) \wedge x \ge 1 \wedge x \le 4 \wedge y = x + 30 \wedge y \ge 31 \wedge y \le 34$?

giving the result:

Answer: $x = 1 \wedge y = 31 \vee x = 2 \wedge y = 32 \vee x = 3 \wedge y = 33 \vee x = 4 \wedge y = 34$

1.1.3   Meta-level

PLL has a metalevel capability where expressions can be stored in variables. These can then be rewritten by directly calling the PLL interpreter with an in-built predicate *rewrite*.

In principle, we can put the expression "$x = 2 * 3 + 7$" into a variable t_{in}. We can then rewrite:
$$(\exists t_{in})(t_{in} = \text{``}x = 2 * 3 + 7\text{''} \wedge t_{out} = rewrite(t_{in}))$$
into another variable t_{out} :
$$t_{out} = \text{``}x = 13\text{''}$$
Because t_{out} is also a string, we could if necessary, complete the reduction elsewhere.

For efficiency, PLL actually stores PLL expressions as list structures. However, the above illustrates the basic idea.

1.1.4 Mathematical Logic view of PLL

The scheme of work [2] is as follows: Given a database Δ, Δ is translated via some logical or non-monotonic rules M into a set of PLL rewrites Π. (Π is supposed to represent Δ where for example, we may adopt some closed world assumption). Given any logical query Q from Δ, Π applies to Q and rewrites to Q'. Therefore, Q' is logically equivalent to Q under Π.

$$\Pi \vdash Q \Leftrightarrow Q'$$

or equivalently:

$$\Delta \vdash Q \Leftrightarrow Q'$$

The PLL rewrite machine will return Q' as the simplified query. It is up to us, namely the user, to extract an answer set from Q'.

> For example, suppose:
> $$\Delta = P(a), P(b)$$
> $$M = \text{Non-Monotonic mechanism}$$
> where a, b, c are all the constant elements involved and where we may adopt the closed world assumption.
> Therefore:
> $$M(\Delta) = \Pi$$
> and
> $$\Pi = P(x) \stackrel{rewrite}{\rightarrow} x = a \vee x = b$$
> If we ask the query:
> $$P(c)?$$
> PLL will rewrite:
> $$\Pi P(c) \text{ to } c = a \vee c = b \text{ and so to } False$$
> However, the undefined Q(c) rewrites to itself:
> $$\Pi Q(c) \text{ to } Q(c)$$

Let the mechanism for extracting an answer from the Q' answer set be N. N could be a failure mechanism for saying no to queries whenever possible. N applied to $False$ is $false$. N applied to $Q(c)$ is up to us. We may decide N makes things $False$ hence we answer $false$.

By comparison, in Prolog one takes $M =$ closed world assumption and N = Fail any query if we cannot solve to a disjunction $\phi_1 \vee \phi_2 \vee ... \vee \phi_n$ or TRUE, where ϕ_i is solved if ϕ_i is of the form $x_1 = c_1 \wedge ... \wedge x_m = c_m$.

1.2   Design Strategy

In summary, therefore, PLL was designed [6] [8] according to the following ideas:

1. Logic expressions Q should rewrite to simpler logic expressions Q'.
   $\Pi \vdash Q \Leftrightarrow Q'$ [4]

2. *Unsolvable expressions* should be designed [5] to terminate using suitable guards.

3. Separate metalevel and object level variables and environment should be available.

The resulting language is PLL. This paper concentrates on giving a users view of the language. The reader should refer to the accompanying paper [15] for a more detailed explanation of the computational model and the C implementation.

2   Basic Features of PLL

PLL has two broad classes of rewrites:

- Atomic formula rewrites which apply to *atomic formulas* involving data structures such as numbers, strings and lists.

- Compound formula rewrites which apply to a *set of formulas*.

2.1   Notation

Before continuing, it is worth noting some of the notations used in PLL. A query or definition [15] is written after the prompt *Query:* and is terminated by a question mark. The question mark "?" also closes off all unmatched brackets. The answer is written after the word *Answer:* In addition the *rewrite* symbol $-R->$ is used to show that something is rewritten using a rewrite definition. The greek letter ϕ is used to denote a PLL expression such as *(x = 2 * 3)*. The letter c is used to represent bound variables or constants such as the number *12* or the list *[1,2]*. Comments in PLL programs follow a % sign. The function $rewrite_{PLL}(\phi)$ rewrites the expression ϕ using the PLL interpreter.

---

[4]By contrast traditional logic languages obeys the weaker $\Pi \vdash Q \Leftarrow Q'$

2.2 Atomic Formula Rewrites

These rewrites apply to *atomic formulas* and try to reduce them to the solution *atomic formula* of the form $x_1 = c_1 \wedge ...x_m = c_m$

2.2.1 Arithmetic

We can write the following query in PLL:

```
Query: 1.84*pounds = 14?
  -R-> pounds = 14/1.84
Answer: pounds = 7.608696
```

As can be seen, PLL gives an answer even though the variable *pounds* is not placed in a conventional assignment. Currently no equation solver is built into PLL. Therefore, the problem solving power on an individual atomic arithmetic formula is limited to dynamically rearranging the expression into pairwise terms such as $6 + 3$, $6 * 3$, $6 - 3$ and $6/3$ that can be replaced by their corresponding values 9, 18, 3 and 2. Hence, we can also rewrite the earlier query in several equivalent forms and still get the same answer:

```
Query: 1.84*pounds-14 = 0?
Answer: pounds = 7.608696

Query: 14/1.84 = pounds?
Answer: pounds = 7.608696
```

In each case, an attempts is made to find a value for the variable *pounds*[5]. This flexibility in the language, means that the user can use his natural style, rather than the machines.

2.2.2 Lists

Like other logic languages, the language allows operations on list structures. To split a list into its *head* and *tail* we use the equation *list* = *headoflist* :: *tailoflist*. Thus:

---

[5] Because PLL is based on logic, we only assign to the variable *pounds* once

```
Query: ["ros","daf","dai"] = head :: tail?
Answer: head = "ros" & tail = ["daf","dai"]
```

splits the list of quoted values *["ros", "daf", "dai"]* into the head *"ros"* and tail *["daf", "dai"]*. Alternatively, we can equate [6] two list structures where some of the elements are variables:

```
Query: [x, "daf", "dai"] = ["ros", y, "dai"]?
Answer: x = "ros" &  y = "daf"
```

2.2.3   Ranges

The equation x *in* S, corresponding to $x \in S$, allows us to generate or test membership of a list:

```
Query: x in ["ros", "daf", "dai"]?
Answer: x = "ros" or  x = "daf" or x = "dai"
```

or range of numbers:

```
Query: x in [1 .. 10]?
Answer: x = 1 or  x = 2 or x = 3 or ... x = 10
```

2.2.4   Unsolvable Problems

Atomic formulas contain guards [4] [17] [18] [19] to trap situations that would lead to infinite solution sets. If this occurs, then the elementary predicate simply rewrites to itself in the manner illustrated below:

```
Query: x = y + 20?
Answer: x = y + 20
```

The expression $x = y + 20$ is unsolvable because there is an infinite set of values of x and y that satisfy this equation. In all cases, unsolvable problems are just rewritten to themselves and not to FALSE.

Alternatively, part of the problem can be solved:

---

[6] The solution of sets of equations involving list structures is the equivalent of unification

```
Query: y-4 = 3*7 & x = w*77?
Answer: (y=25 & x=w*77)
```

In this case $y - 4 = 3 * 7$ is reduced to $y = 25$, but $x = w * 77$ is left unchanged because of the internal guards on an arithmetic expression.

2.3 Compound Formula Rewrites

Compound formula rewrites operate on sets of atomic formulas.

2.3.1 Conjunction

Consider a conjunction of atomic formulas:

$$\phi_1 \wedge ...\phi_i \wedge ... \wedge \phi_n$$

Execution is performed by reducing each formula ϕ_1 ... ϕ_n in turn until some definite or improved binding for a variable occurs. If this happens, all the other formulas are executed again. Execution then continues until a set of formulas is left that cannot be further reduced in any order.

The constraint technology, described later, in PLL tries to perform this reduction in an optimal order - such as, reducing the smallest disjunction first. Furthermore, expressions reducing to TRUE or FALSE either disappear or eliminate other terms according to the rewrites:

$$\phi \wedge TRUE \quad -R- > \quad \phi$$
$$\phi \wedge FALSE \quad -R- > \quad FALSE$$

In the example below, line 1 cannot be reduced but line 2 can be reduced to the definite value *dollars* = 14. Lines 1 and 3 are now re-examined. Because of this new binding, line 1 now reduces to *pounds* = 7.6087 and then the remaining term can be reduced to *cost* = 439.087.

```
Query:  1.  1.84*pounds=dollars  &
        2.  dollars=10+4  &
        3.  cost-13=56*pounds?
Answer:  dollars=14 & pounds=7.608696 & cost=439.086957
```

In fact we can think of a PLL computation continuing until a formula ϕ is obtained with the property that $\phi = rewrite_{PLL}(\phi)$.

2.3.2   Disjunction

For a disjunction:

$$\phi_1 \vee ...\phi_i \vee ... \vee \phi_n$$

each expression ϕ_i. is reduced independently. A simplification occurs as follows:

$$\phi \vee TRUE \quad -R- > \quad TRUE$$
$$\phi \vee FALSE \quad -R- > \quad \phi$$

A false arm is ignored and a true arm causes all the other arms to be ignored. When a conjunction contains a disjunction:

$$\phi_1 \wedge (\phi_2 \vee \phi_3)$$

the strategy is to execute ϕ_1 first and then $(\phi_2 \vee \phi_3)$. However, if ϕ_1 is unsolvable then ϕ_1 is delayed and the above is converted using the rewrite:

$$(\phi_2 \vee \phi_3) \wedge \phi_1 -R- > \quad (\phi_2 \wedge \phi_1 \vee \phi_3 \wedge \phi_1)$$

The resulting expression is then executed in the normal manner.

2.3.3   Existential Quantification

Existential quantification is a way of introducing local variables into an expression ϕ. In logic we write $(\exists x_1, x_2...)\phi$ and it means do there exist any binding for the variables $x_1, x_2...$ that make the formula true.

To the user, the expression ϕ is locally reduced with the prevailing bindings. The complication is that we must restore the quantifier if we haven't bound all the variables mentioned in the list. Thus we have the rewrites:

$$\exists X \phi(Y) \qquad -R- > \quad \exists (X \cap Y')\phi'(Y'))$$

where $\phi'(Y') = rewrite_{PLL}(\phi(Y))$
and X, Y and Y' are sets of variables

$$\exists x (x = c \vee f(x,y)) \ -R-> \quad TRUE$$

$$\exists x (x = c \wedge f(x,y)) \ -R-> \quad f(c,y)$$

In the example below, $X = \{x,y\}$, $Y = \{y,z\}$ and $Y' = \{x,y\} \cap \{y,z\}$ giving $\{y\}$ for the quantified variable.

$$(\exists x, y) f(y,z) - R-> \exists y f(y,z)$$

In the next example:

$$(\exists x)(x = 2 * 3 \vee x = y * z + 7) - R-> TRUE$$

x gets bound to 6 and so the whole expression becomes $TRUE$

$$(\exists x)(x = 3 * 3 \wedge x = y * z + 7) - R-> (2 = y * z)$$

In this case x gets bound to 9 and so the quantifier disappears.

Below is some actual PLL. The variable y is not mentioned in the final reduced expression and so y is removed from the quantifier:

```
Query: some(y)(x = y + 3 & y = 2 + 2)?
 -R-> some(y)(x = 4 + 3)?
 -R-> some(y)(x = 7)?
Answer: (x=7)
```

Below, z is not mentioned and so is removed even though the query is not completely reduced.

```
Query: some(x,y,z)(x = y + 3 * 3 & ~ f(x,y))?
Answer: some (x y)( x=y+9 & ~ f(x,y) )
```

In the next example, all the variables are bound to constants and so all the quantifiers can be removed.

```
Query: some(x,y)(x = y + 3 * 3 & ~ f(x,y) & y = 0)?
Answer: ~ f(9,0)
```

2.3.4   Universal Quantification and Implies

Universal quantification, such as $\forall x f(x, y)$, allows the testing of the universal truth of $f(x, y)$ over all values of x - giving the values of y for which this is true. Implication $\phi_1 \Rightarrow \phi_2$ allows a test on ϕ_2 to be conditional on whether ϕ_1 is true. A practical use of this quantifier and implication is given later where we ask which suppliers make all the parts in a set of parts - formalised in logic as $\forall p(part(p) \Rightarrow sp(sp))$

In PLL, *universal quantifiers* and *implies* are immediately written to a negative existential quantifier and a disjunction:

$$\forall x \phi \qquad -R-> \qquad \neg \exists x \neg \phi$$
$$\phi_1 \Rightarrow \phi_2 \qquad -R-> \qquad \neg \phi_1 \vee \phi_2$$

Execution then proceeds as usual for existential quantifiers, negation and disjunctions.

2.3.5   Classical Negation

In the case of negation, the approach is more subtle than PROLOG *Negation As Failure*. In PLL we use standard tautologies of logic as rewrites:

1. Try to remove double negations:

$$\neg \neg \phi \qquad -R-> \qquad \phi$$

2. Try to move any not on a disjunction inwards to turn the expression into a conjunction:

$$\neg(\phi_1 \vee \phi_2) \qquad -R-> \qquad (\neg \phi_1 \wedge \neg \phi_2)$$

Conjunctions are good because they allow the variables in say $(\phi_1 \wedge \phi_2)$ to influence each other.

3. Try to rewrite the argument of any remaining *not*:

$$\neg \phi \qquad -R-> \qquad \neg rewrite_{PLL}(\phi)$$

where rewrite is the PLL interpreter.

4. If the repeated application of the above causes no change in the expression, then try to move a *not* on a conjunction inwards:

$$\neg(\phi_1 \wedge \phi_2) \quad -R-> \quad (\neg\phi_1 \vee \neg\phi_2)$$

5. In addition, try all queries that cannot be reduced further in negated form - currently unimplemented except as metalevel construct:

$$\phi \qquad -R-> \qquad \neg rewrite_{PLL}(\neg\phi_1)$$

Here are a few simple examples using these rewrites:

```
Query:   ~~(x = 10 + 10)?          % Rule 1
Answer:  (x = 20)

Query:   ~(~x = 1 or ~x = 2)?      % Rule 2
-R-> x=1 & x=2
Answer:  FALSE

Query:   ~some(x) (x = 1 & x = 2)? % Rule 3
-R-> ~some(x) (FALSE)
-R-> ~FALSE
Answer:  TRUE

Query:   ~(~x = 1+2 & ~x = 2*5)?   % Rule 4
Answer:  x = 3 or x = 10

Query:   ~x = 1 or ~x = 4?         % Rule 5
-R-> ~(x = 1 & x = 4)
-R-> ~ FALSE
Answer:  TRUE
```

2.3.6   Definitions

A typical predicate, defined by the user, has an atomic head formula, followed by a guard expression, and then a body formula:

define <atomic head formula> <guard expression> tobe ϕ ?

Thus any expression matching the atomic head formula is replaced by the body formula ϕ with dummy parameters in the definition being replaced by the parameters in the corresponding position of the original atomic formula. Only if the variables mentioned in the guard expression are bound does the rewrite occur, otherwise the *<atomic head formula>* remains unrewritten. The guard expression has the form $(x)or(y)$ if one must be bound or $(x\,y)$ if both must be bound. It is up to the predicate designer to include this basic trap on infinite looping[4] and provide a specification of what the resulting predicate can do in terms of problem solving.

For example:
$define f(x, z)\ guard(x)or(z)\ tobe\ some(y)(g(x, y)\ \&\ h(y, z))$?
defines:
$f(1, 2)$ to be rewritten to $some(y)(g(1, y)\ \&\ h(y, 2))$
or:
$f(w, 2)$ to be rewritten to $some(y)(g(w, y)\ \&\ h(y, 2))$
but with neither variable bound:
$f(w, x)$ rewrites to itself $f(w, x)$.

3   Scientific Applications

3.1   Introduction

The electrical and mechanical systems have been chosen to illustrate the operation of the language in practical applications.

3.2   Electrical Circuit

An electrical circuit, Figure 1, consists of two resistances *r1* and *r2* in parallel, followed by a single resistance *r3* in series with these. Across this circuit is a 4 volt lead-acid accumulator. Such a system can be modelled by a set of equations.

3.2.1   Parallel Circuit

First, we define the resistance of any pair of parallel resistances *r1* and *r2*:

```
define parallel(r,r1,r2) tobe 1/r = 1/r1 + 1/r2?
```

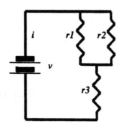

Figure 1: Electrical Network

Using this definition we can compute the resistance of a *3 ohm* and a *6 ohm* resistance connected in parallel:

```
Query: parallel(r,3,6)?
  --R--> 1/r = 1/3 + 1/6
  --R--> 1/r = 0.5
  --R--> 1/0.5 = r
Answer: r = 2.000000 (ohms)
```

As this detailed reduction shows, the predicate *parallel* is rewritten to *1/r = 1/3 + 1/6*. A *3* and a *6* have been substituted for *r1* and *r2* in the definition. The formula is then further reduced to its simplest form *r = 2*.

Unlike a traditional computer language, which computes in only one direction, the language can often operate reversibly. Thus, if we know the value of one of the two parallel resistances - namely *6 ohms* and we know the total resistance is *2 ohms*, then the language can still obtain the value of the other resistance:

```
Query: parallel(2,rx,6)?
  --R--> 1/2 = 1/rx + 1/6
```

```
  --R--> 1/rx = 1/2 - 1/6
  --R--> 1/rx = 2/6
  --R--> rx = 6/2
Answer: rx = 3.000000 (ohms)
```

Reduction takes place as before, except that a slightly different order is now taken.

3.2.2   Complete Circuit

Next we define the resistance of any two series resistors:

```
define series(r,r1,r2) tobe r = r1 + r2?
```

The total resistance is given by using these parallel and series predicates to form a single expression representing the complete circuit resistance:

```
define network(R,r1,r2,r3) tobe
    some(rx) (parallel(rx,r1,r2) &
    series(R,rx,r3))?
```

In this definition, we define *rx* from *r1* and *r2* using the parallel predicate. We then use the series predicate to combine *rx* with *r3* to obtain the total resistance *R*. The quantifier *some* declares *rx* as a local variable—invisible outside its scope. The complete circuit is then modelled by including Ohm's law and this *network* predicate:

```
define circuit(v,i,r1,r2,r3)  tobe
    some (R) (v = i * R & network(R,r1,r2,r3))?
```

Because the total resistance is not required in the model it is also made local with a *some(R)* quantifier.

3.2.3   Using the Electrical Circuit

We can now use this 5 variable electrical model to calculate the current given a 4 volt accumulator and values of 3, 6 and 2 ohms for *r1*, *r2* and *r3* respectively:

```
Query: circuit(4,i,3,6,2)?
  --R-->     some (R) (4 = i * R & network(R,3,6,2))
  --R-->     some (R) (4 = i * R & R = 4)
  --R-->             4 = i * 4
Answer: i = 1.000000
```

or to obtain the value of *r3* assuming we know the current *i* is *1 ampere*:

```
Query: circuit(4,1,3,6,r3)?
Answer: r3 = 2.000000 (ohms)
```

However, suppose the two resistances are unknown but the voltage is 4 volts and the current is 1 amp:

```
Query: circuit(4,1,r1,r2,2)?
Answer: 0.500000=1/r1+1/r2
```

The query is now rewritten to an equation relating *r1* and *r2*, rather than a definite numerical solution. Now suppose, we know all the resistances values but not the voltage and current:

```
Query: circuit(v,i,3,6,2)?
Answer: v=i*4 (volts)
```

In this case, we get the relationship between the voltage and the current as our answer. If we now decide the voltage is 8 volts we can then use this incremental equation $v=i*4$ rather than the original circuit predicate to answer our question. Thus we have avoided the unnecessary recomputation needed when starting from the circuit predicate.

Each of these queries would need a separate algorithm in a conventional programming language. The conciseness of PLL means that we need only *one* definition.

3.3 Mechanical System

A mechanical system consists of two gear wheels connected to a connecting rod driving a piston in the manner shown in Figure 2. This first gear is 1 cm radius, the second is R cms radius and this drives a connecting rod of L cms in length with a piston at its end.

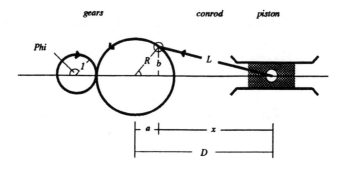

Figure 2: Mechanical System

This is represented by an equation:

```
define piston(Phi,R,L,D) tobe
  some(a b x)
    a=R*cos(Phi/R) &
    b=R*sin(Phi/R) &
    L*L=x*x+b*b &
    D=a+x &
    L>0  &
    D>0?
```

Starting from *Phi* in Figure 2, the value of *a* and *b* are obtained using $a = R*cos(Phi/R)$ and $b = R*sin(Phi/R)$. Pythagoras, $L*L = x*x+b*b$ gives x and b from the connecting rod length L . The position of the piston D is then the sum of x and a.

Using this mechanical model we can ask a variety of questions such as *what is the position of the piston?*

```
Query: piston(20,2,4.5,D)?
Answer: (D=6.45619)
```

or *what is the length of the connecting rod?*

```
Query: piston(20,2,L,6.0)?
Answer: (L=4.04532)
```

4 Advanced Features of PLL

4.1 Recursion

4.1.1 Reversible Factorial

This is a reversible definition of factorial defined as *If x = 0 then y = 1 else y = x*fact(x-1)*. PLL doesn't support functional notation and so this is written:

```
define fact(n,y) guard(n)or(y) tobe
n=0 & y=1
or some (n1,y1)
     ( n in [1 .. 20]
     & n=n1+1
     & y=n*y1
     & fact(n1,y1) ) ?
```

As the queries below show, *fact* can go forwards or backwards. The guards check that either n or y are bound before making the actual rewrite thus preventing the infinite *fact(n y)* being actually computed.

```
Query:   fact(3,y)?
Answer:  y=6

Query:   fact(n,6)?
Answer:  n=3

Query:   fact(n,y)?
Answer:  fact(n,y)
```

In the complex case below, *not fact(n y)* is delayed until *fact(3 y)* is rewritten to y = 6. This value is then used in *fact(n 6)* to n = 3 giving the answer shown.

```
Query:   ~fact(n,y) & fact(3,y)?
Answer:  ~n=3 & y=6
```

4.1.2   Reversible Perm

This example illustrates how a version of *perm* can be defined that permutes
from x to y but also from y to x.

The *ins* predicate splits a list such as $x = [c_1\ c_2\ c_3]$ into its elements:

For example $y = c_1$ & $z = [c_2\ c_3]$ or $y = c_2$ & $z = [c_1\ c_3]$ or $y = c_3$ & $z =$
$[c_1\ c_2]$ by recursively dismantling the list into its elements.

```
define ins(x,y,z) guard (x) or (y,z) tobe
   x=y::z
or some(xhead,x1,z1)
        ( x=xhead::x1
        & z=xhead::z1
        & ins(x1,y,z1))?
```

The *perm* predicate recursively dismantles the list x into its head *xhead* and
tail *x*1. This tail is then permuted recursively to give all permutations in *y*1.
xhead is then inserted into all positions of *y*1 to give all the permutations
in *y*.

```
define perm(x,y) guard (x) or (y) tobe
        x=[] & y=[]
        or some (xhead,x1,y1)
           ( x=xhead::x1
           & ins(y,xhead,y1)
           & perm(x1,y1))?
```

The above predicate then gives the following results on the queries below:

```
Query:   perm(x,y)?
Answer:  perm(x,y)

Query:   perm(x,[1,2])?
Answer:  ( x=[1,2] or x=[2,1] )

Query:   perm([1,2],y)?
```

```
Answer: ( y=[1,2] or y=[2,1] )

Query:  ~perm([1,2],y)?
Answer: ( ~ y=[1,2] & ~ y=[2,1] )

Query:  perm([1,2],y) & ~perm(y,[8,9])?
Answer: ( y=[1,2] or y=[2,1] )
```

4.2   Debugging

Despite the fact that the order of execution of atomic formulas in PLL is
unknown until execution, PLL is surprisingly easy to debug. There are two
techniques:

- Include dummy predicates which behave like *print* statements in a
  conventional language

- Incrementally execute the language by making recursive calls to atomic
  formulas temporarily undefined.

4.2.1   Debugging using Dummy Predicates

Dummy predicates can be added to definitions to give the effect of a print
statement in a conventional language.

```
define fact(n,y) guard(n)or(y) tobe
print_fact(n,y) &   % trace predicate
(n=0 & y=1
or some (n1,y1)
    ( n in [1 .. 20]
    & n=n1+1
    & y=n*y1
    & fact(n1,y1) )) ?
```

The language then returns an expression tracing the computation so far:

```
Query:  fact(3,y)?
Answer: print_fact(3, 6)
   & print_fact(2, 2)
   & print_fact(1, 1)
```

```
& print_fact(0, 1)
& (y = 6)
```

4.2.2   Incremental Debugging

Another method of debugging the *fact* predicate is to rename the recursive call as *xxxfact* thus making it undefined:

```
define fact(n,y) guard (n) or (y) tobe
    n=0  & y=1
    or   some (a,b)
    (n in [1..20] &
    n=a+1 &
    y=n*b &
    xxxfact(a,b) )?  % temporarily undefined
```

Execution can now proceed by changing *xxxfact* back to *fact* and reentering the previous answer as a query.

```
Query:  fact(3,y)?
Answer: some(b)(y = 3 * b & xxxfact(2,b))
```

Now replace *xxxfact* by *fact* to give successive new queries to further check the operation of *fact*:

```
Query:  some(b)(y=3*b & fact(2,b))?
Answer:
 some(b,b1)(y=3*b1 & b1=2*b & xxxfact(1,b))

Query:
 some(b,b1)(y=3*b1 & b1=2*b & fact(1,b))?
Answer:
 some(b,b1,b2)(y=3*b2 & b2=2*b1
  & b1=1*b & xxxfact(0,b))

Query:
 some(b,b1,b2)(y=3*b2 & b2=2*b1
  & b1=1*b & fact(0,b))?
Answer: (y=6)
```

As you can see this is also a useful way of discovering what PLL does!

4.3 Meta level

PLL allows an expression tree to be put into a metavariable and the tree in this metavariable reduced by rewrites to a new tree. This process is potentially very powerful. For example, given some query ϕ_1 we can first use a special metapredicate *simplify* to examine ϕ for redundant or contradictory subexpressions such as $\phi \wedge \neg\phi$ to give ϕ_1. We can then test if the result ϕ_1 definitely solves our problem by testing that the expression contains no undefined atomic formulas. If ϕ_1 is unsolved we can then further reduce this expression by applying the PLL interpreter. We can then repeat these two steps until a fixed point or unchanging expression is reached.

In summary, the reduction can either be performed by:

- Predicate called *rewrite* which uses the normal PLL interpreter plus object level rewrites to reduce an expression.

- A metapredicate which uses metalevel rewrites to reduce an expression tree.

- An external problem solving system called by PLL that can transform expression trees to simpler expression trees.

4.3.1 Expression Trees

PLL expressions are stored in tree structure form, such as:
```
tree = ["x","=" , [3,"+",7]].
```
If we wish to include metavariables such as *subtree* within an expression we simply include an appropriate variable:
```
some(subtree)
    (tree = [[["x","=",1],"or",["x","=",2]] , "or",subtree]
    & subtree = ["x","=",3] )?.
```
Because constants such as $=, 2, TRUE,$ and *or* have the same interpretation at all levels they could be left unquoted:
```
tree = [[["x",=,1],or,["x",=,2]],or,subtree]
    & subtree = ["x",=,3].
```

Suppose we issue the earlier expression as a query:

```
Query:   some(subtree)
  (tree = [[["x","=",1],"or",["x","=",2]] , "or",subtree]
    & subtree = ["x","=",3] )?
Answer:
 tree = [[["x","=",1],"or",["x","=",2]],"or",["x","=",3]]
```

Then the contents of *subtree* are included in the value of *tree*.

An important operation on trees is to see if a PLL expression is a solution expression containing only atomic formulas of the form TRUE, FALSE or $(x = c)$. The predicate *soluble* below recursively winds down through the expression tree to achieve this result.

```
define soluble(tree) guard(tree) tobe
       tree = ["TRUE"]
   or
       tree = ["FALSE"]
   or
       some(v1,v2) (tree = [v1,"=",v2]
       & variable(v1)
       & number(v2))
   or
       some(e1,e2) (tree = e1::[]
       & soluble(e1))
   or
       some(e1,e2) (tree = e1 ::"&" ::e2
       & soluble(e1)
       & soluble(e2))
   or
       some(e1,e2) (tree = e1 ::"or" ::e2
       &  soluble(e1)
       &  soluble(e2))
?
```

This recursive predicate can then examine an expression such as:

```
soluble([["x","=",4],"or",["x","=",2]])?
 -R-> soluble([["x","=",4])&soluble([["x","=",2]])
 -R-> TRUE
soluble([["x","=",["y","+",4]],"or",["x","=",2]])?
 -R-> soluble([["x","=",["y","+",4]])
      &  soluble([["x","=",2]])
 -R-> FALSE
```

and determine if they are completely reduced.

Other important predicates would check if one expression had more bound variables than another so that a fixed point in a computation could be found. This is useful in halting a metalevel program that is trying a repertoire of problem solvers when we wish to know that none of them is improving on the solution.

4.3.2 Execution of Expression Trees

Expressions in PLL can be reduced by reentering the PLL interpreter with a metapredicate called *rewrite*:

$$t' = rewrite(t, pi)$$

where $pi = \phi_{rewrite\ definitions}$

In general, this predicate takes an expression t as its argument and applies the rewrites in the expression pi to give a simplified expression t'.

Here is a simple example to show how *rewrite* handles expression trees:

```
Query:   some(tree) (tree = "x = 2 + 6"
              & answer = rewrite(tree)) ?
Answer:  answer = ["x" ,"=",8]
```

PLL can be used to simplify an expression such as **"y=2*z + 5*z"** to **"y=7*z"** and then to execute this simplified expression with a value of 28 being given to y:

```
define atom(x) guard(x) tobe
    ~x=[] & ~some(x1,x2)  x = x1::x2 ?

define makestring(n,h) tobe
   number(n) & string(h,n)
   or ~ number(h)  & n=h ?

define flat(x,y) tobe
   x = [] & y=""
   or atom(x) & y=x
   or x = h::x1
      & flat(h,h1)
```

```
      & flat(x1,h2)
      & makestring(h1,s1)
      & makestring(h2,s2)
      & y=s1+s2 ?

define simpler(ei,eo)   tobe
some (y,x,a,b)
        (ei=[y,"=",[a,"*",x],"+",[b,"*",x]]
        & n = a + b
        & eo = [y,"=",[n,"*",x]] )
      or
        ~ some(y,x,a,b)
        ei=[y,"=",[a,"*",x],"+",[b,"*",x]] & eo=ei
?
```

Below, we put the simplified expression into variable eo, bind the quoted metavariable y to 28 and get the answer $z = 4$.

```
Query:  simpler(["y","=",4],eo)?
Answer: eo = ["y","=",4]

Query:  some(eo,eo1,eo2,ans1)
    (simpler(["y","=",[2,"*","z"],"+",[5,"*","z"]],eo)
            & eo1=[["y","=",28],"&",eo]
            & flat(eo1,eo2)
            & ans1 = rewrite(eo2)
            & flat(ans1,ans) )?
Answer:  ans = "z=4 & y=28"
```

4.4   Incremental Execution

Suppose we have a big problem $\phi(\alpha)$ that takes several hours to run and has to be run with different definitions for a predicate α. Instead of executing $\phi(\alpha_1)$, $\phi(\alpha_2)$, ... PLL allows the execution of $\phi(\alpha)$ with α undefined to give an incremental expression $\phi'(\alpha)$:

$$\phi'(\alpha) = rewrite(\phi(\alpha), \ \Pi)$$

where the rewrites in Π do not include α.

This incremental expression can be used with the definition of each α_i to obtain a corresponding answer:

$$\phi_i'' = rewrite(\phi'(\alpha_i), \Pi(\alpha_i))$$

where Π_i includes the definition of α_i.

The cutting problem, described later, illustrates this process, where we attempt to use PLL to return a general formula representing the positions of a number of templates. However, possibly the most important commercial use of incremental execution is in database integrity checking. The integrity query usually takes days to run over a large database and so it is actually run incrementally as each update occurs on the assumption that the system was consistent before the update.

More specifically, if ϕ depends on a predicate α and we wish to insert $\Delta\alpha$ into or delete $\Delta\alpha$ from α. Then the corresponding incremental queries $\phi_{insert}(\Delta\alpha)$ and $\phi_{delete}(\Delta\alpha)$ are given below:

$$\phi'_{insert}(\Delta\alpha) = rewrite(\phi(\alpha \vee \Delta\alpha), \Pi(\alpha))$$

$$\phi'_{delete}(\Delta\alpha) = rewrite(\phi(\alpha \wedge \neg\Delta\alpha), \Pi(\alpha)))$$

Each time we further update a predicate we can include a another increment $\Delta'\alpha$ in the result of the last query:

$$\phi''_{insert}(\Delta'\alpha) = rewrite(\phi'(\Delta\alpha \vee \Delta'\alpha), \Pi(\Delta\alpha))$$

$$\phi''_{delete}(\Delta'\alpha) = rewrite(\phi'(\Delta\alpha \wedge \neg\Delta'\alpha), \Pi(\Delta\alpha)))$$

so that the original query need never be recomputed.

4.4.1 Example of Incremental Execution

In the example below, the query:
$$\forall p(h(x) \Rightarrow f(x))$$
corresponds to checking that the set represented by h and f are subsets such that $h \subset f$.

Suppose we have a rewrite h in the database. We can obtain the query needed to check an incremental update to h by *oring* a dummy predicate dh to h:

```
define h(x) tobe x = "a" ?
```

```
define f(x) tobe x = "a" ?

Query:    all(x)((h(x) or dh(x)) -> f(x))?
Answer:   ~ ( some(x) (dh(x) & ~ x = "a" ))
```

The answer to this query is an incremental query with *dh* being defined as the insert. Thus if we update *h* with the element "*a*" by including this in *dh* the incremental query gives the answer TRUE:

```
define dh(x) tobe x = "a" ?

Query:    ~(some (x) (dh(x) & ~ x = "a" ))?
Answer:   TRUE
```

However, if we update *h* with the element "*b*" by including this in *dh* the incremental query correctly gives the answer FALSE:

```
define dh(x) tobe x = "b" ?        % Insert

Query:    ~(some (x) (dh(x) & ~ x = "a" ))?
Answer:   FALSE
```

The next incremental query is obtained by including a predicate *ddh* in the definition *dh* to cover the possibility of a further insert to *h*:

```
define dh(x) tobe x = "a" ?

Query:    ~(some (x) ((ddh(x) or dh(x)) & ~ x = "a" ))?
Answer:   ~ (some (q0)( ddh(q0) & ~ q0="a")  )
```

The answer is the query that should be asked in order to check another insert.

Similarly we can obtain a simple expression for checking deletions to the predicate *f*:

```
define h(x) tobe x = "a"  or  x = "c"?
define f(x) tobe x = "a"  or  x = "b"  or  x = "c"?

Query:    all(x)(h(x) -> (f(x) & ~df(x)) )?
Answer:   ( ~ df("a") & ~ df("c") )
```

Thus for deletions we need only ask if (~ df("a") & ~ df("c")) is true.

```
define df(x) tobe x = "a" ?
Query:   ~ df("a") & ~ df("c")?
Answer: FALSE

define df(x) tobe x = "b" ?
Query:   ~ df("a") & ~ df("c")?
Answer: TRUE
```

4.5   Constraint Technology

The constraint technology in PLL is based on the ECRC [12] work on Finite Domains and Intervals. Because PLL is a rewrite language the implementation [1] is different but the resulting performance is very similar. However, because PLL can return general expressions, it can reason and give answers about infinite domains.

The following are some of the rewrites that are implemented as an integral part of the interpreter.

4.5.1   Simplifying Interval Domains

$$x \geq c_1 \land x \geq c_2 \; \text{-R->} \; x \geq c_1 \qquad \text{if } c_1 \geq c_2$$

$$x \geq c_1 \land x \geq c_2 \; \text{-R->} \; x \geq c_2 \qquad \text{if } c_1 < c_2$$

4.5.2   Propagating Interval Domains through Linear Equations

$$x \geq c_1 \land x \leq c_2 \land y = ax + b$$

$$\text{-R->}$$

$$x \geq c_1 \land x \leq c_2 \land$$

$$y \geq (ac_1 + b) \land y \leq (ac_2 + b) \land$$

$$y = ax + b$$

4.5.3   Restricting Real to Integer Domains

if $integer(x) \land x \geq c_1 \land x \leq c_2$

```
-R->
```

$x \in \{$set of integers encoded as bitmap from c_1 to $c_2\}$

4.5.4   Propagating Finite Domains through Linear Equations

$x \in \{c_1, c_2, ...\ c_n\} \land y = x + b$

```
-R->
```

$x \in \{c_1, c_2, ...\ c_n\} \land y \in \{c_1 + b, c_2 + b, ...c_n + b\} \land y = x + b$

4.5.5   Restricting Finite Domains with $\neq$

The sets of constants are encoded by their upper and lower limit and by a bitmap:

$x \in \{c_1, c_2, ...\ c_i, ...c_n\} \land x \neq c_i$

```
-R->
```

$x \in \{c_1, c_2, (\text{without } c_i\ )\ c_n\}$

The actual method of coding is very similar to the methods used in database query optimisation [7].

4.5.6   Constraint Technology Examples

```
QUERY:  x >= 5 & x >= 2 ?
ANSWER: (5 <= x & x <= MAXFLOAT)

QUERY:  x  >= 2 & x <= 7 & y = x + 6 ?
ANSWER: ( 8 <= y & y <= 13
        & 2 <= x & x <= 7
        & ( y - x = 6 ) )

QUERY:  x in [1,2,3] & y = x + 2 ?
```

```
ANSWER: ( ( y = 3  & x = 1  )
        or ( y = 4  & x = 2  )
        or ( y = 5  & x = 3  ) )

QUERY:  x >= 5 & x <= 8 & integer(x)?
ANSWER: ( x = 5 or x = 6 or x = 7 or x = 8)
```

The earlier example *Using the Electrical Circuit* can now be repeated with some latitude in the value of current between 2 and 10 amperes.

```
QUERY:  circuit(v,i,3,6,2) & i >= 2 & i <= 10?
ANSWER:" ( 2 <= i & i <= 10
        & 8 <= v & v <= 40
        & ( v - 4*i = 0 ))
```

or some latitude in the value of $r3$:

```
QUERY:  circuit(4 i 3 6 r3)
        & r3 >= 4.0 & r3 <= 5.0 ?
ANSWER: some(R)
        ( 6.9 <= R & R <= 7.1
        & 4.9 <= r3 & r3 <= 5.1
        & R - r3 = 2
        & 4 = i*R )
```

This shows an important feature of logic rewrite. Traditional logic language queries often just return FALSE with no explanation. However, as this example shows, this formula gives us the chance to obtain a possible range of currents corresponding to R at 6.9 and 7.1 amps giving the range of current as 4/6.9 to 4/7.1 amps. Now if we decide the current is 4/7 amps we can compute the value of r3:

```
QUERY: some(i) (i = 4/7 & some(R)
       ( 6.9 <= R & R <= 7.1
       & 4.9 <= r3 & r3 <= 5.1
       & R - r3 = 2
       & 4 = i*R   )
ANSWER: r3 = 5
```

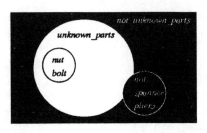

Figure 3: Venn Diagram of Parts

5   Commercial Applications

5.1   Introduction

Two applications described later, involve commercial databases and show
how complex data and queries can be represented in a Pure Logic Language. A simple application of the Constraint Technology in PLL is given
by applying it to the problem of cutting templates from a sheet of tin.

Often we are faced with the problem of handling uncertain information especially in the early stages of planning. One use for the PLL is for supporting
a temporal database capability where uncertain facts about people's holiday dates are stored. We can then use this in deciding on dates of meetings
or in persuading people to provide more definite information.

All these applications clearly need a natural front end and PLL should be
seen as the formalism for such a front end to map to.

5.2   Open and Negative Database Information

Most databases use a closed world assumption where facts that are not true are assumed false. Pure Logic Language allows a more subtle representation to be used where this is appropriate. In the Venn diagram in Figure 3, there are parts *nuts* and *bolts, unknown parts* and definite non parts such as *pliers* and *spanners*. This information is represented as follows:

```
define part_db(part) tobe
   ((part ="nut" or part = "bolt") or
   unknownpart(part))
&
   ~(part = "spanner" or part = "pliers")?
```

If we now ask questions of this database, we get a more natural response. Thus, *Is nut a part?* is TRUE. *Is spanner a part?* is FALSE and most important *Is gear a part?* is unknown rather than FALSE.

```
Query:    part_db("nut")?
Answer:   TRUE

Query:    part_db("spanner")?
Answer:   FALSE

Query:    part_db("gear")?
Answer:   unknownpart("gear")
```

This corresponds to the natural answer we might get, if we asked the above question of a user. In fact, even negated queries such as *Is a nut not a part?* give the correct answer:

```
Query:    ~part_db("nut")?
Answer:   FALSE

Query:    ~part_db("spanner")?
Answer:   TRUE

Query:    ~ part_db("gear")?
Answer:   ~ unknownpart("gear")
```

This representation, avoids the problem of answers to identical queries that were false becoming true after an update.

5.3   Complex Database Query

Consider the following small database of suppliers and parts:

```
define part(p) tobe
     p = "nut" or p = "bolt"?

define sp(s,p) tobe
     [s,p] = ["s1","nut"]
  or [s,p] = ["s1","bolt"]
  or [s,p] = ["s2","nut"]?
```

Using this database it is possible to ask questions using the standard *Predicate Calculus* universal quantification. Many database query languages are based on Predicate Calculus but use only *tuple variables* rather than *domain variables*. Even though PLL can use both, domain variables are usually the most natural: Thus we can ask [7] *Which supplier makes all parts?*:

```
Query:   all(p) (part(p) -> sp(s,p))?
Answer:  s = "s1"
```

Examination of the above database should show that indeed *s1* is the only supplier of *all* the parts. Alternatively we can ask [8] *Which suppliers do* not *make all parts?*.

```
define supplier_all_parts(s) tobe
        all(p) (part(p) -> sp(s,p))?

Query:   some(p) (sp(s,p) & ~supplier_all_parts(s))?
Answer:  s = "s2"
```

Again, it must be emphasised that PLL is not really intended for direct end user usage - rather it is meant as a language for interfacing to some natural interface system with this formalism usually being hidden away!

5.3.1   Universal Quantifier Execution

Briefly the rewrites described in the section *Compound Rewrites* are used to obtain the answer $s = "s1"$ as follows:

---

[7] $\forall p(part(p) \Rightarrow sp(s,p))$ in predicate calculus

[8] $sp(s,p) \wedge \neg\forall p(part(p) \Rightarrow sp(s,p))$ in predicate calculus

Query: ∀ (p) (part(p) ⇒ sp(s,p))

–R–> ¬∃(p) ¬ (¬ part(p) ∨ sp(s,p))

–R–> ¬∃(p)(part(p) ∧¬sp(s,p))

–R–> ¬∃(p)((p = "nut" ∨p = "bolt") ∧ ¬sp(s,p))

–R–> ¬∃(p)(p = "nut"∧¬sp(s,p)∨p = "bolt"∧¬sp(s,p))

–R–> ¬ (¬ sp(s,"nut") ∨¬ sp(s,"bolt"))

–R–> sp(s,"nut") ∧ sp(s,"bolt"))

–R–> (s = "s1" ∨ s = "s2") ∧ s = "s1"

Answer: s = "s1"

First we translate the universal quantifier to a negative existential quantifier. The negative disjunction is changed to a conjunction. The positive definition is expanded -for clarity *sp* is not expanded. The ∃*p* now disappears because there are now definite bindings for *p*. The resulting disjunction is again converted to a conjunction. Finally *sp* is expanded to give the final answer.

5.4 Cutting Problem

In this placement problem we wish to know the alternative ways of cutting templates from an area of material. In Figure 4 are three templates a,b,c which we wish to cut from a sheet of tin plate.

The rectangular templates etc are described by the coordinates of their lower and upper corners. Thus (x1 y1) represents the lower corner and (x2 y2) represents the upper corner of a template.

The predicate *intinplate* constrains the templates to be within the area of the tin plate - 8cm by 8cm. The next two predicates define the rectangles *a* and *b* to be 7 x 4 and 6 x 3 respectively. The predicate *notoverlap* then checks that any two templates do not overlap. Finally, the predicates *sheetc1* and *sheetc2* defines the irregular shape shown as two rectangles constrained to move together.

```
define intinplate(x1,x2,y1,y2) tobe
x1 >= 0 & x2 <= 8 &
y1 >= 0 & y2 <= 8 ?

define sheeta(x1,x2,y1,y2) tobe
```

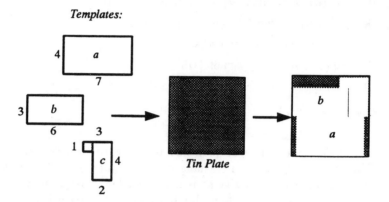

Figure 4: Cutting problem with tin plate that almost exactly fits

```
x2 = x1+7 & y2 = y1+4 &
intinplate(x1,x2,y1,y2) ?

define sheetb(x1,x2,y1,y2) tobe
x2 = x1+6 & y2 = y1+3 &
intinplate(x1,x2,y1,y2)?

define notoverlap(ax1,ax2,ay1,ay2,bx1,bx2,by1,by2) tobe
bx1 >= ax2 or bx2 <= ax1 or   by1 >= ay2 or   by2 <= ay1 ?

define sheetc1(x1,x2,y1,y2) tobe
x2 = x1+1 & y2 = y1+1 &
intinplate(x1,x2,y1,y2) ?

define sheetc2(x1,x2,y1,y2) tobe
x2 = x1+2 & y2 = y1+4 &
intinplate(x1,x2,y1,y2) ?
```

When these definitions are used in a query we obtain what is effectively a
new constraint representing the manner in which these templates can move
around. To reduce the size of the answer, the position of template *a* is
fixed to the bottom of the tin plate otherwise reading this should be fairly

straight forward.

```
Query:
ay1 = 0 &
sheeta(ax1,ax2,ay1,ay2) &
sheetb(bx1,bx2,by1,by2) &
notoverlap(ax1,ax2,ay1,ay2,bx1,bx2,by1,by2) &
sheetc1(cx1,cx2,cy1,cy2) &
sheetc2(dx1,dx2,dy1,dy2) &
cx2 = dx1 & cy1 = dy1 + 3 &
notoverlap(ax1,ax2,ay1,ay2,cx1,cx2,cy1,cy2) &
notoverlap(ax1,ax2,ay1,ay2,dx1,dx2,dy1,dy2) &
notoverlap(bx1,bx2,by1,by2,cx1,cx2,cy1,cy2) &
notoverlap(bx1,bx2,by1,by2,dx1,dx2,dy1,dy2) ?
```

After execution this query gives an answer which shows the only solution is as shown in Figure 5. However, importantly PLL has been able to show the uncertainty in the position of template a as movement in the x direction of 1 cm. This is because we have returned the constraint between ax1 and ax2 namely $(ax2 = ax1 + 7)$.

```
ANSWER:
  ( ay1 = 0
  & ay2 = 4
  & 0 <= ax1 & ax1 <= 1
  & 7 <= ax2 & ax2 <= 8
  & ( ax2 =  ax1 + 7)
  & bx1 = 0   & bx2 = 6   & by1 = 4   & by2 = 7
  & cx1 = 5   & cx2 = 6   & cy1 = 7   & cy2 = 8
  & dx1 = 6   & dx2 = 8   & dy1 = 4   & dy2 = 8
  )
```

If the value of ax1 is fixed to zero then a definite value for ax2 is obtained if the answer above is reissued as a query with say $ax1 = 0$ included. Now, if the size of the tin plate is now slightly enlarged to 8.9cms X 9cms then the answer becomes a more complex expression:

```
define intinplate(x1,x2,y1,y2) tobe
x1 >= 0 & x2 <= 8.9 &
y1 >= 0 & y2 <= 9 ?
```

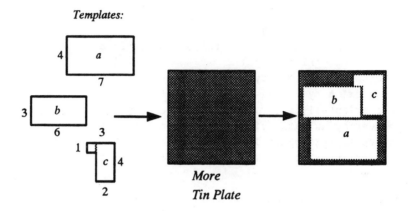

Figure 5: Cutting problem with more tin plate

```
Query: ... same as before ...

Answer:
( 8 <= dy2 & dy2 <= 9      & 4 <= dy1 & dy1 <= 5
& 8 <= dx2 & dx2 <= 8.9    & 6 <= dx1 & dx1 <= 6.9
& 8 <= cy2 & cy2 <= 9      & 7 <= cy1 & cy1 <= 8
& 6 <= cx2 & cx2 <= 6.9    & 5 <= cx1 & cx1 <= 5.9
& 7 <= by2 & by2 <= 8      & 4 <= by1 & by1 <= 5
& 6 <= bx2 & bx2 <= 6.9    & 0 <= bx1 & bx1 <= .9
& ay2 = 4  & ay1 = 0 & 7 <= ax2 & ax2 <= 8.9
& 0 <= ax1 & ax1 <= 1.9 & cy1 >= by2    & dx1 >= bx2
& ( cy1 - dy1 = 3 ) & ( cx2 - dx1 = 0 )
& ( ax2 - ax1 = 7 ) & ( dy2 - dy1 = 4 )
& ( dx2 - dx1 = 2 ) & ( cy2 - cy1 = 1 )
& ( cx2 - cx1 = 1 ) & ( by2 - by1 = 3 )
& ( bx2 - bx1 = 6 ) )
```

The effect of even slightly attempting to obtain definite solutions can be illustrated by defining all variables to be integers in the *intinplate* predicate:

```
define intinplate(x1,x2,y1,y2) tobe
```

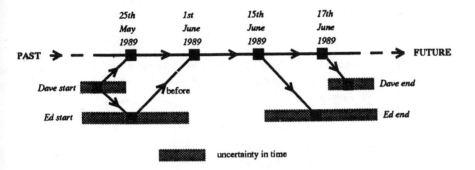

Figure 6: Uncertain Holiday Dates

```
integer(x1) &integer(x2) &integer(y1) &integer(y2) &
x1 >= 0 & x2 <= 8.9 &
y1 >= 0 & y2 <= 9 ?

Query: ... same as before ...

Answer:
((dy2 = 8 & dy1 = 4 & dx2 = 8 & dx1 = 6
 & cy2 = 8 & cy1 = 7 & cx2 = 6 & cx1 = 5
 & by2 = 7 & by1 = 4 & bx2 = 6 & bx1 = 0
 & ay2 = 4 & ax2 = 7 & ax1 = 0 & ay1 = 0)
 ... 6 more solutions
```

The problem with such an enumeration is that if we make the quantisation too coarse we are likely to lose all solutions and simply give the answer FALSE. Too fine a quantisation and the answer is too voluminous!

5.5 Temporal Logic

PLL has a temporal database capability based on Interval Quantification *IQ* [20] [11]. A simple example, for this temporal logic, is to model data about holidays in a small office. It can handle the usual uncertain information that normally precedes a definite entry in a holiday planner. Figure 6 shows that early in the year, we only know the following about Ed and Dave's holidays.

> Dave goes on holiday before Ed. Dave takes his holiday before May 25th. Ed must go on holiday before 1st June. Ed must return to work after 15th June and Dave must return after 17th June.

Figure 6 represents the slack in the position of these dates by the shaded areas. In PLL, this time sequence is asserted by the following *add date1 before date2* commands:

```
Query:
add 'Davestart before 890525?
add 'Edstart before 890601?
add 'Davestart before 'Edstart?
add 890615 before 'Edend?
add 890617 before 'Daveend?
```

A predicate called *iand* which will perform high speed intersection of intervals is used to find *if both Ed and Dave are on leave between the 8th June and 13th June*:

```
Query:   I = iand([["Davestart", "Daveend"]
                   ["Edstart", "Edend"][890608, 890613]])?
Answer:  I = [890608, 890613]
```

or *when are both Dave and Ed on leave before the 13th June?*

```
Query:   I = iand([["Davestart", 890613]
                 ["Edstart", 890613]])?
Answer:  I = ["Edstart", 890613]
```

showing that the answer is some time between Edstart and the 13th June. Next *when are both Dave and Ed on leave?*

```
Query:
 I = iand([["Davestart", "Daveend"]["Edstart", "Edend"]])?
Answer:
 I = iand([["Edstart", "Edend"] ["Davestart", "Daveend"]])
```

In this case we can see from the diagram above that there is no definite answer. The finish date of Dave's leave can be either before or after the finish date of Ed's leave. Rather than return a complicated conditional expression[9], the original query is returned[10]. The user then can either alter his query or add more definite temporal information in the time sequence database.

6 Discussion

6.1 Background

The major concern of PLL was to improve the match between an application builder's problem and the language used to describe his problem. Most programming languages use control structures and data structures that obscure the definition of the problem even though there is an underlying logic to the program. The perfect PLL would contain no control structures with all high speed algorithms being hidden in the system. In practice, PLL needs some control and should really be considered as a language for the creation of such a system. The metalevel of PLL would orchestrate the passing of problems to various specialised external systems. These might be traditional theorem provers which can look for contradictions in expressions - to high performance deductive database systems able to operate on large scale volumes of data.

The role of PLL is to make the creation of systems cheaper by saving the end user time rather than necessarily offering improved execution speeds. High performance is best achieved by writing a specialised module in an algorithmic language and using it from PLL.

6.2 Brief State of the Art

Lloyd [14] in his Bristol report refers to many problems [24] with traditional traditional logic language. A typical problem is that $p(x), q(x)$ *fails* whereas changing the order to $q(x), p(x)$ may cause it to succeed. In fact the metalevel system in PLL was inspired by Lloyd's ideas.

ECRC in Munich have augmented traditional logic language with an optimiser *CHIP* meaning *Constraint Handling in PROLOG* [12]. Many prob-

---

[9] which can be done

[10] or a simplified form if some of the intersections can be unconditionally performed

lems that involve searching use many variables. If each variable ranges over many states, the search space quickly becomes impossibly large. CHIP avoids such coarse searching by essentially reasoning about the domains of values in a similar way to that described in this paper but without PLL's rewrite capability.

IBM in York Town Heights have a language called CLP($\mathcal{R}$) [13]. This is another enhanced version of PROLOG which includes an equation solver - they say *solving constraints in the domain of uninterpreted functors over real arithmetic terms.*

The Pure Logic Language described in this paper aims to solve some of Lloyd's objections to traditional logic languages and to include some of the constraint satisfaction ideas in the ECRC and IBM work. However, unlike these systems PLL is a rewrite language and has an altogether more general expressive power than traditional logic languages with its reliance on Horn Clause syntax and Negation As Failure [10].

6.3 Temporal Logic

The previous section on temporal logic essentially performed temporal logic by a series of predicates operating at the metalevel. However, when the object level contains temporal constraints, many of the temporal operators currently implemented as specialised metalevel rewrites can be replaced by a call to the object level. Below, the earlier queries are reworked to show how they would appear in PLL with temporal constraints.

We include in the database *pi* the temporal relationships between the variables which now become global constants. The queries are then standard PLL expressions except that the time variable *t* explicitly appears.

```
pi = ["Davestart" < 890525
      & "Edstart" < 890601
      & "Davestart" < "Edstart"
      & 890615 < "Edend"
      & 890617 < "Daveend" ]

Query:  tree = rewrite("(Davestart <= t
                & t <= Daveend
                & Edstart <= t & t <= Edend
                & 890608 <= t & t <= 890613)",pi) ?
Answer: tree = "(890608  <= t & t <= 890613)"
```

```
Query:  tree = rewrite("(Davestart <= t & t <= 890613
                 & Edstart  <= t & t <= 890613)",pi) ?
Answer: tree = "(Edstart <=t & t <= 890613)"


Query:  tree = rewrite("(Davestart <= t & t <= Daveend
                 & Edstart <= t & t <= Edend)",pi) ?
Answer: tree = "(Edstart <= t
                 & t <= Edend & t <= Daveend)"
```

The big advantage over the previous system is that arithmetic can now easily be performed between these time variables using PLL.

6.4   Negation as Failure

Negation as Failure [10] [21] in mathematical logic can be formalised as: $(\vdash \neg(\vdash \phi))$ meaning that it is provable that ϕ *is not provable*, where ϕ has no free variables. In PLL this can be defined using the metalevel predicate *rewrite*. We first define provable in PLL as a rewrite that rewrites an expression *query* to TRUE assuming that *query* contains no free variables. *Negation as failure* in PLL is then the same as the mathematical logic definition:

```
define provable(query) tobe  ["TRUE"] = rewrite(query) ?

define naf(query) tobe
   query1 = "\"" + query + "\""
   & metaquery = "~ provable(" + query1 + ")"
   & provable(metaquery) ?
```

For this expression to be TRUE, *query* must rewrite to anything but TRUE. Furthermore, for this expression to be computable, all the free variables in *query* must be bound or quantified. These examples:

```
naf("some(x, y) f(x, y)")?        -R->   TRUE
naf("some(x, y) (x = y + 20)")?   -R->   TRUE
naf("2 = 2")?                     -R->   FALSE
naf("2 = 3")?                     -R->   TRUE
naf(x)                            -R->   naf(x)
```

illustrate how this kind of negation doesn't distinguish between something that is never true like $2 = 3$ and something which is simply undefined like $some(x, y)f(x, y)$. The classical negation in PLL allows this distinction. The closed world assumption, that all things that are undefined are false moves this negation closer to classical negation. However, the closed world assumption in traditional logic languages forces the system to be non-monotonic so that answers that were previously FALSE become true as past undefined definitions become defined in the future.

6.4.1 Monotonic PLL

PLL supports a monotonic database. Thus, the situation need never occur where a predicate that is altered changes from giving false to true answers. If our definitions are never to be updated, like factorial, then predicates are defined by closed rewrites as usual in this paper. However, if we know the predicate contains undefined positive or negative information, then we must include a dummy predicate to represent this unknown knowledge.

6.5 Implementation and Performance

If you tried to run $x = y + 10 \& x = 3$ in a traditional logic languages version without delays it would take for ever. Thus PLL could claim a tremendous speed advantage! To achieve the equivalent effect requires much careful programming—especially when constraint technology is used in PLL.

Currently, PLL expressions are represented internally by tree structures. This structure is then interpreted by a C program. Where the operations are large-scale there is no advantage in compilation. However, where arithmetic is involved then the overhead of interpretation becomes large compared with execution and a mapping to an instruction set close to that of the computer becomes essential.

6.6 General Comparison of PLL with other Logic Languages

The table below crudely compares PLL with traditional and new logic languages. Only PLL supports classical negation, expression rewrite, incremental execution, conjunction, separate metalevel and monotonic updating. The others can do all these but not as part of the language. For example, traditional logic language can sometimes return unsolvable list expressions.

Directly Supports:	PLL	PROLOG/CLP($\mathcal{R}$)/CHIP
Classical Negation	YES	NO
Negation by failure	YES	YES
rewrite expressions	YES	Very limited
Constraints	YES	YES
Classical Conjunction	YES	NO
Incremental Execution	YES	NO
Separate Metalevel	YES	NO
Monotonic Updating	YES	NO
Quantifiers	YES	LIMITED
Large Constraints	NOT YET	YES

6.7 PLL and Theorem Proving

The purity of PLL means that programs can be either reduced at the object level, by the PLL rewrite system, or simplified at the metalevel. Because the tautologies of predicate calculus apply, tautologies such as $\forall x \exists y f(xy) \Rightarrow \exists x y f(xy)$ can be used at the metalevel to simplify a PLL expression. Currently, this would be written using metalevel rewrites where the quantifiers are possibly encoded as skolem functions.

7 Conclusion

The original Alvey project aimed to investigate the foundations of logic programming languages and to improve their relationship to the end user. The most tangible result of this study is the Pure Logic Language. The role of PLL is to make the creation of systems cheaper by saving the end user time rather than necessarily offering improved execution speeds. To this end, it currently offers classical logic, incremental execution and constraints.

Whilst PLL cannot solve all problems, it is intended to be the platform from which more specialised problem solvers can be evoked. These could be anything from mundane algorithms for computing a factorial and used at the object level to powerful resolution theorem provers called from the metalevel. Since PLL was never intended for high-speed algorithms the intention is that these would be provided in a suitable library.

ICL intend to exploit this research in the Visible Logic *Eureka* project called VisiLog. This aims to use the improved expressibility provided by mathematical logic as the language underpinning a spreadsheet/icon based system for helping people solve problems.

8 Acknowledgement

PLL is based on work performed mainly under Alvey contracts *IKBS 084 Pure Logic Language* and *IKBS 092 Logic Database Demonstrator*. These contracts involved Imperial College, Edinburgh University, Bradford University and the Turing Institute. The funding by Alvey and ICL and the important contributions of Ian Nairn [16], Peter McBrien[11], David Cooper[12], Pete Slessenger [22], Koos Rommelse[13], Joachim Achtzehnter [1][14] and Joan Travis is gratefully acknowledged. In addition, we received background help from Bill O'Riordan Manager Strategic Systems Technology ICL, and from groups led by Professor B Richards at Edinburgh University, Professor Dov Gabbay at Imperial College and Professor Imad Torsun at Bradford University.

References

[1] J. Achtzehnter. Interval reduction in the pure logic language. Internal report, ICL.

[2] K. R. Apt and M. H. van Emden. Contributions to the theory of logic programming. *JACM*, 29:841–863, 1982.

[3] E. Babb. Performing relational operations by means of specialised hardware. *ACM TODS*, March 1979.

[4] E. Babb. Finite computation principle: An alternative method of adapting resolution for logic programming. In *Proceedings of Logic Programming 83*, Portugal, June 1983.

---

[11] Prototype implementation in C
[12] prototype temporal logic [11]
[13] Engineered implementation in C - mainly used in this paper
[14] prototype constraint technology

[5] E. Babb. The logic language PrologM in database technology and intelligent knowledge based systems. *ICL Technical Journal*, November 1983.

[6] E. Babb. Requirements for large knowledge bases. In *ACM 84—The challenge of the 5th generation*, San Francisco, September 1984.

[7] E. Babb. File correlation unit. *ICL Technical Journal*, November 1985.

[8] E. Babb. Mathematical logic in the large practical world. *ICL Technical Journal*, November 1986.

[9] E. Babb. Pure logic language. *ICL Technical Journal*, May 1989.

[10] K. L. Clark. Negation as failure. In H. Gallaire and J. Minker, editors, *Logic and Data Bases*, pages 293–322. Plenum Press, 1978.

[11] D. Cooper. Temporal operators in PLL. Future systems report, ICL.

[12] The CHIP group. *CHIP version 2.1 Reference manual*. ECRC, Arabella str. 17, D-8000 Munchen 81, West Germany.

[13] J. Jaffar, Michaylov, P. J. Stuckey, and R. H. C. Yap. The CLP($\mathcal{R}$) language and system.

[14] J. W. Lloyd. Directions for metaprogramming. Technical report, Bristol University.

[15] P.J. McBrien. Implementing logic languages by graph rewriting. In A. Dodd, R. Owens, and S. Torrance, editors, *Expanding the horizons: proceedings of the 1st United Kingdom Logic Programming Conference*. Intellect.

[16] I. A. Nairn. Pure logic language based on a rewrite technique. Future systems report, ICL.

[17] Lee Naish. *MuPROLOG Reference manual*.

[18] Lee Naish. Automating control for logic programs. *Journal of Logic Programming*, 2(3), October 1985.

[19] M. J. O'Donnell. *Equational Logic as a programming language*. MIT Press, 1985.

[20] B. Richards and I. Bethke. Temporal databases: an IQ approach. Research Paper EUCCS/RP-19, Edinburgh University, March 1988.

[21] J. C Shepherdson. Negation as failure. II. *Journal of Logic Programming*, 2(3), October 1985.

[22] P. H. Slessenger. Trial distribution manager implementation in PLL. Future systems report, ICL.

[23] Leon Sterling and Ehud Shapiro. *The Art of Prolog*. MIT Press.

[24] M. H. van Emden and J. W. Lloyd. The logical reconstruction of PROLOG II. *Journal of Logic Programming*, 1(2), August 1984.

[25] Pascal van Hentenryck. *Constraint Satisfaction in Logic Programming*. MIT Press.

PR: a Logic for Practical Reasoning

Tim Flannagan

Abstract

We construct a formal logic for practical reasoning (PR) from an analysis of Kenny's informal 'logic of satisfactoriness' [4], which is intended to preserve 'satisfactoriness' in passing from premises to conclusions just as deductive logic preserves logical truth. PR is intended primarily but not solely as a logic for 'planning' in artificial intelligence.

Whereas Kenny's logic argues to sufficient means to ends, PR argues to both necessary means and to sufficient means. It models intuitive sufficiency as material implication and satisfactoriness as relative consistency. Unlike Kenny's logic it has a precise definition of defeasibility.

PR extends first order logic with the following rule of inference which we call *co-modus ponens*. From G (understood as a goal) and $C \rightarrow G$, infer C, provided that C and G are jointly consistent relative to X (the non-logical axioms). PR has the following properties.

1. If A is a deductive consequence of X, then it is derivable in PR from X but the converse is false.

2. If A is derivable from X in PR, then it is consistent with X, and the converse is false.

3. PR is thus complete and consistent, and, on account of 2, we say that it is *relatively sound*.

4. The separate derivability in PR of two sentences from a set X does not imply that their conjunction is derivable. It is thus possible for A and $\neg A$ to be derivable without this resulting in a contradiction.

5. PR is a non-enthymematic, defeasible logic and hence strongly non-monotonic.

1   Introduction

We construct a formal logic for practical reasoning (PR) from an analysis
of Kenny's informal 'logic of satisfactoriness' [4]. The origin of Kenny's
logic is with Aristotle for whom it was a logic for deriving actions, as in the
argument

> Men are to march
> I am a man
> Therefore I march

as well as a logic for deriving decisions to act, as in the following variant of
one of Kenny's examples.

> I want to be in San Francisco by noon
> If I take the 11.30 train, I'll be in San Francisco by noon
> So I'll take the 11.30 train

Now there is clearly a difference between an action and a decision to act
but Aristotle considered both of the above conclusions to represent actions.
In fact, he considered them to *be* actions, so if he considered that the
conclusion of a piece of practical reasoning must always be an action, as
it seems that he did [1], then he was surely wrong because something may
prevent an action from taking place immediately but not limit the feasibility
of a decision to act at some future time. Kenny ([4] p.98) maintains that
'the correct account (of Aristotle's position) seems to be that the conclusion
of a piece of practical reasoning is the description of an action to be done'.
However, whatever difference there is between an action and a decision to
act seems to be inessential to Aristotle's account of practical reasoning.
For example, the conclusion of the second argument above could equally
well have the same form as the conclusion of the first argument: it could
be 'I do A' instead of 'I will do A'. For the sake of simplicity, then, PR
makes no formal distinction between actions and decisions to act. What
interests us about the above arguments is their clear difference of form and
the difference in the relationships between the premises and the conclusions.
By analogy with the standard terminology of formal logic, Hare [3] describes
the conclusion of the first argument as a necessary condition to fulfilling
the given command or want and he describes the conclusion of the second
argument as a sufficient condition for fulfilling it.

2   Kenny's Logic of Satisfactoriness

Consider the second argument. If, like Kenny ([4] p.70), we ignore modalities and loosely translate the 'if...then' of the second premise as a material implication, the argument can be written as an instance of the following schematic rule of inference.

$$\frac{G, C \rightarrow G}{C}$$

We call this schema *co-modus ponens* because it is a kind of converse of *modus ponens*. It is intended to indicate that one passes from the premises G and $C \rightarrow G$ to the conclusion C, where G is considered as a goal.

Kenny takes this form of practical reasoning as the basis of his 'logic of satisfactoriness', which is designed to preserve 'satisfactoriness' in passing from premises to conclusions, just as deductive logic preserves truth. Thus he refers to *co-modus ponens* as the '*modus ponens* of practical reasoning' ([4] p.70) but neither he nor Hare has a name for it as a formal rule of inference perhaps because the logic of satisfactoriness is not a formal (mathematical) system.

In deductive logic, of course, *co-modus ponens*, as stated above, is invalid. It is called the *fallacy of affirming the consequent*. However, neither Kenny's logic nor our logic PR is based entirely on deduction. In fact, deduction has no part at all in Kenny's logic.

In PR, therefore, *co-modus ponens* is only to be applied under a certain proviso which we describe in the section below on the formal properties of PR.

Now, given the premise $C \rightarrow G$, the conclusion C is deductively sufficient for G but it is not deductively necessary for G since $G \rightarrow C$ is not explicitly a premise. However, there is another, less formal sense in which C is not necessary to G, namely, the sense that it is not necessarily the only condition which is deductively sufficient for G. This can be seen informally from the train example above. The conclusion of the argument (I'll take the 11.30 train) is sufficient to achieve the goal but it isn't necessary because if there is a 10.30 train, I could take it and still be in San Francisco by noon.

In contrast to the formal notion of sufficiency, as expressed in a sentence of the form

$$C \rightarrow G,$$

let us say that a sentence like

If I take the 11.30 train, I'll be in San Francisco by noon.

expresses the intuitive sufficiency of the antecedent

> I take the 11.30 train

for the consequent

> I'll be in San Francisco by noon.

Conversely, we obtain intuitive necessity.

There is thus a parallel between formal sufficiency and necessity on the one hand and intuitive sufficiency and necessity on the other. The logic of satisfactoriness can therefore be described as a logic for deriving intuitively sufficient practical means to given practical ends[1]. Likewise, *co-modus ponens* can be described as a rule for deriving formally sufficient conditions for sentences which are to be intuitively understood as goals.

Now both Kenny ([4] pp. 89, 95) and Hare ([3] pp.59–73) are clear that the logic of satisfactoriness is only a part of practical reasoning and that, among other things such as the ability to weight pros and cons and reasoning about commands ([4] p. 90), practical reasoning in real life involves reasoning to necessary means to ends, as in the following example.

> I am to catch a plane at 7.00
> If I am to catch a plane at 7.00, I must be at the airport before 7.00
> So I will be at the airport before 7.00

Reasoning to necessary means or the 'logic of satisfaction' as Kenny calls it ([4] p. 98), is analogous to deductive reasoning. For example, leaving aside modalities etc., the plane argument above could be formalised as an instance of modus ponens:

$$\frac{G, G \rightarrow C}{C}.$$

Kenny, however, is not concerned with reasoning about pros and cons, the logic of commands or deductive logic, which he calls *theoretical logic*, for he holds that the essence of practical (as opposed to theoretical) reasoning is to argue, as in the train example, from satisfactory goals to satisfactory

---

[1] The use of the word 'practical' here is not meant to suggest that actual actions are derived. Accuracy dictates therefore that we should perhaps follow Kenny and talk about 'descriptions of practical means'. Brevity, on the other hand, dictates that we shouldn't.

(and sufficient) means to goals. Thus, he calls his logic a logic for practical reasoning.

Now it is clear from Kenny's account of the logic of satisfactoriness that there is more to practical reasoning and the notion of satisfactoriness than the derivation of intuitively sufficient means.

3 Satisfactoriness and Consistency

Kenny does not define satisfactoriness but that in itself is not a bad thing, for truth and falsity are not defined in classical logic either. However, their assignments to propositional truth tables and hence to model-theoretic interpretations of sentences are defined in classical logic and Kenny provides no way of assigning satisfactoriness to goals or conclusions. He writes ([4] p. 82):

> It is impossible to base the logic of satisfactoriness on satisfactoriness-tables, because satisfactoriness, unlike truth, is a relative notion[2].

Actually, a formal assignment to sentences of satisfactoriness or unsatisfactoriness (to imitate the true-false contrast of classical logic) would seem to require Kenny's logic to be a formal, mathematical system but Kenny does not even provide an informal account of how satisfactoriness is to be attributed to sentences in general. He merely argues that if a goal is satisfactory in relation to given facts, then a piece of practical reasoning, as typified by the train example, preserves satisfactoriness if it results in a conclusion which is known from the facts to be a sufficient means for the attainment of the goal and if the conclusion is consistent with the facts. In this case, he argues, the conclusion is necessarily satisfactory in relation to the facts and the goal together.

Thus, satisfactoriness does not exist *simpliciter*. A goal is satisfactory only in relation to a given body of information and may be unsatisfactory in relation to another body of information, particularly a more extensive one. Similarly, a means to a goal is only satisfactory in relation to the goal and the given information together. It may be unsatisfactory in relation to the same goal and different information or vice versa. Of course, if the goal

---

[2] On the face of it, this is an astonishing thing to say about truth. However, Kenny is speaking about logical truth and he seems to mean that the logical truth of a proposition does not depend on the logical truth of a set of premises. Whilst this is true, it is not true in general to say that logical truth is not a relative notion, for the truth of a sentence is not defined except in relation to a given model.

is unsatisfactory in relation to the given information, then every sufficient means to the goal and, for that matter, every necessary means to it is unsatisfactory in relation to the information combined with the goal, but it is not necessarily unsatisfactory in relation only to the information.

For example, imagine yourself consulting a timetable of trains between Palo Alto and San Francisco and that you want to be in San Francisco by noon. The timetable might show that a train leaves Palo Alto at 11.30 a.m. In this case, your goal is satisfactory because it is achievable according to the timetable, and a decision to take the 11.30 train would be a satisfactory conclusion because the timetable allows it and because it would enable you to achieve your goal. On the other hand, if the 11.30 were to stop at every station and you wanted to take a non-stop train, then a decision to take the 11.30 would be unsatisfactory relative to your goal but not unsatisfactory relative to the timetable.

In the above example, the informal notion of one thing being consistent relative to another or, as we often say, consistent *with* it can clearly be substituted for satisfactoriness. For instance, the goal of being in San Francisco by noon is consistent with the given timetable but not necessarily consistent with an extension of it. Likewise the decision to take the 11.30 train is consistent with the timetable and the goal together but although a decision to take the 1p.m. train might not be inconsistent with the timetable, it is inconsistent with the goal. Similarly, a decision to take a non-stop train at 11.30 is consistent with the goal but it might be inconsistent with the timetable because there might not be such a train.

By considering the timetable and the goals and possible conclusions as being sentences in some formal mathematical language, it is a trivial matter to translate this informal notion of relative consistency, and hence the notion of satisfactoriness, into the formal notion of relative consistency. This is defined as follows. If X and Y are sets of sentences in classical logic, then Y is consistent relative to X if the consistency of X implies the consistency of Y.

Thus, relative consistency captures much of Kenny's intuitive sense of satisfactoriness and seems the obvious and natural formal analogue of it. This, then, is how we model satisfactoriness in PR.

As Hare and Kenny agree, material implication is also the obvious analogue of the intuitive 'if...then' relation. In general, of course, this analogy has limitations, particularly because 'if...then' often involves the notion of cause. On the other hand, practical reasoning often, if not always, involves cause, as in sentences like

If I take the 11.30 train, I'll be in San Francisco by noon

A fuller account of 'if...then' versus material implication can be found in [2].

As explained in [2], the inexactness of the mathematical modelling of intuitive concepts is to be expected in the light of the imprecision of the one and the limitation on appropriate formalisms for the other. It is not only common mathematical practice, it is precisely through being inexact and not capturing all the intuitions of the intuitive notion that mathematics is able to proceed and even increase our understanding of the intuitive concepts. For example, the real number line is used to represent time as well as numbers, and though some lingustic considerations, for example, indicate that it might not be the perfect representation of time, it has proven an extremely valuable one in mathematics generally. Similarly, if Newton had not ignored many of the philosophical and religious intuitions of infinity and provided his elegant, finitary definitions of an infinite limit, the calculus would likely not exist as we know it.

Kenny himself acknowledges ([4] p. 82), though he does not admit theoretical reasoning to a central place in practical reasoning, that

> ...because of the mirror image relation between the logics of satisfaction and satisfactoriness (between *modus ponens* and *co-modus ponens*) it is possible to test the validity of inferences in the logic of satisfactoriness by appeal to truth tables and quantificational truths.

PR therefore models 'if...then' as material implication and satisfactoriness as relative consistency. Now the latter, in fact, assumes the former, so the adequacy of relative consistency as a model of satisfactoriness accordingly justifies the modelling of 'if...then' by material implication, at least in the context of PR.

4   Defeasibility

In the train example, the conclusion (I'll take the 11.30), and thus the logic itself, is said to be *defeasible* because the addition of new premises or goals can force the withdrawal of the conclusion in the sense of preventing it from being drawn. To take another of Kenny's examples, if we add the premises

I want to be sure of a seat
P: If I take the 11.30, I won't be sure of a seat
If I take the 10.30, I'll be in San Francisco by noon

then I would not conclude that I'll take the 11.30 because it would be inconsistent with the new premises. Instead, I would conclude that I'll take the 10.30 train. Defeasibility thus makes the logic non-monotonic because non-monotonicity requires that there are extensions of the premises from which the previous conclusions cannot be drawn.

Now defeasibility is not a property of deductive reasoning because if a sentence A can be deduced from a set of premises X, then it can be deduced from every extension of X. This is another reason why Kenny considers the logic of satisfactoriness to be central to practical reasoning. He also argues that it is important to considerations of the freedom of the will, which is one of his principal concerns, but that is another issue.

Kenny's account of the logic of satisfactoriness is initially plausible but he is not fully explicit about his interpretations of either satisfactoriness, consistency or defeasibility. Moreover, the exclusion of deduction from his logic leads to intuitive anomalies.

Consider satisfactoriness. It follows from his account of it that the satisfactoriness of a sentence in relation to a set of premises is non-monotonic downwards but this simply isn't brought out. Take the train example again. If there is an 11.30 train from Palo Alto to San Francisco, then the decision to take it is satisfactory in relation to the timetable and the goal together. However, if the 11.30 were scratched from the timetable, then, taking the 11.30 is no longer sufficient for arriving in San Francisco by noon. For this reason alone, the decision to take the 11.30 would be unsatisfactory in relation to the reduced timetable.

Thus, Kenny assumes that defeasibility arises only from the addition of premises, not their removal.

Taking the example further, the decision to take the 11.30 train would surely be unsatisfactory on the grounds that there is no such train in the reduced timetable, but, in Kenny's sense, the decision is not unsatisfactory on that score because it is not logically inconsistent with the timetable. For that matter, of course, the sentence

If I take the 11.30 train, I'll be in San Francisco by noon

is also logically consistent with the timetable and the goal together, assuming, that is, that modalities are omitted. On the other hand, if Kenny were to require, for example, that, in order to figure in an application of *co-modus ponens*, the above sentence were not to be merely consistent with the timetable but deducible from it, then the sentence would fail that requirement, and the decision to take the 11.30 would cease to be a satisfactory conclusion. In fact, it could not be drawn. It is therefore unclear what Kenny intends to be the logical relationship between premises X and the specified conditionals $C \rightarrow G$ in applications of *co-modus ponens*.

Kenny's interpretation of the notion of logical consistency is also incomplete. He insists that deduction has no part in the logic of satisfactoriness but, if this be so, then he may regard a set of sentences as inconsistent in the model-theoretic sense that there is no model of it, but he cannot regard an inconsistency as enabling, within his logic, the derivation of every sentence, for such a derivation implies *modus ponens*. For example, let us suppose we have a semantic contradiction in the form of a pair of sentences $\{A, \neg A\}$. Certainly the implication

$$A \wedge \neg A \rightarrow B$$

is classically valid for every B. In order to derive B within the logic, however, *modus ponens* would need to be used with $A \wedge \neg A$ as the antecedent. We would also need to know that $A \wedge \neg A$ could be derived from the pair $\{A, \neg A\}$, as it is in classical logic.

Given his exclusion of deduction, there is an anomalous aspect of Kenny's notion of defeasibility. Consider again the premises **P** above. Certainly the sentence

I'll take the 11.30 train

is intuitively inconsistent with **P** and, if we ignore modalities and represent **P** as

$$A$$
$$B \rightarrow \neg A$$
$$C \rightarrow G$$

then B is model-theoretically inconsistent with $\{A, B \rightarrow \neg A\}$. However, although we cannot therefore infer B (I'll take the 11.30 train) in Kenny's logic, and although we can infer C (I'll take the 10.30 train), we cannot infer $\neg B$ (I will not take the 11.30 train) because deduction is prohibited. Kenny does not bring this out. Clearly no inconsistencies would be introduced by admitting deduction.

Given that deductive logic is considered by both Kenny and Hare to be a legitimate part of practical reasoning, we have decided that the logic PR should extend Kenny's logic by admitting deduction. PR thus includes the logic of satisfactoriness and the logic of satisfaction. It argues to sufficient means to ends and to necessary means to ends. It also permits a precise definition of defeasibility and is defeasible in those terms.

5   The Logic PR

PR ignores the modalities of goals and conclusions not in the mistaken belief that they are unimportant but because we wish to formulate a simple but sound formal logic for practical reasoning which can handle *co-modus ponens* as well as *modus ponens.*

PR thus extends first order logic by the addition of the *co-modus ponens* rule

$$\frac{G, C \to G}{C} \operatorname{mod} X$$

which is now to be read as follows. If G and $C \to G$ are both in the set X and if C is consistent relative to X, then, since G is considered a goal, conclude C as a subgoal of G and add it to X so as to be able to derive subgoals of C by further applications of the rule. Unlike *modus ponens,* therefore *co-modus ponens* can only be used under a proviso, namely,

$$rel - con(X, C),$$

which says that C is consistent relative to X, that is, if X is consistent, then so is $X \cup \{C\}$.

We are not concerned to merely deduce G from X for G follows trivially from X since it is a member of it, that is, $X \vdash_{PC} G$, where PC denotes the predicate calculus. Intuitively speaking, applications of *co-modus ponens* yield, on the basis of X, sufficient and satisfactory means to satisfactory goals in X. Thus, a sufficient means C for a goal G must not only be sufficient for G relative to X but C and G must be jointly consistent relative to X. That is, the set $\{G, C\}$ ust be consistent relative to X. Now G is assumed to be a member of X, so it is certainly consistent relative to X and $rel - con(X, C)$ implies $rel - con(X, \{G, C\})$. The fact that $C \to G$ is also in X declares C to be a sufficient means to G relative to X but we need to know that C is consistent relative to X before adopting it as a satisfactory means to G. Hence the proviso that C must be consistent relative to X.

Notation 1   *1. A sentence C is a* sufficient means *to G relative to X if $C \to G$ is consistent relative to X, i.e. $rel - con(X, C \to G)$;*

2. A sentence A is satisfactory *in relation to X if $rel - con(X, A)$.*

Instead of being the fallacy of affirming the consequent, as it was in the un-provisional form in which it was introduced earlier, *co-modus ponens* is now logically valid and the proof of its validity is trivial, for if $rel - con(X, C)$, then it is logically permissible to assume C, provided X is consistent. Furthermore, if $C \to G$ is in X, then

$$X \cup \{C\} \vdash_{\text{PC}} G.$$

If X is inconsistent, then this is vacuously true.

We now define a derivation in PR.

Definition 2 *Let X be a set of sentences in a first order language $\mathcal{L}$ and let A be a sentence in $\mathcal{L}$. A finite sequence $\mathbf{D} = \langle A_1, \ldots, A_n \rangle$ is called a* derivation *of A from X in PR if A_n is A and for each $i = 1 \ldots n$ one of the following holds.*

1. *A_i is a logical axiom;*

2. *A_i is a member of X;*

3. *A_i follows by* modus ponens *from A_j and A_k for some j and $k < i$;*

4. *A_i follows by* co-modus ponens *from A_j and $A_i \to A_j$ for some $j < i$, where $A_i \to A_j$ is a member of $X \cap \mathbf{D}_{i-1}$, $\mathbf{D}_{i-1} = \{A_1, \ldots, A_{i-1}\}$, and $rel - con(X \cup \mathbf{D}_{i-1}, A_i)$.*

We now establish some elementary properties of PR. $X \vdash_{\text{PR}} A$ will denote that there is a derivation of A from X in PR.

First, note that A's being derivable from X in PR does not imply that it is derivable from X in the predicate calculus PC. It does, however, imply what it should imply in the context of practical reasoning, namely, that A is a sufficient or necessary means to a goal which is derivable from X and that, being consistent with X, it is also a satisfactory conclusion. We thus note the following two facts.

Fact 1 *If A is a deductive consequence of X, i.e. $X \vdash_{PC} A$, then $X \vdash_{PR} A$ but the converse is false.*

The proof is immediate from the definition of PR.

Since the predicate calculus is complete, that is, if every model of X is a model of A, then $X \vdash_{PC} A$, it follows trivially from the first fact that PR is also complete.

Fact 2 *If $\langle A_1 \ldots A_n \rangle$ is a derivation of A from X in PR, then $\{A_1, \ldots, A_n\}$ is consistent with X. In particular, A is consistent with X. Taking X as the empty set, it follows trivially that PR is consistent.*

Proof: Let $\mathbf{D}_i = \{A_1 \ldots A_i\}$. We show by induction on i that $rel - con(X, \mathbf{D}_i)$. The rest follows trivially.

If $i = 1$ or $i = 2$, the result is trivial since A_1 and A_2 are either logical axioms or members of X. Assume the result for $i - 1$, i.e. that $rel - con(X, \mathbf{D}_{i-1})$, and consider A_i.

If A_i is a member of X, then $X \cup \mathbf{D}_i = X \cup \mathbf{D}_{i-1}$ and the result is trivial. Now the union of a consistent set of sentences with any set of logical axioms is consistent, so if A_i is a logical axiom and $X \cup \mathbf{D}_{i-1}$ is consistent, then $X \cup \mathbf{D}_i$ is also consistent. Thus, $rel - con(X, \mathbf{D}_{i-1})$ implies $rel - con(X, \mathbf{D}_i)$. By the induction hypothesis it follows that $rel - con(X, \mathbf{D}_i)$. If A_i follows by *modus ponens* from A_j and A_k for some j and $k < i$, then A_j and A_k are members of D_{i-1}, and, trivially, $rel - con(X \cup \mathbf{D}_{i-1}, X \cup \mathbf{D}_{i-1} \cup \{A_i\})$ i.e. $rel - con(X \cup \mathbf{D}_{i-1}, X \cup \mathbf{D}_i)$. Since $rel - con(X, \mathbf{D}_{i-1})$, it follows that $rel - con(X, \mathbf{D}_i)$. Now suppose that A_i follows by *co-modus ponens* from A_j and $A_i \rightarrow A_j$ for some $j < i$, where $A_i \rightarrow A_j$ is a member of $X \cap \mathbf{D}_{i-1}$ and $rel - con(X \cup \mathbf{D}_{i-1}, A_i)$. By the induction hypothesis, $rel - con(X, \mathbf{D}_{i-1})$, so $rel - con(X, \mathbf{D}_{i-1} \cup \{A_i\})$, i.e. $rel - con(X, \mathbf{D}_i)$, as required.   □

6   The relative soundness of PR

Fact 2 does not imply that PR is sound, i.e. that if $X \vdash_{PR} A$, then every model of X is a model of A. It tells us that if $X \vdash_{PR} A$ and X has a model $\mathcal{M}$, then there is also a model $\mathcal{M}^*$ of $X \cup \{A\}$, but Fact 2 says nothing about a relationship between $\mathcal{M}$ and $\mathcal{M}^*$. We thus say that PR is *relatively sound*.

The proof of Fact 2 shows that, in a derivation $\langle A_1, \ldots, A_n \rangle$ of A from X, $\mathbf{D}_{i-1}$ is consistent relative to X for each $i = 1, \ldots n$, and that A_i is consistent relative to $X \cup \mathbf{D}_{i-1}$. A_i is thus consistent relative to X and extends $\mathbf{D}_{i-1}$ consistently to $\mathbf{D}_i$. In addition, if A_i follows by *modus ponens* from members A_j and $A_j \rightarrow A_i$ of $\mathbf{D}_{i-1}$, then, relative to $X \cup \mathbf{D}_{i-1}$ and hence relative to X, A_i is a necessary consequence of A_j. Similarly, if A_i follows by *co-modus ponens* from A_j and $A_i \rightarrow A_j$, where $A_i \rightarrow A_j$ is a member of $X \cap \mathbf{D}_{i-1}$ and $rel - con(X \cup \mathbf{D}_{i-1}, A_i)$, then, relative to X, A_i is a sufficient condition for A_j. Intuitively, then, each A_i is satisfactory or feasible relative to X. We use the words 'feasible' and 'satisfactory' interchangeably but note, incidentally, that Kenny means more by 'satisfactory' than we do because he is concerned not only with sufficiency but with the satisfactoriness of *fiats*, that is, commands, imperatives or expressions of intention.

Notice that Fact 2 leaves the way open for both a sentence A and its negation $\neg A$ to be derivable from X and, in general, for incompatible statements to be derivable from X. This does not mean, however, that everything that is consistent with X is derivable from it.

Fact 3 *The consistency of A with X does not imply that $X \vdash_{PR} A$.*

Proof: Take X as $\{B\}$. Then A is consistent with X but it is not derivable from it since X contains no sentence of the form $A \rightarrow C$. $\qquad\square$

Since it reasons to satisfactory conclusions which are either sufficient or necessary means to satisfactory ends, PR seems to be an appropriate logic for 'planning' in AI. Fact 2 means, incidentally, that PR illuminates what McDermott[5] claims is a common misunderstanding about the nature of AI planning, namely, that it is the business of planning to deduce outright that goals will succeed.

A goal G is not simply deduced in PR from a set of premises X but it can be deduced from a consistent extension of X on the basis of the join consistency with X of G and a set of sufficiency statements of the form $A \rightarrow B$. For example, let Y be the set of sentences

$$
\begin{aligned}
&G \\
&C \rightarrow G \\
&B \rightarrow C \\
&G \rightarrow F
\end{aligned}
$$

and assume that Y is consistent with X. Then

$$X \cup Y \vdash_{PR} C,$$

provided C is consistent with $X \cup Y$,

$$X \cup Y \cup \{C\} \vdash_{PR} B,$$

provided B is consistent with $X \cup Y\{C\}$, and although it is certainly true that

$$X \cup Y \cup \{B\} \vdash_{\text{PC}} G,$$

all these steps involve meta-level inferences of relative consistency.

Thus, a belief that goals can be deduced outright in PR would overlook the important and ubiquitous role of relative consistency in mathematical logic and confuse logical inference with object-level deduction.

Definition 3 *Sentences A and B are* jointly derivable *from X if there is a derivation of a sentence C from X in which both A and B appear. Of course, C could be A or B.*

Fact 4 *Sentences A and $\neg A$ may be separately derivable from a set X in PR but they are not jointly derivable. Nor is their conjunction $A \wedge \neg A$ derivable.*

Proof: Take X as the set of propositions

$$G$$
$$A \;\rightarrow\; G$$
$$\neg A \;\rightarrow\; G$$

Each of the sets $X \cup \{A\}$ and $X \cup \{\neg A\}$ is clearly consistent so by *co-modus ponens*, with G as a goal, we can conclude both A and $\neg A$ separately.

On the other hand, if A and $\neg A$ are jointly derivable from X, then there is a derivation **D** in which they both appear. This is impossible by Fact 2. Similarly, $A \wedge \neg A$ is inconsistent with every set of sentences, so it cannot be derived from any set X.   □

Note that, independently of Fact 2, A and $\neg A$ are jointly derivable from a set X if and only if $A \wedge \neg A$ is derivable from X. Thus, suppose A and $\neg A$ are jointly derivable from X and appear together in **D**. By using the logical axiom

$$A \rightarrow (\neg A \rightarrow (A \wedge \neg A))$$

and applying *modus ponens* twice, **D** can be extended to a derivation of $A \wedge \neg A$. Conversely, if $A \wedge \neg A$ is derivable, then by using *modus ponens* and the logical axioms

$$(A \wedge \neg A) \rightarrow A$$

and

$$(A \wedge \neg A) \rightarrow \neg A$$

A and $\neg A$ are jointly derivable.

PR is thus a logic in which contradictory conclusions are derivable from a set X without this leading to deductive contradictions.

Intuitively speaking, the above example would mean that if G were a goal, then it could be achieved whether one were to do A or $\neg A$, i.e., it could be achieved irrespective of what other actions were taken.

Fact 3 has the following corollary.

Corollary 1 *In general, the separate derivability of A and B does not imply the joint derivability of A and B or the derivability of $A \wedge B$.*

This situation should be contrasted with the fact of classical logic that the separate consistency of two sentences A and B with a set of sentences X does not imply their joint consistency with X. That is, the existence of a model of $X \cup \{A\}$ and of a model of $X \cup \{B\}$ does not imply the existence of a model of $X \cup \{A, B\}$. This was one of the main facts motivating the development of PR. The other key facts were that relative consistency plays a vital part in formal logic and that it is non-monotonic. That is, $rel - con(X, A)$ does not imply $rel - con(X', A)$ when $X' \supset X$.

Fact 5 *The derivability relation in PR is* non-monotonic (upwards). *That is, $X \vdash_{PR} A$ does not imply $X' \vdash_{PR} A$ when $X' \supset X$.*

Proof: By Fact 2, $X \vdash_{PR} A$ implies that A is consistent with X but it does not imply that A is consistent with X'. It therefore doesn't imply that A is derivable from X'. □

Fact 6 *The derivability relation in PR is* non-monotonic downwards. *That is, $X' \vdash_{PR} A$ does not imply $X \vdash_{PR} A$ when $X' \supset X$.*

Proof: Take X as $\{C\}$ and X' as $\{C, A \to C\}$. Then $X \vdash_{PR} A$ but A is not a consequence of X. □

Fact 5 can also be proven from the definition of a derivation in PR. The critical case is when A_i follows by *co-modus ponens*. In this case, A_i is consistent $X \cup \mathbf{D_{i-1}}$ but this doesn't imply that it is consistent with $X \cup X' \cup \mathbf{D_{i-1}}$ when X' is non-empty.

Intuitively, then, A being a consequent of X means that, on the basis of X alone, A is a feasible course of action to ensure a given goal but this feasibility may not only cease in the face of more or fewer premises or goals but may be strongly denied in the sense that the negation of A might then be feasible.

We now define defeasibility.

Definition 4 *If $X \vdash_{PR} A$, then A is a* defeasible *consequence of X if there is a set of sentences X' such that $X' \supset X$, X' is consistent relative to X and A is inconsistent with X'. We say that X' defeats A.*

Note that if $X \vdash_{PC} A$, $X' \supset X$ and A is inconsistent with X', then $X' \vdash_{PC} \neg A$, A is not derivable from X' by Fact 2 and X' must be a proper extension of X, for otherwise $X \vdash_{PC} \neg A$ and, by Fact 2, A is not derivable from X.

Notice also that it would not be enough to define the defeasibility of A by saying that there is a relatively consistent extension X' of X such that $X' \vdash_{PR} \neg A$, for by Fact 4 the derivability of $\neg A$ does not by itself imply that A is not derivable, and we certainly want A to be non-derivable in X'.

We could, of course, adopt a weaker definition of defeasibility by saying that A is a defeasible consequence of X if $X \vdash_{PR} A$ and if there is a set of sentences X' such that $X' \supset X$, X' is consistent relative to X and A is not a consequence of X'. This is analogous to Kenny's notion of defeasibility. It is a strictly weaker notion than the one we have adopted because not being a consequence of X' does not imply being inconsistent with it. The inconsistency of A with X' is not even implied by A not being derivable from X' and $\neg A$ being derivable from X'.

Definition 5 *X is PR-complete with respect to A if $X \vdash_{PR} A$ and A is not a defeasible consequence of X.*

Fact 7 *If $X' \vdash_{PR} A$ for every relatively consistent extension X' of X, including X itself, then X is PR-complete w.r.t. A.*

Proof: If $X' \vdash_{PR} A$, then A is consistent with X' by Fact 2, so it cannot be a defeasible consequence of X.   □

We use the prefix 'PR' before the word 'complete' in order to avoid confusion with the notion of completeness in classical logic. By contrast, a set of sentences X is complete in the predicate calculus with respect to a sentence A if either $X \vdash_{PC} A$ or $X \vdash_{PC} \neg A$. Thus, X being PR-complete w.r.t. A does not mean that either $X \vdash_{PR} A$ or $X \vdash_{PR} \neg A$, for both are possible simultaneously. Intuitively it means that X contains no unstated premises with which A is inconsistent and that X also presupposes nothing with which A is inconsistent. For example, there must be no unstated goals to be satisfied by A. By an unstated premise we mean, of course, a statement which does not yet appear in X and cannot be deduced from X but is nevertheless consistent with it. If there were such a premise, it could be consistently added to X and, by Fact 2, A could no longer be derived.

Notice that A being a defeasible consequence of X does not mean that X is enthymematic w.r.t. A. X being enthymematic w.r.t. A means that it has a non-empty set X' of presuppositions or unstated premises and that X is deducible from $X \cup X'$. Certainly, if $X \vdash_{PR} A$ there is a trivially consistent extension of X from which A is deducible, namely, $X \cup \{A\}$ but A being derivable from X does not mean that it is an unspoken premise or a presupposition. It is simply unnecessary to seek a consistent extension of X from which C is non-trivially deducible. For example, if X is a set $\{G, C \rightarrow G\}$, then C is consistent with X and this consistency is a logically sufficient reason to conclude C. C being explicitly sufficient for G is a further reason to conclude it.

Of course, consequences of a set X are not necessarily defeasible. In particular, deductive consequences of X are not defeasible, for if $X \vdash_{PC} A$, then A is consistent with every relatively consistent extension of X. Here too, of course, there is no sense in which X is enthymematic w.r.t. A.

Note that there generally do exist defeasible consequences of a set X because X can generally be consistently extended to include goals or information with which previous conclusions are inconsistent. Again, the train example illustrates this. From the set of sentences

> I want to be in San Francisco by noon
> If I take the 11.30 train, I'll be in San Francisco by noon

we could conclude by *co-modus ponens* that I'll take the 11.30 train. On the other hand if, à la Kenny, we add to the premises the statements

> I want to be sure of a seat
> If I take the 11.30 I won't be sure of a seat

then, in contrast to what is permissible in Kenny's logic, we could deduce that I won't take the 11.30. By Fact 2, we could therefore not conclude from the extended premises that I would take the 11.30 train. A formal analogue of this is as follows.

Let X be the set of statements

$$G$$
$$C \;\rightarrow\; G$$

Then $X \cup \{C\}$ is consistent and $X \vdash_{PR} C$. If X' is obtained from X by adding the sentences

$$S$$
$$C \;\rightarrow\; \neg S$$

then $X' \vdash_{PC} \neg C$ so $X' \vdash_{PR} \neg C$ and, by Fact 2, C is not derivable from X.

Since given premises generally have defeasible consequences, we say that PR is a *defeasible* logic. Notice that the defeasibility of PR comes about essentially through *co-modus ponens* and because derivability is defined in terms of relative consistency.

Defeasibility is clearly stronger than non-monotonicity because the latter only requires that $X \vdash_{PR} A$ does not imply $X' \vdash_{PR} A$ when $X' \supset X$.

PR is thus a non-monotonic logic but since defeasibility means that conclusions can not only be withdrawn from relatively consistent extensions of the premises but that their negations may be deducible from them, we say that PR is *strongly non-monotonic*.

7 Conclusion

PR is not intended only as a logic for AI planning. It has implications for AI generally where sufficient means and necessary means to given ends are at issue. It is a strongly non-monotonic logic, stronger in fact than other non-monotonic logics such as negation as failure, which withdraws conclusions without being able to negate them except enthymematically. Roughly speaking, Negation as Failure has the property that if a query Q succeeds in a program P and fails in $P' \supset P$, then $\neg Q$ cannot be derived from P' except enthymematically, though we do know exactly what is the set of sentences that is consistent with P' and can be added to it so as to derive $\neg Q$. PR is fully first order and, unlike circumscription, it is only first order. It is non-enthymematic and it allows the derivation of incompatible sentences without this leading to inconsistency. It also has an ancient beginning.

References

[1] Aristotle. *De Motu Animalium*.

[2] T. B. Flannagan. Fiat lux: A reply to McDermott's 'a critique of pure reason'. *Computational Intelligence*. To appear.

[3] R. M. Hare. *Practical Inference*. London, 1971.

[4] A. Kenny. *Will, Freedom and Power*. Blackwell, 1975.

[5] D. McDermott. A critique of pure reason. Manuscript.

A Temporal Logic Programming Machine [Modal and Temporal Logic Programming, Part 2]

D. M. Gabbay*

Abstract

This paper introduces a sensible practical logic programming approach to handling time and modality. The approach is based on direct use of time operators rather than on simulation. Intuitively we propose an indexed system of Prolog programs controlled by a master metaprogram which handles their relationships and interactions.

1 Introduction and Background

This paper is a continuation of Modal and Temporal Logic Programming I [7]. It can however be read independently. The essential features needed are summarised in this introduction.

The purpose of this paper is twofold:

1. To present a practical sensible logic programming machine for handling time and modality.

2. To present a general framework for extending logic programming to non-classical logics.

*Research partially supported by SERC project "Metatem" GR/F 28526 and by Esprit Cost 13 project "Logical Techniques in Knowledge Representation". I am grateful to A. Galton and L. Lazarte for helpful criticism.

(1) is the main task of this paper. It is done within the framework of (2). The ideas behind our approach have already been discussed in Part 1 of this paper and the reader is referred to Part 1 for a fuller discussion.

Horn clause logic programming has been generalised in essentially two major ways;

1. Using the metalevel features of ordinary Horn clause logic to handle time while keeping the syntactical language essentially the same.

2. Enriching the syntax of the language with new symbols and introducing additional computation rules for the new symbols.

The first method is basically a simulation. We use the expressive power of ordinary Horn clause logic to talk about the new features. The *Demo* predicate, the *Hold* predicate and other metapredicates play a significant role.

The second method is more direct. The additional computational rules of the second method can be broadly divided into two:

(2.1) Rewrites

(2.2) Subcomputations

The rewrites have to do with simplifying the new syntax according to some rules (basically eliminating the new symbols and reducing goals and data to the old Horn clause language) and the subcomputations are the new computations which arise from the reductions.

Part 1 of this paper [7] examined the possibilities of handling time in Logic Programming. It examined the first approach and compared it with the second approach.

We summarise the conclusions of Part 1 in the following:

Given a temporal set of data, this set has the intuitive form:

"$A(x)$ is true at time t",

This can be represented in essentially two ways (in parallel to the two methods discussed):

1. Adding a new argument for time to the predicate A and writing $A^*(t, x)$ and working within an ordinary Horn clause computational environment

2. Leaving time as an external indicator and writing "$t : A(x)$", to represent the above temporal statement.

To compare the two approaches, imagine now that we want to say the following:
"If $A(x)$ is true at t, then it will continue to be true".

The first approach will write it as:

$$\forall s(A^*(t,x) \land t < s \to A^*(s,x))$$

The second approach has to talk about t. It would use a special temporal connective "G" for "always in the future". Thus the data item becomes

$$t : A(x) \to GA(x)$$

It is equivalent to the following in the first approach:

$$A^*(t,x) \to \forall s[t < s \to A^*(s,x)]$$

The statement "GA is true at t" is translated as

$$\forall s(t < s \to A^*(s)).$$

Part 1 of this paper introduced temporal connectives and wanted to discover what kind of temporal clauses for the new temporal language arise in ordinary Horn clause logic when we allow time variables in the atoms (eg $A^*(t,x), B^*(s,y)$) and allow time relations like $t < s$, $t = s$ for time points. This would give us a clue to what kind of temporal Horn clauses to allow in the second approach. The computational tractability of the new language is assured, as it arises from Horn clause computation. Skolem functions have to be added to the Horn clause language, to eliminate the F and P connectives which are existential. All we have to do is change the computational rules to rely on the more intuitive syntactical structure of the second approach. The following definition of temporal clauses was arrived at:

Definition D0: (Compare section 2 of part 1.) The language contains $\land, \to, F$ (it will be the case) P (it was the case) and $\Box$ (it is always the case).

We define the notions of:
Ordinary Clauses
Always Clauses

Heads
Bodies
Goals

1. A *Clause* is either an always clause or an ordinary clause.

2. An *Always Clause* is $\Box A$ where A is an ordinary clause.

3. An *Ordinary Clause* is a Head or an $A \to H$ where A is a Body and H is a Head.

4. A *Head* is either an atomic formula or FA or PA, where A is a conjunction of ordinary clauses.

5. A *Body* is either an atomic formula, a conjunction of Bodies, an FA or a PA, where A is a body.

6. A goal is any body.

Example E1
$$a \to F((b \to Pq) \land F(a \to Fb))$$
is an acceptable clause.
$$a \to \Box b$$
is not an acceptable clause.

The reason for not allowing $\Box$ in the head is computational and not conceptual. The difference between a (temporal) Logic Programming Machine and a (temporal) Automated Theorem Prover is *tractability*. Allowing disjunctions in Heads or $\Box$ in heads crosses the boundary of tractability. We can give computational rules for richer languages and we will in fact do so in later sections, but we will lose tractability; what we will have then is a theorem prover for full temporal logic.

From now on we continue to develop the temporal logic programming machine. At this point we conclude our revision from Part 1 and begin Part 2 proper. The reader can read Part 1 for further background, but this is not necessary.

2   LDS - Labelled Deduction Systems

This section will present the labelled deduction methodology which serves as a framework for developing the temporal Prolog machine. We begin by asking ourselves what is a temporal database? Intuitively, looking at existing real temporal problems, we can say that we have information about things happening in different times and some connections between them. Here is an example:

Example E2: A Temporal Configuration

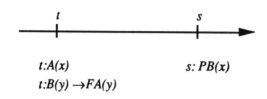

Figure 1

The diagram shows a finite set of points of time and some labelled formulas. These are supposed to hold at the times indicated by the labels. Notice that we have not only labelled assertions but also Horn clauses showing dependencies across times. Thus at time t it may be true that B will be true. We represent that as $t : FB$. The language we are using has F and P as connectives. It is possible to have more connectives and still remain within the Horn clause framework. Most useful among them are "$t : F^s A$" and "$t : P^s A$" reading "$t < s$ and $s : A$" and "$s < t$ and $s : A$", in words: " A will be true at time $s > t$".

The temporal configuration consists of two components.

1. A (finite) graph $(\rho, <)$ of time points and the temporal relationships between them.

2. With each point of the graph we associate a (finite) set of clauses and assertions, representing what is true at that point.

In Horn clause computational logic, there is an agreement that if a formula of the form $A(x) \rightarrow B(x)$ appears in the database with x free then it is understood that x is universally quantified. Thus we assume $\forall x(A(x) \rightarrow B(x))$ is in the database. The variable x is then called universal (or type 1). In the case of modal and temporal logics, we need another type of variable, called type 2 or a Skolem variable. To explain the reason, consider the item of data

"$t : FB(x)$".

This reads, according to our agreement,
"$\forall x F B(x)$ true at t."

For example it might be the sentence: t: "Everyone will leave."

The time in the future in which $B(x)$ is true depends on x. In our example, the time of leaving depends on the person x. Thus, for a given unknown (uninstantiated) u, that is for a given person u which we are not yet specifying, we know there must be a point t_1 of time (t_1 is dependent on u) with $t_1 : B(u)$. This is the time in which u leaves.

This u is by agreement not a type 1 variable. It is a u to be chosen later. Really u is a Skolem constant and we do not want to and cannot read it as $t_1 : \forall u B(u)$. Thus we need two types of variables. The other alternative is to make the dependency of t_1 on u explicit and to write

$$t_1(x) : B(x)$$

with x a universal type 1 variable, but then the object language variable x appears in the world indices as well. The world indices, ie the t's, are external to the formal clausal temporal language, and it is simpler not to mix the t's and the x's. We chose the two type of variable approach. Notice that when we ask for a goal $?G(u)$, u is a variable to be instantiated, ie a type 2 variable. So we have these variables anyway, and we prefer to develop a systematic way of dealing with them.

To explain the rôle of the two types of variables, consider the following classical Horn clause database and query:

$$A(x,y) \rightarrow B(x,y) \quad ?B(u,u)$$
$$A(a,a)$$

This means "Find an instantiation u_0 of u such that $\forall x, y[A(x,y) \rightarrow B(x,y)] \wedge A(a,a) \vdash B(u_0, u_0)$". There is no reason why we cannot allow for the following

$$A(u,y) \rightarrow B(x,u) \quad ?B(u,u)$$
$$A(a_j a)$$

In this case we want to find a u_0 such that

$$\forall x, y[A(u_0, y) \rightarrow B(x, u_0)] \wedge A(a,a) \vdash B(u_0, u_0)$$

or to show

$$\vdash \exists u\{[\forall x, y[A(u,y) \rightarrow B(x,u)] \wedge A(a,a) \rightarrow B(u,u)]\}$$

u is called type 2 (Skolem) variable and x, y are universal type 1 variables. Given a database and a query of the form $\Delta(x, y, u)?Q(u)$, success means $\vdash \exists u[\forall x, y \Delta(x, y, u) \rightarrow Q(u)]$.

The next sequence of definitions will develop the syntax of the Temporal Prolog Machine. A lot depends on the flow of time. We will give a general definition, (definition D2 below), which includes the following connectives:

☐ Always

F It will be the case

P It was the case

G It will always be the case (not including now)

H It has always been the case (up to now and not including now)

$\bigcirc$ Next moment of time (in particular it implies that such a moment of time exists)

⊙ Previous moment of time (in particular it implies that such a moment of time exists).

Later on we will also deal with S (Since) and U (Until).

The flows of time involved are mainly three.

- General partial orders $(T, <)$.

- Linear orders

- The integers or the natural numbers.

The logic and theorem provers involved, even for the same connectives, are different for different partial orders. Thus the reader should be careful to note in which flow of time we are operating. Usually the connectives $\bigcirc$ and $\otimes$ assume we are working in the flow of time of integers.

Having fixed a flow of time $(T, <)$, the Temporal Machine will generate finite configurations of points of time according to the information available to it. These are denoted by $(\rho, <)$. We are supposed to have $\rho \subseteq T$ (more precisely ρ will be homomorphic into T), and the ordering on ρ be the same as the ordering on T. The situation gets a bit complicated if we have a new point s and we do not know where it is supposed to be in relation to known points. We will need to consider all possibilities. Which possibilities do arise depend on $(T, <)$, the background flow of time we are working with. Again we should watch for variations in the sequel.

Definition D1

Let $(\rho, <)$ be a finite partial order. Let $t \in \rho$ and let s be a new point. Let $\rho' = \rho \cup \{s\}$, and let $<'$ be a partial order on ρ'. Then $(\rho', <', t)$ is said to be a (one new point) *future* (respectively *past*) *configuration of* $(\rho, <, t)$ iff $t <' s$ (respectively $s <' t$) and $\forall xy \in \rho(x < y \leftrightarrow x <' y)$.

Example E3

Consider a general partial flow $(T, <)$ and consider the subflow $(\rho, <)$.

The possible future configurations (relative to $T, <)$) of one additional point s are:

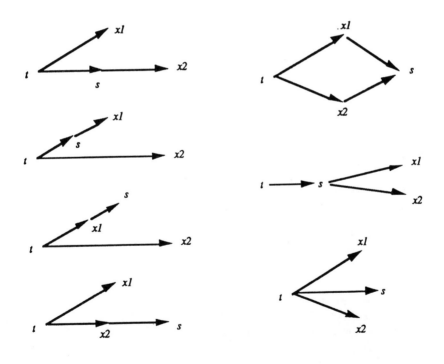

Figure 2

For a finite $(\rho, <)$ there is a finite number of future and past non-isomorphic configurations. This finite number is exponential in the size of ρ. So in the general case without simplifying assumptions we will have an intractable exponential computation. A configuration gives all possibilities of putting a point in the future or past.

In case of an ordering in which a next element or a previous element exists (like $t + 1$ and $t - 1$ in the integers) the possibilities for configurations are different. In this case we must assume that we know the *exact* distance between the elements of $(\rho, <)$.

For example in the configuration $\{t < x_1, t < x_2\}$ of the figure above we may have the further following information as part of the configuration:

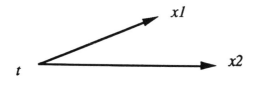

Figure 3

$$t = \otimes^{18} x_1$$

$$t = \otimes^6 x_2$$

so that we have only a finite number of possibilities for putting s in.

Note that although $\otimes$ operates on propositions, it can also be used to operate on points of time, denoting the predecessor function.

Definition D2
Consider a Temporal Prolog Language with the following connectives and predicates:

1. Atomic predicates.

2. Function symbols and constants

3. Two types of variables:
   Universal variables (Type 1) $V = \{x_1, y_1, z_1, x_2, y_2, z_2, \ldots\}$
   and Skolem variables (Type 2) $U = \{u_1, v_1, u_2, v_2, \ldots\}$.

4. The connectives $\wedge, \rightarrow, \vee, F, P, \mathcal{O}, \otimes, \square$ and $\neg$.

FA reads: it will be the case that A.

PA reads: it was the case that A.

$\mathcal{O}A$ reads: A is true tomorrow (if a tomorrow exists, if tomorrow does not exist then it is false).

$\otimes A$ reads: A was true yesterday (if yesterday does not exist then it is false).

$\neg$:   represents negation by failure.

We define now the notions of an *Ordinary Clause*, an *Always Clause*, a *Body*, a *Head* and a *Goal*.

1. A *Clause* is either an always clause or an ordinary clause.

2. An *Always Clause* has the form $\Box A$, where A is an ordinary clause.

3. An *Ordinary Clause* is a Head or an $A \rightarrow H$, where A is a body and H is a Head.

4. A *Head* is either an atomic formula or an FA or a PA or an $\mathcal{O}A$ or an $\otimes A$ where A is a finite conjunction of ordinary clauses.

5. A *Body* is either an atomic formula or an FA or a PA or an $\mathcal{O}A$ or an $\otimes A$ or $\neg A$ or a conjunction of bodies where A is a body.

6. A *Goal* is a body whose variables are *all* Skolem variables.

7. A disjunction of goals is also a goal.

Remark R1

Definition D2 included all possible temporal connectives. In practice different systems may contain only some of these connectives. For example a modal system may contain only $\Diamond$ (corresponding to F) and $\Box$. A future discrete system may contain only $\mathcal{O}$ and F etc.

Depending on the system and the flow of time, the dependencies between the connectives change. For example we have the equivalence

$$\Box(a \rightarrow \mathcal{O}b) \text{ and } \Box(\otimes a \rightarrow b)$$

whenever both $\otimes a$ and $\mathcal{O}b$ are meaningful.

Definition D3

Let $(T, <)$ be a flow of time. Let $(\rho, <)$ be a finite partial order. A *labelled temporal database* is a set of labelled ordinary clauses of the form $(t_i : A_i), t \in \rho$ and always clauses of the form $\Box A_i$, A_i a clause. A labelled goal has the form $t : G$, where G is a goal.

Δ is said to be a labelled temporal database over $(T, <)$ if $(\rho, <)$ is homomorphic into $(T, <)$.

Definition D4
We now define the computation procedure for the temporal Prolog for the language of definitions D2 and D3. We assume a flow of time $(T, <)$. $\rho \subseteq T$ is a finite set of points of time involved so far in the computation. The exact computation steps depend on the flow of time. It is different for branching, discrete linear etc. We will give the definition for linear time, though not necessarily discrete. Thus the meaning of $\mathcal{O}A$ in this logic is that there exists a next moment and A is true at this next moment. Similarly for $\otimes A$. $\otimes A$ reads there exists a previous moment and A was true at that previous moment.

We define the success predicate $\mathbf{S}(\rho, <, \Delta, G, t, G_0, t_0, \Theta)$ where $t \in \rho, (\rho, <)$ is a finite partial order and Δ is a set of labelled clauses $(t : A), t \in \rho$.

$\mathbf{S}(\rho, <, \Delta, G, t, G_0, t_0, \Theta)$ reads: The labelled goal $t : G$ succeeds from Δ under the substitution Θ to all the type 2 variables of G and Δ in the computation with starting labelled goal $t_0 : G_0$.

When Θ is known, we write $\mathbf{S}(\rho, <, \Delta, G, t, G_0, t_0)$ only.

We define the simultaneous success and the failure of a set $\mathbf{\Pi}$ of metapredicates of the form $\mathbf{S}(\rho, <, \Delta, G, t, G_0, t_0)$ under a substitution Θ to type 2 variables. To explain intuitive the meaning of success or failure, assume first that Θ is a substitution which grounds all the Skolem type 2 variables. In this case $(\mathbf{\Pi}, \Theta)$ succeeds if by definition all $\mathbf{S}(\rho, <, \Delta, G, t, G_0, t_0, \Theta) \in \mathbf{\Pi}$ succeed and $(\mathbf{\Pi}, \Theta)$ fails if at least one of $\mathbf{S} \in \mathbf{\Pi}$ fails. The success or failure of $\mathbf{S}$ for a Θ as above has to be defined recursively. For a general $\Theta, (\mathbf{\Pi}, \Theta)$ succeeds, if for some Θ' such that $\Theta\Theta'$ grounds all type 2 variables $(\mathbf{\Pi}, \Theta\Theta')$ succeeds. $(\mathbf{\Pi}, \Theta)$ fails if for all Θ' such that $\Theta\Theta'$ grounds all type 2 variables we have that $(\mathbf{\Pi}, \Theta\Theta')$ fails. We need to give recursive procedures for the computation of the success and failure of $(\mathbf{\Pi}, \Theta)$. In the case of the recursion, a given $(\mathbf{\Pi}, \Theta)$ will be changed to a $(\mathbf{\Pi}', \Theta')$ by taking $\mathbf{S}(\rho, <, \Delta, G, t, G_0, t_0) \in \mathbf{\Pi}$ and replacing it by $\mathbf{S}(\rho', <', \Delta', G', t', G_0, t_0)$. We will have several such changes and thus get several $\mathbf{\Pi}'$ by replacing several $\mathbf{S}$'s in $\mathbf{\Pi}$. We write the several possibilities as $(\mathbf{\Pi}'_i, \Theta'_i)$. If we write $(\mathbf{\Pi}, \Theta)$ to mean $(\mathbf{\Pi}, \Theta)$ succeeds and $\sim (\mathbf{\Pi}, \Theta)$ to read $(\mathbf{\Pi}, \Theta)$ fails, then our recursive computation rules have the form: $(\mathbf{\Pi}, \Theta)$ succeeds (or fails) if some boolean combination of $(\mathbf{\Pi}'_i, \Theta'_i)$ succeed (or fail). The rules allow us to pick an element in $\mathbf{\Pi}$, eg $\mathbf{S}(\rho, <, \Delta, G, t, G_0, t_0)$ and replace it with one or more elements to obtain the different $(\mathbf{\Pi}'_i, \Theta'_i)$, where Θ'_i is obtained from Θ. In case of failure we require that Θ grounds all type 2 variables. We do not define failure for a nongrounding Θ.

To summarise the general structure of the rules is:

$(\mathbf{\Pi}, \Theta)$ succeeds (or fails) if some boolean combination of the successes and failures of some $(\mathbf{\Pi}'_i, \Theta'_i)$ holds and $(\mathbf{\Pi}, \Theta)$ and $(\mathbf{\Pi}'_i, \Theta'_i)$ are related according to one of the following cases:

I If $\mathbf{\Pi} = \emptyset$ then $(\mathbf{\Pi}, \Theta)$ succeeds, (ie the boolean combination of $(\mathbf{\Pi}_i, \Theta_i)$ is *truth*.

II $(\mathbf{\Pi}, \Theta)$ fails if for some $\mathbf{S}(\rho, <, \Delta, G, t, G_0, t_0)$ in $\mathbf{\Pi}$ we have G is atomic and for all $\square(A \to H) \in \Delta$ and for all $(t : A \to H) \in \Delta, H\Theta$ does *not* unify with $G\Theta$. Further, for all Ω and s such that $t = \Omega s$ and for all $s : A \to \Omega H$ and all $\square(A \to \Omega H)$ we have $H\Theta$ does not unify with $G\Theta$, where Ω is a sequence of $\mathcal{O}$ and $\otimes$.

Remark R2

We must qualify the conditions of the notion of failure. If we have a goal $t : G$, with G atomic, we know for sure that $t : G$ finitely fails under a substitution Θ, if $G\Theta$ cannot unify with any head of a clause. This is what the condition above says. What are the candidates for unification? These are either clauses of the form $t : A \to H$, with H atomic or $\square(A \to H)$, with H atomic.

Do we have to consider the case where H is not atomic? The answer depends on the flow of time and on the configuration $(\rho, <)$ we are dealing with. If we have eg $t : A \to FG$ then if $A \to FG$ is true at t, G would be true (if at all) in some s, $t < s$. This s is irrelevant to our query $?t : G$. Even if we have $t' < t$ and $t' : A \to FG$ and A true at t', we still can ignore this clause because we are not assured that any s such that $t' < s$ and G true at s would be the desired t (ie $t = s$).

The only case we have to worry about is when the flow of time and the configuration are such that we have for example $t' : A \to \mathcal{O}^5 G$ and $t = \mathcal{O}^5 t'$.

In this case we must add the following clause to the notion of failure:

For every s such that $t = \mathcal{O}^n s$ and every $s : A \to \mathcal{O}^n H$, $G\Theta$ and $H\Theta$ do not unify.

We also have to check what happens in the case of always clauses.

Consider an integer flow of time and the clause $\square(A \to \mathcal{O}^5 \otimes^{27} H)$, This true at the point $s = \otimes^5 \mathcal{O}^{27} t$ and hence for failure we need that $G\Theta$ does not unify with $H\Theta$.

The above explains the additional condition on failure.

The following conditions (1) - (10), (12) - (13) relate to the success of $(\mathbf{\Pi}, \Theta)$ if $(\mathbf{\Pi}'_i, \Theta'_i)$ succeed. Condition (11) uses the notion of failure, to give the success of negation by failure. Conditions (1)-(10), (12)-(13) give certain alternatives for success. They give failure if each one of these alternatives end up in failure.

1. **Success rule for atomic query:**
   $\mathbf{S}(\rho, <, \Delta, G, t, G_0, t_0) \in \mathbf{\Pi}$ and G is atomic and for some head H, $(t : H) \in \Delta$ and for some substitutions Θ_1 to the universal variables of H and Θ_2 to the existential variables of H and G we have $H\Theta_1\Theta\Theta_2 = G\Theta\Theta_2$ and $\mathbf{\Pi}' = \mathbf{\Pi} - \{\mathbf{S}(\rho, <, \Delta, G, t, G_0, t_o)\}$ and $\Theta' = \Theta\Theta_2$.

2. **Computation rule for atomic query:**
   $\mathbf{S}(\rho, <, \Delta, G, t, G_0, t_o) \in \mathbf{\Pi}$ and G is atomic and for some $(t : A \rightarrow H) \in \Delta$ or for some $\square(A \rightarrow H) \in \Delta$ and for some Θ_1, Θ_2, we have $H\Theta_1\Theta\Theta_2 = G\Theta\Theta_2$ and $\mathbf{\Pi}' = (\mathbf{\Pi} - \{\{\mathbf{S}(\rho, <, \Delta, G, t, G_0, t_o)\}\}) \cup \{\mathbf{S}(\rho, <, \Delta, A\Theta_1, t, G_0, t_o)\}$ and $\Theta' = \Theta\Theta_2$.

The above rules dealt with the atomic case. Rules (3), (4) and (4*) deal with the case the goal is FG. The meaning of (3), (4) and (4*) is the following:
we ask FG at t. How can we be sure that FG is true at t? There are two possibilities, (a) and (b)

(a) We have $t < s$ and at $s : G$ succeeds. This is rule (3).

(b) Assume that we have the fact that $A \rightarrow FB$ is true at t. We ask for A and succeed and hence FB is true at t. Thus there should exist a point s' in the future of t where B is true. Where can s' be? We don't know where s' is in the future of t. So we consider all future configurations for s'. This gives us all future possibilities where s' can be. We assume for each of these possibilities that B is true at s' and check whether either G follows at s' or FG follows at s'. If we find that for all future constellations of where s' can be $G \vee FG$ succeeds in s' from B, then FG holds at t. Here we use the transitivity of $<$. (4a) gives the possibilities where s' is an old point s in the future of t. (4b) gives the possibilities where s' is a new point forming a new configuration. Success is needed from *all* possibilities.

3. **Immediate rule for F:**
   $\mathbf{S}(\rho, <, \Delta, FG, t, G_0, t_o) \in \mathbf{\Pi}$ and for some $s \in \rho$ such that $t < s$ we have $\mathbf{\Pi}' = (\mathbf{\Pi} - \{\mathbf{S}(\rho, <, \Delta, FG, t, G_0, t_o)\}) \cup \{\mathbf{S}(\rho, <, \Delta, G, s, G_0, t_o)\}$ and $\Theta' = \Theta$.

4. **First configuration rule for** F:
$\mathbf{S}(\rho, <, \Delta, FG, t, G_0, t_o) \in \mathbf{\Pi}$ and some $(t : A \to F \wedge_j B_j) \in \Delta$ and some Θ_1, Θ_2 we have both (a) and (b) below are true. A may not appear in which case we pretend $A = truth$.

(a) For *all* $s \in \rho$, such that $t < s$ we have that

$$\mathbf{\Pi}'_s = (\mathbf{\Pi} - \{\mathbf{S}(\rho, <, \Delta, FG, t, G_0, t_0)\}) \cup \\ \{\mathbf{S}(\rho, <, \Delta, E\Theta_1, t, G_0, t_0)\} \cup \\ \{\mathbf{S}(\rho, <, \Delta \cup \{(s : B_j \Theta_1) \mid j = 1, 2, \ldots\}, D, s, G_0, t_0\}$$

succeeds with $\Theta'_s = \Theta \Theta_2$ and $D = G \vee FG$ and $E = A$.

(b) For all future configurations of $(\rho, <, t)$ with a new letter s, denoted by the form $(\rho_s, <_s)$ we have that

$$\mathbf{\Pi}'_s = (\mathbf{\Pi} - \{\mathbf{S}(\rho, <, \Delta, FG, t, G_0, t_o)\}) \cup \\ \{\mathbf{S}(\rho, <, \Delta, E\Theta_1, t, G_0, t_o)\} \cup \\ \{\mathbf{S}(\rho_s, <_s, \Delta \cup \{(s : B_j) \mid j = 1, 2, \ldots\}, D, s, G_0, t_0)\}$$

succeeds with $\Theta'_s = \Theta \Theta_2$ and $D = G \vee FG$ and $E = A$.

The reader should note that conditions (3), (4a) and (4b) are needed only when the flow of time has some special properties. To explain by example, assume we have the configuration

Figure 4

and $\Delta = \{t : A \to FB, t' : C\}$ as data and our query is $?t : FG$.

Then according to rules (3), (4) we have to check and succeed in all the following cases:

1. From rule (3) we check $\{t' : C, t : A \to FB\}?t' : G$

2. From rule (4a) we check $\{t' : C, t : A \to FB, t' : B\}?t' : G$

3. From rule (4b) we check $\{t' : C, t : A \to FB, s : B\}?s : G$

for the three configurations below

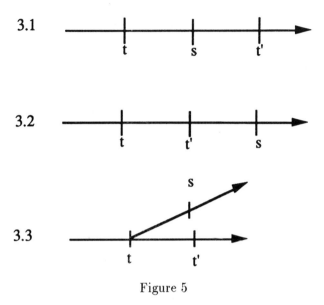

3.1

3.2

3.3

Figure 5

If time is linear configuration 3.3 does not arise and we are essentially checking 3.1, 3.2 and the case 4a corresponding to $t' = s$.

If we do not have any special properties of time, success in case 3.2 is required. Since we must succeed in all cases and 3.2 is the case with *least* assumptions, it is enough to check 3.2 alone.

Thus for the case of no special properties of the flow of time, case 4 can be replaced by case 4 general below:

4 *general.* $\mathbf{S}(\rho, <, \Delta, FG, t, G_0, t_0) \in \Pi$ and for the future configuration $(\rho_1, <_1)$ defined as $\rho_1 = \rho \cup \{s\}$ and $<_1 = < \cup \{t < s\}$, s a new letter we have that:
$\Pi's = (\Pi - \{\mathbf{S}(\rho, <, \Delta, FG, t, G_0, t_0)\}) \cup \{\mathbf{S}(\rho, <, \Delta, E\Theta_1, t, G_0, t_0)\} \cup \{\mathbf{S}(\rho_1, <_1, \Delta \cup \{(s : B_j) \mid j = 1, 2, \ldots\}, D, s, G_0, t_0)\}$ succeeds with $\Theta'_s = \Theta\Theta_1$ and $D = G \vee FG$ and $E = A$.

    4*. **2nd Configuration rule for** F:
For some $\mathbf{S}(\rho, <, \Delta, FG, t, G_0, t_0)$ and some $\square(A \rightarrow F \wedge_j B_j) \in \Delta$ and some $\Theta_1 \Theta_2$ we have both cases 4a and 4b above true with $E = A \vee FA$ and $D = G \vee FG$.

4*general Similar to (4 *general*) for the case of general flow.

5. This is the the mirror image of (3) with "*PG*" replacing "*FG*" and "$s < t$" replacing "$t < s$".

6; 6* This is the mirror image of (4) and (4*) with "*PG*" replacing "*FG*", "$s < t$" replacing "$t < s$" and "past configuration" replacing "future configuration".

general This is the image of (4 *general*).

We give now the computation rules (7)-(10) for $\mathcal{O}$ and $\otimes$ for orderings in which a next point and/or previous points exist. If $t \in T$ has a next point we denote this point by $s = \mathcal{O}t$. If it has a previous point we denote it by $s = \otimes t$. For example, if $(T, <)$ is the integers then $\mathcal{O}t = t + 1$ and $\otimes t = t - 1$. If $(T, <)$ is a tree then $\otimes t$ always exists, except at the root, but $\mathcal{O}t$ may or may not exist. For the sake of simplicity we must assume that if we have $\mathcal{O}$ or $\otimes$ in the language then $\mathcal{O}t$ or $\otimes t$ always exist. Otherwise we can sneak negation in by putting $(t : \mathcal{O}A) \in \Delta$ when $\mathcal{O}t$ does not exist!

7. **Immediate rule for $\mathcal{O}$:**
   $\mathbf{S}(\rho, <, \Delta, \mathcal{O}G, t, G_0, t_o) \in \mathbf{\Pi}$ and $\mathcal{O}t$ exists and $\mathcal{O}t \in \rho$ and $\Theta' = \Theta$ and $\mathbf{\Pi}' = (\mathbf{\Pi} - \{\mathbf{S}(\rho, <, \Delta, \mathcal{O}G, t, G_0, t_o)\}) \cup \{\mathbf{S}(\rho, <, \Delta, G, \mathcal{O}t, G_0, t_o)\}$

8. **Configuration rule for $\mathcal{O}$:**
   $\mathbf{S}(\rho, <, \Delta, \mathcal{O}G, t, G_0, t_o) \in \mathbf{\Pi}$ and some Θ_1, Θ_2 some $(t : A \twoheadrightarrow \mathcal{O} \wedge_j B_j) \in \Delta$ and
   $\mathbf{\Pi}' = (\mathbf{\Pi} - \{\mathbf{S}(\rho, <, \Delta, \mathcal{O}G, t, G_0, t_o)\}) \cup \{\mathbf{S}(\rho, <, \Delta, A\Theta_1, t, G_0, t_o)\}$ $\cup \cup$ $\{\mathbf{S}(\rho \cup \{\mathcal{O}t\}, <', \Delta \cup \{(\mathcal{O}t : B_j)\}, G, \mathcal{O}t, G_0, t_0)\}$ succeeds with $\Theta' = \Theta\Theta_2$, and $<'$ is the appropriate ordering closure of $< \cup \{(t, \mathcal{O}t)\}$

   Notice that case 8 is parallel to case 4. We do not need 8a and 8b because of $\mathcal{O}t \in \rho$ then what would be case (8b) becomes (7).

9. The mirror image of (7) with "$\otimes$" replacing "$\mathcal{O}$".

10. The mirror image of (8) with "$\otimes$" replacing "$\mathcal{O}$".

11. **Negation as failure rule:**
    $\mathbf{S}(\rho, <, \Delta, \neg G, t, G_0, t_0) \in \mathbf{\Pi}$ and Θ grounds every type 2 variable and the computation for success of $\mathbf{S}(\rho, <, \Delta, G, t, \Theta)$ ends up in failure.

12. **Disjunction rule:**
    $\mathbf{S}(\rho, <, \Delta, G_1 \vee G_2, t, G_0, t_o) \in \mathbf{\Pi}$ and $\mathbf{\Pi}' = (\mathbf{\Pi} - \{\mathbf{S}(\rho, <, \Delta, G_1 \vee G_2, t, G_0, t_o)\}) \cup \{\mathbf{S}(\rho, <, \Delta, G_i, t, G_0, t_o)\}$ and $\Theta' = \Theta$ and $i \in \{1, 2\}$.

13. **Conjunction rule:**
    $\mathbf{S}(\rho, <, \Delta, G_1 \wedge G_2, t, G_0, t_o) \in \mathbf{\Pi}$ and $\mathbf{\Pi}' = (\mathbf{\Pi} - \{\mathbf{S}(\rho, <, \Delta, G_1 \wedge G_2, t, G_0, t_o)\}) \cup \{\mathbf{S}(\rho, <, \Delta, G_i, t, G_0, t_o) \mid i \in \{1, 2\}\}$

14. **Restart Rule**
    $\mathbf{S}(\rho, <, \Delta, G, t, G_0, t_o) \in \mathbf{\Pi}$ and $\mathbf{\Pi}' = (\mathbf{\Pi} - \{\mathbf{S}(\rho, <, \Delta, G, t, G_0, t_o)\}) \cup$
    $\{\mathbf{S}(\rho, <, \Delta, G_1, t_0, G_0, t_0)\}$ where G_1 is obtained from G_0 by substituting completely new type 2 variables u_i' for the type 2 variables u_i
    of G_0, and where Θ' extends Θ by giving $\Theta'(u_i') = u_i'$ for the new
    variables u_i'.

15. **To Start the Computation:**
    Given Δ and $t_0 : G_0$ and a flow $(T, <)$, we start the computation
    with $\mathbf{\Pi} = \{\mathbf{S}(\rho, <, \Delta, G_0, t_0, G_0, t_0)\}$, where $(\rho, <)$ is the configuration
    associated with Δ, over $(T, <)$ (definition D3).

Let us check some examples

Example E4
Data:

1. $t : a \rightarrow Fb$

2. $\Box(b \rightarrow Fc)$

3. $t : a$

Query: $?t : Fc$

Configuration: $\{t\}$

Using rule (4*) we create a future s with $t < s$ and ask the two queries:
(the notation $A?B$ means that we add A to the data (1), (2), (3) and ask
$?B$).

4. $?t : c \vee Fb$
   and

5. $s : c?s : c \vee Fc$

   (5) succeeds and (4) splits into two queries by rule (4).

6. $?t : a$
   and

7. $s' : b?s' : b$.

The above computation is the same as the one in Figure 3 of part 1 of this
paper. The only difference is that since our data are labelled we do not

have to keep copying the database. More significant differences will show in the next example.

Example E5
Data:

(1) $t : FA$

(2) $t : FB$

Query: $t : F\varphi$ where $\varphi = (A \wedge B) \vee (A \wedge FB) \vee (B \wedge FA)$.

The query will fail in any flow of time in which the future is not linear. The purpose of this example is to examine what happens when time is linear. Using (1) we introduce a point s, with $s : A$ and query from s the following:

$$?s : \varphi \vee F\varphi$$

If we do not use the restart rule, the query will fail. Now that we are at a point s there is no way to go back to t. We therefore cannot reason that we also have a point $s' : B$ and $t < s$ and $t < s'$ and that because of linearity either $s = s'$ or $s < s'$ or $s' < s$. However, if we are allowed to restart, we can continue and ask $t : F\varphi$ and now use the clause $t : FB$ to introduce s'. We now reason using linearity in rule (4) that the configurations are

either $t < s < s'$
or $t < s' < s$
or $t < s = s'$.

and φ succeeds at t for each configuration.

The reader should note the reason for the need to use the restart rule. When time is just a partial order, the two assumptions $t : FA$ and $t : FB$ do not interact. Thus when asking $t : FC$, we know that there are two points $s_1 : A$ and $s_2 : B$.

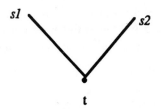

$$t$$

Figure 6

and C can be true in either one of them. $s_1 : A$ has no influence on
$s_2 : B$. When conditions on time (such as linearity) are introduced, s_1 does
influence s_2 and hence we must introduce both at the same time. When one
does forward deduction one can introduce both s_1 and s_2 going forward.
The backward rules do not allow for that. That is why we need the restart
rule. When we restart, we keep all that has been done (with, for example
s_1) and have the opportunity to restart with s_2. The restart rule can be
used to solve the linearity problem for classical logic only. Its side effect
is that it turns intuitionistic logic into classical logic, see my paper on N-
Prolog. In theorem proving based on intuitionistic logic where disjunctions
are allowed, forward reasoning cannot be avoided. See next example.

It is instructive to translate the above into Prolog and see what happens
there.

Example E6

1. $t : FA$ translates into $(\exists s_1 > t)A^*(s_1)$

2. $t : FB$ translates into $(\exists s_2 > t)A^*(s_2)$.
   The query translates into the formula $\psi(t)$:
   $\psi = \exists s > t[A^*(s) \wedge B^*(s)] \vee \exists s_1 > t[A^*(s_1) \wedge \exists s_2 > s_1 B^*(s_2)] \vee \exists s_2 > t[B^*(s_2) \wedge \wedge \exists s_1 > s_2 A^*(s_2)]$
   which is equivalent to the disjunction of

   (a) $[t < s \wedge A^*(s) \wedge B^*(s)]$

   (b) $t < s_1 \wedge s_1 < s_2 \wedge A^*(s_1) \wedge B^*(s_2)$

   (c) $t < s_1 \wedge s_2 < s_1 \wedge A^*(s_1) \wedge B^*(s_2)$.

all of (a), (b), (c) fail from the data, unless we add to the data the disjunction

$$\forall x y(x < y \vee x = y \vee y < x)$$

Since this is not a Horn clause, we are unable to express it in the database.

The Logic Programmer might add this as an integrity constraint. This is
wrong as well. As an integrity constraint it would require the database to
indicate which of the three possibilities it adopts, namely

either $x < y$ is in the data
or $x = y$ is in the data
or $y < x$ is in the data

This is stronger than allowing the disjunction in the data.

The handling of the integrity constraints corresponds to our meta handling of what configurations $(\rho, <)$ are allowed depending on the ordering of time. By labelling data items we are allowing for the metalevel considerations to be done separately on the labels.

This means that we can handle properties of time which are not necessarily expressible by an object language formula of the logic. In some cases (finiteness of time) because they are not first order, in other cases (irreflexivity) because there is no corresponding formula (axiom) and in other cases because of syntactical restrictions (linearity).

We can now make clear our classical versus intuitionistic distinction. If the underlying logic is classical then we are checking whether $\Delta \vdash \psi$ in classical logic. If our underlying logic is intuitionistic, then we are checking whether $\Delta \vdash \psi$ in intuitionistic logic where Δ and ψ are defined below:

Δ is the translation of the data together with the axioms for linear ordering namely, the conjunction of:

1. $\exists s_1 > t A^*(s_1)$

2. $\exists s_2 > t B^*(s_2)$

3. $\forall xy(x < y \lor x = y \lor y < x)$

4. $\forall x \exists y(x < y)$

5. $\forall x \exists y(y < x)$

6. $\forall xyz(x < y \land y < z \rightarrow x < z)$

7. $\forall x \neg(x < x)$.

ψ is the translation of the query as given above.

The computation of example E5, using restart, answers the question $\Delta \vdash ? \psi$ in classical logic. To answer the question $\Delta \vdash ? \psi$ in intuitionistic logic we cannot use restart, we must use forward rules as well.

Example E7
Example E5 for the case that the underlying logic is intuitionistic. *Data* and *Query* as in Example E5.

Going forward, we get:

(3) $s : A$ from   (1)
(4) $s' : B$ from   (2)

By linearity, either

$$t < s < s'$$

$$\text{or } t < s' < s$$

$$\text{or } t < s = s'$$

ψ will succeed for each case.

Our language does not allow us to ask queries of the form $\Box G(x)$, where x are all universal variables (ie $\forall x \Box G(x)$). However such queries can be computed from a database Δ. The *only* way to get *always* information out of Δ for a general flow of time is via the always clauses in the database. Always clauses are true everywhere, so if we want to know what else is true everywhere, we ask it from the always clauses: Thus to ask:

$$?\Box G(x), x \text{ a universal variable.}$$

we first skolemise and then ask

$$\{X, \Box X \mid \Box X \in \Delta\}?G(c)$$

where c is a Skolem constant.

We can add a new rule to definition D4:

15. Always Rule
$\mathbf{S}(\rho, <, \Delta, \Box G, t, G_0, t_0) \in \mathbf{\Pi}$ and $\mathbf{\Pi}' = (\mathbf{\Pi} - \{\mathbf{S}(\rho, <, \Delta, \Box G, t, G_0, t_0)\}) \cup \{\mathbf{S}(\{s\}, \emptyset, \Delta', G', s, g', s)\}$ where s is a completely new point and G' is obtained from G by substituting new Skolem constants for all the universal variables of G and

$$\Delta' = \{B, \Box B \mid \Box B \in \Delta\}.$$

We can use (15) to add another clause to the computation of Definition D4, namely

16. $\mathbf{S}(\rho<, \Delta, F(A \wedge B), t, G_0, t_0) \in \mathbf{\Pi}$ and $\mathbf{\Pi}' = (\mathbf{\Pi} - \{\mathbf{S}(\rho, <, \Delta, F(A \wedge B), t, G_0, t_0)\}) \cup \{\mathbf{S}(\rho, <, \Delta, FA, t, G_0, t_0), \mathbf{S}(\rho, <, \Delta, \Box B, t, G_0, t_0)\}$

Example E8.

Data	Query	Configuration
$\Box a$	$t : F(a \wedge b)$	$\{t\}$
$t : Fb$		

First Computation.
Create $s, t < s$ and get

Data	Query	Configuration
$\square a$	$s : a \wedge b$	$t < s$
$t : Fb$		
$s : b$		

$s : b$ succeeds from the data. $s : a$ succeeds by rule 2, definition D4.

Second Computation
Use rule 16. Since $?\square a$ succeeds ask for Fb and proceed as in the first computation.

3   Different Flows of Time

We now check the effect of different flows of time on our logical deduction (computation). We consider a typical example:

Example E9:

Data	Query	Configuration
$t : FFA$	$?t : FA$	$\{t\}$

The possible world flow is a general binary relation.

We create by rule (4b) of definition D4, a future configuration $t < s$ and add to the database $s : FA$
we get:

Data	Query	Configuration
$t : FFA$	$?t : FA$	$t < s$
$s : FA$		

Again we apply rule (4a) of definition D4 and get the new configuration with $s < s'$ and the new item of data $s' : A$. We get

Data	Query	Configuration
$t : FFA$	$?t : FA$	$t < s$
$s : FA$		$s < s'$
$s' : A$		

whether or not we can proceed from here depends on the flow of time. If $<$ is transitive, then $t < s'$ holds and we can get $t : FA$ in the data by rule 3.

Actually by rule (4*) we could have proceeded along the following sequence of deduction. Rule (4*) is especially geared for transitivity.

Data	Query	Configuration
$t : FFA$	$t : FA$	t

using rule (4*) we get

Data	Query	Configuration
$t : FFA$	$s : FA \lor FFA$	$t < s$
$s : FA$		

The first disjunct of the query succeeds.

If $<$ is not transitive, rule 3 does not apply, since $t < s'$ does not hold.

Supose our query were $?t : FFFA$.

If $<$ is reflexive then we can succeed with $?t : FFFA$ because $t < t$.

If $<$ is dense (ie $\forall xy(x < y \rightarrow \exists z(x < z \land z < y))$) we should also succeed because we can create a point z with $t < z < s$.

$z : FFA$ will succeed and hence $t : FFFA$ will also succeed.

Here we encounter a new rule (density rule), whereby points can always be "landed" between existing points in a configuration.

We now address the flow of time of the type natural numbers, $\{1, 2, 3, 4, \ldots\}$. This has the special property that it is generated by a function symbol **s**.

$$\{1, \mathbf{s}(1), \mathbf{ss}(1) \ldots\}.$$

Example E10.

Data	Query	Configuration
$\Box(q \rightarrow \mathcal{O}q)$	$1 : F(p \land q)$	$\{1\}$
$1 : \mathcal{O}q$		
$1 : Fp$		

If time is the natural numbers, the query should succeed from the data. If time is not the natural numbers but, for example $\{1, 2, 3, \ldots w, w + 1, w + 2, \ldots\}$ then the query should fail.

How do we represent the fact that time is the natural numbers in our computation rule? What is needed is the ability to do some induction. We can use rule (4b) and introduce a point t with $1 < t$ into the configuration and even say that $t = n$, for some n. We thus get:

Data	Query	Configuration
$\Box(q \rightarrow \mathcal{O}q)$	$1 : F(p \wedge q)$	$1 < n$
$1 : \mathcal{O}q$		
$1 : Fp$		
$n : p$		

Somehow we want to derive $n : q$ from the first two assumptions. The key reason for the success of $F(p \wedge q)$ is the success of $\Box q$ from the first two assumptions. We need an induction axiom on the flow of time.

To get a clue as to what to do, let us see what Prolog would do with the translations of the data and goal.

Translated Data
$\forall t[1 \leq t \wedge Q^*(t) \rightarrow Q^*(t+1)]$
$Q^*(1)$
$\exists t P^*(t)$

Translated Query
$\exists t(P^*(t) \wedge Q^*(t))$

After we skolemise, the database becomes:

1. $1 \leq t \wedge Q^*(t) \rightarrow Q^*(t+1)$

2. $Q^*(1)$

3. $P^*(c)$

and the query is
$$P^*(s) \wedge Q^*(s)$$

We proceed by letting $s = c$. We ask $Q^*(c)$ and have to ask after a slightly generalised form of unification $?1 \leq c \wedge Q^*(c-1)$.

Obviously this will lead nowhere without an induction axiom. The induction axiom should be that for *any* predicate $PRED$
$$PRED(1) \wedge \forall x[1 \leq x \wedge PRED(x) \rightarrow PRED(x+1)] \rightarrow \forall x PRED(x)$$

written in Horn clause form this becomes:

$$\exists x \forall y[PRED(1) \wedge [1 \leq x \wedge PRED(x) \rightarrow PRED(x+1)] \rightarrow PRED(y)].$$

Skolemising gives us

4. $PRED(1) \wedge (1 \leq d \wedge PRED(d) \rightarrow PRED(d+1)) \rightarrow PRED(y)$

d is a skolem constant.

Let us now ask the query $P^*(s) \wedge Q^*(s)$ from the database with (1)-(4). We unify with clause (3) and ask $Q^*(c)$. We unify with clause (4) and ask $Q^*(1)$ which succeeds and ask for the implication

$$?1 \leq d \wedge Q^*(d) \rightarrow Q^*(d+1)$$

This should succeed since it is a special case of clause (1) for $t = d$.

The above shows that we need to add an induction axiom of the form

$$\mathcal{O}x \wedge \square(x \rightarrow \mathcal{O}x) \rightarrow \square x$$

Imagine that we are at time t, and assume $t' < t$. If A is true at t' and $\square(A \rightarrow \mathcal{O}A)$ is true, then A is true at t.

We thus need the following rule:

17. **Induction Rule:**

$t : F(A \wedge B)$ succeeds from Δ at a certain configuration if the following conditions all hold.

1. $t : FB$ suceed.

2. For some $s < t, s : A$ succeeds.

3. $m : \mathcal{O}A$ succeeds from the database Δ', where $\Delta' = \{X, \square X \mid \square X \in \Delta\} \cup \{A\}$ and m is a completely new time point and the new configuration is $\{m\}$.

The above shows how to compute when time is the natural numbers. This is not the best way of doing it. In fact, the characteristic feature involved here is that the ordering of the flow of time is a Herbrand universe generated by a finite set of function symbols. FA is read as "A is true at a point generated by the function symbols". This property requires a special study. See our METATEM paper, [2].

4 A Theorem Prover for Modal and Temporal Logics

This section will briefly indicate how our temporal Horn clause computation can be extended to be an automated deduction system for full modal and temporal logic. We present computation rules for propositional temporal logic with $F, P, \mathcal{O}, \otimes, \wedge \rightarrow$ and $\perp$. We approach predicate logic in a subsequent paper as it is relatively complex. The presentation will be intuitive:

Definition D5:
We define the notions of a *Full Clause*, a *Body* and a *Head*.

(a) A *Full Clause* is either an atom q or $\perp$ or $B \rightarrow H$, or H where B is a body and H is a head.

(b) A *Body* is a conjunction of full clauses.

(c) a *Head* is either an atom q or $\perp$ or FH or PH or $\mathcal{O}H$ or $\otimes H$, where H is a body.

Notice that negation by failure is not allowed. We used the connectives $\wedge, \rightarrow$, $\perp$. The other connectives, $\vee$ and $\sim$ are definable in the usual way $\sim A = A \rightarrow \perp$ and $A \vee B = (A \rightarrow \perp) \rightarrow B$. The reader can show that every formula of the language with the connectives $\{\sim, \wedge, \vee, F, G, P, H\}$ is equivalent to a conjunction of full clauses. We use the following equivalences:

$$A \rightarrow (B \wedge C) = (A \rightarrow B) \wedge (A \rightarrow C)$$

$$A \rightarrow (B \rightarrow C) = A \wedge B \rightarrow C$$

$$GA = F(A \rightarrow \perp) \rightarrow \perp$$

$$HA = P(A \rightarrow \perp) \rightarrow \perp$$

Definition D6:
A database is a set of labelled full clauses of the form $(\Delta, \rho, <)$, where $\rho = \{t \mid t : A \in \Delta,$ for some $A\}$. A query is a labelled full clause.

Definition D7:
The following is a definition of the predicate $\mathbf{S}(\rho, <, \Delta, G, t, G_0, t_0)$, which reads:
The labelled goal $t : G$ succeeds from $(\Delta, \rho, <)$ with parameter (initial goal) $t_0 : G_0$.

1(a). $\mathbf{S}(\rho, <, \Delta, q, t, G_0, t_0)$ for q atomic or $\perp$ if for some
$t : A \to q$, $\mathbf{S}(\rho, <, \Delta, A, t, G_0, t_0)$.

(b). If $t : q \in \Delta$ or $s : \perp \in \Delta$ then $\mathbf{S}(\rho, <, \Delta, q, t, G_0, t_0)$.

(c). $\mathbf{S}(\rho, <, \Delta, \perp, t, G_0, t_0)$ if $\mathbf{S}(\rho, <, \Delta, \perp, s, G_0, t_0)$.
This rule says that if we can get a contradiction from any label, it
would be considered a contradiction of the whole system.

2. $\mathbf{S}(\rho, <, \Delta, G, t, G_0, t_0)$ if for some $s : A \to \perp$, $\mathbf{S}(\rho, <, \Delta, A, s, G_0, t_0)$.

3. $\mathbf{S}(\rho, <, \Delta, t, FG, G_0, t_0)$ if for some $s \in \rho, t < s$ and
$\mathbf{S}(\rho, <, \Delta, G, s, G_0, t_0)$.

4. $\mathbf{S}(\rho, <, \Delta, FG, t, G_0, t_0)$ if for some $t : A \to FB \in \Delta$ we have both (a)
and (b) below hold true:

(a) for all $s \in \rho$ such that $t < s$ we have $\mathbf{S}(\rho, <, \Delta^*, s, D, G_0, t_0)$
and $\mathbf{S}(\rho, <, \Delta, E, t, G_0, t_0)$ hold, where $\Delta^* = \Delta \cup \{s : B\}$ and
$D \in \{G, FG\}$ and $E \in \{A, FA\}$.
Note: The choice of D and E is made here for the case of transitive time. In modal logic, where $<$ is not necessarily transitive,
we take $D = G, E = A$. Other conditions on $<$ correspond to
different choices of D and E.

(b) For all future configurations of $(\rho, <, t)$ with a new letter s, denoted by $(\rho_s, <_s)$ we have $\mathbf{S}(\rho_s, <_s, \Delta^*, s, D, G_0, t_0)$ and
$\mathbf{S}(\rho_s, <_s, \Delta, E, t, G_0, t_0)$ hold, where Δ^*, E, D are as in (a).

5. This is the mirror image of (3).

6. This is the mirror image of (4).

7(a) $\mathbf{S}(\rho, <, \Delta, A_1 \wedge A_2, t, G_0, t_0)$ if both $\mathbf{S}(\rho, <, \Delta, A_i, t, G_0, t_0)$ hold for
$i = 1, 2$

(b) $\mathbf{S}(\rho, <, \Delta, A \to B, t, G_0, t_0)$ if $\mathbf{S}(\rho, <, \Delta \cup \{t : A\}, B, t, G_0, t_0)$.

8. **Restart Rule**
$\mathbf{S}(\rho, <, \Delta, G, t, G_0, t_0)$ if $\mathbf{S}(\rho, <, \Delta, G_0, t_0, G_0, t_0))$.

If the language contains $\mathcal{O}$ and $\otimes$ then the following are the relevant rules.

9. $\mathbf{S}(\rho, <, \Delta, \mathcal{O}G, t, G_0, t_0)$ if $\mathcal{O}t$ exists and $\mathcal{O}t \in \rho$ and
$\mathbf{S}(\rho, <, \Delta, G, \mathcal{O}t, G_0, t_0)$.

10. $\mathbf{S}(\rho, <, \Delta, \mathcal{O}G, t, G_0, t_0)$ if for some $t : A \to \mathcal{O}B \in \Delta$ both
$\mathbf{S}(\rho, <, \Delta, A, t, G_0, t_0)$ and $\mathbf{S}(\rho \cup \{\mathcal{O}t\}, <', \Delta \cup \{\mathcal{O}t : B\}, G, \mathcal{O}t, G_0, t_0)$
hold where $<'$ is the appropriate ordering closure of $< \cup \{t < \mathcal{O}t\}$

11. This is the mirror image of (9) for $\otimes$.

12. This is the mirror image of (10) for $\otimes$.

Example E11:
(Here $\Box$ can be either G or H.)

	Data	Query	Configuration
1.	$t : \Box a$	$?t : \Box b$	$\{t\}$
2.	$t : \Box(a \to b)$		t is a constant

Translation:

	Data	Query	Configuration
1.	$t : F(a \to \bot) \to \bot$	$t : F(b \to \bot) \to \bot$	$\{t\}$
2.	$t : F((a \to b) \to \bot) \to \bot$		

Computation:
The problem becomes

	Additional Data	Current Query	Configuration
3.	$t : F(b \to \bot)$	$?t : \bot$	$\{t\}$
from 2		$?t_0 : F((a \to b) \to \bot)$	

From (3) using ** create a new point s:

	Additional Data	Current Query	Configuration
4.	$s : b \to \bot$	$?s : (a \to b) \to \bot$	$t < s$

add $s : a \to b$ to the database and ask

5.	$s : (a \to b)$	$?s : \bot$

from (4) and (5) we ask:
$$?s : a$$

From computation rule (2) and clause 1 of the data we ask
$$?t : F(a \to \bot)$$

From computation rule (2) we ask
$$?s : a \to \bot$$

We add $s : a$ to the data and ask:

Additional Data	Current Query	Configuration
6. $s : a$	$?s : \bot$	$t < s$

The query succeeds.

5   Modal and Temporal Herbrand Universes

This section deals with the soundness of our computation rules. In conjunction with soundness it is useful to clarify the notion of modal and temporal Herbrand models. For simplicty we deal with temporal logic with P, F only and transitive irreflexive time or with modal logic with one modality $\Diamond$ and a general binary accessibility relation $<$. We get our clues from some examples:

Example E12
Consider the database

1. $t : a \rightarrow \Diamond b$

2. $\square(b \rightarrow c)$

3. $t : a$

The constellation is $\{t\}$.

If we translate the clauses into predicate logic we get:

1. $a^*(t) \rightarrow \exists s > t b^*(s)$

2. $\forall x[b^*(x) \rightarrow c^*(x)]$

3. $a^*(t)$

Translated into Horn clauses we get after skolemising:

1.1 $a^*(t) \rightarrow b^*(s)$

1.2 $a^*(t) \rightarrow t < s$

2 $b^*(x) \rightarrow c^*(x)$

3 $a^*(t)$

t, s are Skolem constants.

From this program, the queries

$$a^*(t), \neg b^*(t), \neg c^*(t), \neg a(s), b(s), c^*(s)$$

all succeed. $\neg$ is negation by failure.

It is easy to recognise that $\neg a^*(s)$ succeeds because there is no head which unifies with $a^*(s)$. The meaning of the query $\neg a^*(s)$ in terms of modalities is the query $\Diamond \neg a$.

The question is how do we recognise syntactically what fails in the modal language? The heads of clauses can be whole databases and there is no immediate way of syntactically recognising which atoms are not heads of clauses.

Example E13:
We consider a more complex example:

1. $t : a \rightarrow \Diamond b$

2. $\Box(b \rightarrow c)$

3. $t : a$

4. $t : a \rightarrow \Diamond d$

We have added clause (4) to the database in the previous example. The translation of the first three clauses will proceed as before. We will get

1.1 $a^*(t) \rightarrow c^*(s)$

1.2 $a^*(t) \rightarrow t < s$

2 $b^*(x) \rightarrow c^*(x)$

3 $a^*(t)$

We are now ready to translate clause 4. This should be translated like clause (1) into

4.1 $a^*(t) \rightarrow d^*(r)$

4.2 $a^*(t) \rightarrow t < r.$

The above translation is correct if the set of possible worlds is just an ordering. Suppose we know further that in our modal logic the set of possible worlds is linearly ordered. Since $t < s \land t < r \rightarrow s = r \lor s < r \lor r < s$, this fact must be reflected in the Horn clause database. The only way to do it is to add it as an integrity constraint.

Thus our temporal program translates into a Horn clause program with integrity constraints.

This will be true in the general case. Whether we need integrity constraints or not will depend on the flow of time.

Let us begin by translating from the modal and temporal language into Horn clauses. The labelled wff $t : A$ will be translated into a set of formulas of predicate logic denoted by $Horn\,(t, A)$. $Horn(t, A)$ is supposed to be logically equivalent to A. The basic translation of a labelled atomic predicate formula $t : A(x_1 \ldots x_n)$ is $A^*(t, x_1 \ldots x_n)$. A^* is a formula of a two sorted predicate logic where the first sort ranges over labels and the second sort over domain elements (of the world t).

Definition D8
Consider a temporal predicate language with connectives P and F, and $\neg$ for negation by failure.

Consider the notion of labelled temporal clauses, as defined in definition D2 of Section 2.

Let $Horn(t, A)$ be a translation function associating with each labelled clause or goal a set of Horn clauses in the two sorted language described above. The letters t, s which appear in the translation are Skolem constants. They are assumed to be *all different*.

We assume that we are dealing with a general transitive flow of time. This is to simplify the translation. If time has extra conditions, ie linearity, additional integrity constraints may need to be added. If time is characterised by non-first order conditions, (eg finiteness) then an adequate translation into Horn clause logic may not be possible.

The following are the translation clauses:

1. $Horn\,(t, A(x_1 \ldots x_n)) = A^*(t, x_1 \ldots x_n)$, for A atomic.

2. $Horn\,(t, FA) = \{t < s\} \cup Horn(s, A)$
   $Horn\,(t, PA) = \{s < t\} \cup Horn(s, A)$

3. $Horn\,(t, A \land B) = Horn(t, A) \cup Horn(t, B)$

4. $Horn\,(t, \neg A) = \neg \bigwedge Horn(t, A)$

5. $Horn\,(t, A \rightarrow F \wedge B_j) = \{\wedge Horn(t, A) \rightarrow t < s\} \cup \cup_{B_j} \{\wedge Horn(s, A) \wedge C \rightarrow D \mid (C \rightarrow D) \in Horn(s, B_j)\}$

6. $Horn(t, A \rightarrow P \wedge B_j) = \{\wedge Horn(t, A) \rightarrow s < t\} \cup \cup_{B_j} \{\wedge Horn(s, A) \wedge C \rightarrow D \mid (C \rightarrow D) \in Horn(s, B_j)\}$

7. $Horn(t, \Box A) = Horn(x, A)$ where x is a universal variable.

Example E14

To explain the translation of $t : A \rightarrow F(B_1 \wedge (B_2 \rightarrow B_3))$, let us write it in predicate logic. $A \rightarrow F(B_1 \wedge B_2 \rightarrow B_3))$ is true at t if A true at t implies $F(B_1 \wedge (B_2 \rightarrow B_3))$ is true at t. $F(B_1 \wedge (B_2 \rightarrow B_3))$ true at t if for some s, $t < s$ and $B_1 \wedge (B_2 \rightarrow B_3)$ are true at s.

Thus we have the translation

$$A^*(t) \rightarrow \exists s(t < s \wedge B_1^*(s) \wedge (B_2^*(s) \rightarrow B_3^*(s)))$$

Skolemising on s and writing it in Horn clauses we get the conjunction

$A^*(t) \rightarrow t < s$
$A^*(t) \rightarrow B_1^*(s)$
$A^*(t) \wedge B_2^*(s) \rightarrow B_3^*(s).$

Let us see what the translation *Horn* does:

$Horn\,(t, A \rightarrow F(B_1 \wedge (B_2 \rightarrow B_3))) = \{\wedge Horn(t, A) \rightarrow t < s\} \cup \{\wedge Horn(t, A) \rightarrow Horn(s, B_2\} \cup \wedge \{Horn(t, A) \wedge \wedge Horn(s, B_2) \rightarrow \wedge Horn(s, B_3)\} =$

$\{A^*(t) \rightarrow t < s, A^*(t) \rightarrow B_2^*(s), A^*(t) \wedge B_2^*(s) \rightarrow B_3^*(s)\}$

We prove soundness of the computation of definition D4 of section 2, relative to the Horn clause computation for Horn database in classical logic. In other words if the tranlation $Horn(t, A)$ is accepted as intuitively it should and the computation of $\mathbf{S}(\rho, <, \Delta, G, t, G_0, t_0, \Theta)$ can be translated isomorphically into a Horn clause computation of the form $Horn(t, \Delta)?Horn(t, G)$ then the soundness of the classical Horn clause computation would imply the soundness of our computation.

This method of translation will also relate our temporal computation to that of ordinary Horn clause computation.

The basic unit of our temporal computation is $\mathbf{S}(\rho, < \Delta, G, t, G_0, t_0, \Theta)$. $t : G$ is the current labelled goal and $t_0 : G_0$ is the original goal. $(\rho, <, \Delta)$ is the database and Θ is the current substitution. $t_0 : G_0$ is used in the

Restart rule. For temporal flow of time which is ordinary transitive $<$, we do not need the Restart Rule. Thus we have to translate $(\rho, <, \Delta)$ to classical logic and translate $t : G$ and Θ to classical logic and see what each computation step of **S** of the source translates into the classical logic target.

Definition D9:
Let $(\rho, <)$ be a constellation and let Δ be a labelled database such that

$$\rho = \{t \mid \text{ for some } A, t : A \in \Delta\}$$

Let Horn $((\rho, <), \Delta) = \{t < s \mid t, s \in \rho \text{ and } t < s\} \cup \cup_{t:A \in \Delta} Horn(t, A)$.

Theorem T1 (Soundness)
$\mathbf{S}(\rho, <, \Delta, G, t, \Theta)$ succeeds in temporal logic if and only if in the sorted classical logic $Horn ((\rho, <), \Delta)? Horn(t, G)$ succeeds with substitution Θ.

Proof The proof is by induction on the complexity of the computation tree of $\mathbf{S}(\rho, <, \Delta, G, t, \Theta)$.

We follow the inductive steps of Definition D3 of Section 2. The translation of (Π, Θ) is a conjunction of Horn clause queries, all required to succeed under the same substitution Θ.

I The empty goal succeeds in both cases.

II (Π, Θ) fails if for some $\mathbf{S}(\rho, <, \Delta, G, t)$, we have G is atomic and for all $\Box(A \rightarrow H) \in \Delta$ and all $t : A \rightarrow H \in \Delta$, $G\Theta$ and $H\Theta$ do not unify. The reason they do not unify is because of what Θ substitutes to the variables u_i.

The corresponding Horn clause predicate programs are

$\wedge Horn(x, A) \rightarrow H^*(x)$
and
$\wedge Horn(t, A) \rightarrow H^*(t)$
and the goal is $?G^*(t)$

Clearly since x is a general universal variable, the success of the two sorted unification depends on the other variables and Θ. Thus unification does *not* succeed in the classical predicate case iff it does not succeed in the temporal case.

Rules (1) and (2) deal with the atomic case: The query is $G^*(t)$ and in the database among the data are

$$\wedge Horn(t, A) \rightarrow H^*(t) \text{ and } \wedge Horn(x, A) \rightarrow H^*(x)$$

for the cases of $t : A \to H$ and $\square(A \to H)$ respectively.

For the Horn clause program to succeed $G^*(t)$ must unify with $H^*(t)$. This will hold if and only if the substitution for the domain variables allows unification, which is exactly the condition of definition D3 in Section 2.

Rules (3), (4g) and (4*g) deal with the case of a goal of the form $?t : FG$. The translation of the goal is $t < u \wedge \bigwedge Horn(u, G)$ where u is an existential variable.

Rule (3) gives success when for some $s, t < s \in \Delta$ and $?s : G$ succeeds. In this case let $u = s$, then $t < u$ succeeds and $\wedge Horn(s, G)$ succeeds by the induction hypothesis.

We now turn to the general rules (4g) and (4*g). These rules yield success when for some clause of the form

$$t : A \to F \wedge B_j$$

or

$$\square(A \to F \wedge B_j)$$

$\Delta ?t : A$ succeeds and $\Delta \cup \{(s : B_j)\} ?s : G \vee FG$ both succeed. s is a new point.

The translation $\wedge Horn(t, A)$ succeeds by the induction hypothesis.

The translation of

$$t : A \to F \wedge B_j$$

or

$$\square(A \to F \wedge B_j)$$

contains the following database:

1. $\wedge Horn(t, A) \to t < s$

2. For every B_j and every $C \to D$ in $Horn(s, B_j)$ the clause
   $\wedge Horn(s, A) \wedge C \to D$.

Since $\wedge Horn(t, A)$ succeeds we can assume we have in our database

1* $t < s$

2* $C \to D$, for $C \to D \in Horn(s, B_j)$ for some j.

$(1^*), (2^*)$ were obtained by substituting *truth* in (1) and (2) for $\wedge Horn(t, A)$.

The goal to show is $t < u \wedge \bigwedge Horn(u, G)$.

Again for $u = s, t < u$ succeeds from (1^*) and by the induction hypothesis, since $\Delta \cup \{s : B_j\}?s : G \vee FG$ is successful, we get $\cup_j Horn(s, B_j)? \wedge Horn(s, G) \vee (s < U' \wedge \bigwedge Horn(u', G)$ should succeed, with u' an existential variable.

However, (2^*) is exactly $\cup_j Horn(s, \wedge B_j)$. Therefore we have shown that rules $(4g)$ and (4^*g) are sound.

Rules $(6g)$ and (6^*g) are sound because they are the mirror images of $(4g)$ and (4^*g).

The next relevant rules for our soundness cases are (11) - (13). These follow immediately since the rules for $\wedge, \vee, \neg$ are the same in both computations.

Rule 14, the Restart Rule, is definitely sound. If we try to show in general that $\Delta \vdash A$ then since in classical logic $\sim A \rightarrow A$ is the same as A ($\sim$ is classical negation) it is equivalent to show $\Delta, \sim A \vdash A$.

If $\sim A$ is now in the data, we can *at any time* try to show A instead of the current goal G. This will give us A (shown) and $\sim A$ (in Data) which is a contradiction and this yield *any goal* including the current goal G.

We have thus completed the soundness proof.

6   Tractability and Persistence

We defined a temporal database Δ essentially as a finite piece of information telling us which temporal formulas are true at what times. In the most general case, for a general flow of time $(T, <)$, all a database can do is to provide a set of the form $\{t_i : A_i\}$, meaning that A_i is true at time t_i and a configuration $(\{t_i\}, <)$, giving the temporal relationships among $\{t_i\}$. A query would be of the form $?t : Q$, where t is one of the t_i. The computation of the query from the data is in the general case exponential, as we found in Section 2, from the case analysis of clause 4 of Definition D4 and from example E3. We must therefore analyse the reasons for the complexity and see whether there are simplifying natural assumptions, which will make the computational problem more tractable.

There are three main components which contribute to complexity:

1. The complexity of the temporal formulas allowed in the data and in the query. We allow $t : A$ into the database, with A having temporal operators. So for example, $t : FA$ is allowed and also $t : \mathcal{O}A$. $t : FA$ makes life more difficult because it has in it a hidden Skolem function. It really means $\exists s[t < s$ and $(s : A)]$. This gives rise to case analysis, as we do not know in general where s is. See example E6 of Section 2 and examples E12 and E13 of Section 5. In this respect $t : \mathcal{O}A$ is a relatively simple item. It says $(t + 1) : A$. In fact any temporal operator which specifies the time is relatively less complex. In practice, we do need to allow data of the form $t : FA$. Sometimes we know an event will take place in the future but we do not know when. The mere fact that A is going to be true can affect our present actions. A concrete example where such a case may arise is when someone accepts a new appointment beginning next year, but has not yet resigned from his old position. We know he is going to resign but we do not know when.

2. The flow of time itself gives rise to complexity. The flow of time may be non-Horn clause (eg linear time), which is defined by a disjunctive axiom.
$$\forall xy[x < y \lor y < x \lor x = y]$$
This complicates the case analysis of (1) above.

3. Complexity arises from the temporal behaviour itself. If atomic predicates get truth values at random moments of time, the database can be complex to describe. A very natural simplifying assumption in the case of temporal logic is *persistence*. If atomic statements and their negations remain true for a while then they give rise to less complexity. Such examples are abundant. For example, people usually stay at their residences and jobs for a while. So for example, any payroll or local tax system can benefit from persistence as a simplifying assumption. Thus in databases where there is a great deal of persistence, we can use this fact to simplify our representation and querying. In fact, we shall see that a completely different approach to temporal representation can be adopted when one can make use of persistence.

   Another simplifying assumption is *recurrence*. Saturdays, for example, recur every week, so do paydays. This simplifies the representation and querying. Again, a payroll system would benefit from that.

We said at the beginning that a database Δ is a finitely generated piece of temporal information stating what is true and when. If we do not have any simplifying assumptions, we have to represent Δ in the form $\Delta = \{t_i : A_i\}$ and end up needing the computation rules of Section 2 to answer queries.

Suppose now that we adopt all three simplifying assumptions for our database. We assume that the A_i are only atoms and their negations, we further assume that each A_i is either persistent or recurrent, and let us assume, to be realistic, that the flow of time is linear. Linearity does not make the computation more complicated in this particular case, because we are not allowing data of the form $t : FA$, and so complicated case analysis does not arise. In fact, together with persistence and recurrence, linearity becomes an additional simplifying assumption!

Our aim is to check what form our temporal logic programming machine should take in view of our chosen simplifying assumptions.

First note that the most natural units of data are no longer of the form:

$$t : A;$$

reading: A is true at t

but either of the form:

$$[t, s] : A, [t < s];$$

reading: A is true in the closed interval $[t, s]$

or the form:

$$t \| d : A;$$

reading: A is true at t and recurrently at $t + d, t + 2d, \ldots$
             that is, every d moments of time.

A is assumed to be a literal (atom or a negation of an atom) and $[t, s]$ is supposed to be a maximal interval where A is true. In $t \| d$, d is supposed to be the minimal cycle for A to recur. The reasons for adopting the notation $[t, s] : A$ and $t \| d : A$ are not mathematical but simply intuitive and practical. This is the way we think about temporal atomic data when persistence or recurrence are present. In the literature there has been a great debate whether to evaluate temporal statements at points or intervals. Some researchers were so committed to intervals that they tended, unfortunately, to disregard any system which uses points. Our position here is clear and intuitive. First perform all the computations using intervals. Evaluation at points is possible and trivial. To evaluate $t : A$, ie to ask $?t : A$ as a query from a database, compute the (maximal) intervals at which A is true and see whether t is there. To evaluate $[t, s] : A$ do the same, and check whether $[t, s]$ is a subset.

The query language is left in its full generality. ie we can ask queries of the form $t : A$ where A is unrestricted (eg $A = FB$, etc). It makes sense also to allow queries fo the form $[t, s] : A$, though how exactly we are going to find the answer remains to be seen. The reader should be aware that the data representation language and the query language are no longer the same. This is an important factor. There has been a lot of confusion, especially among the AI community, in connection with these matters. We shall see later that as far as computational tractability is concerned, the restriction to persistent data allows one to strengthen the query language to full predicate quantification over time points.

At this stage we might consider allowing recurrence within an interval, ie we allow something like

"A is true every d days in the interval $[t, s]$."

We can denote this by:
$$[t \| d, s] : A;$$
meaning A is true at $t, t + d, t + 2d$, as long as $t + nd \leq s, n = 1, 2, 3, \ldots$.

We may as well equally have recurrent intervals. An example of that would be taking a two week holiday every year. This we denote by:
$$[t, s] \| d : A, \quad t < s, \quad (s - t) < d;$$
reading A is true at the intervals $[t, s], [t + d, s + d], [t + 2d, s + 2d]$, etc.

The reader should note that adopting this notation takes us outside the realm of first order logic. Consider the integer flow of time. We can easily say that q is true at all even numbers by writing $[0, 0] \| 1$ as a truth set for q and $[1, 1] \| 1$ as a truth set for $\sim q$. (ie q is true at 0 and recurs every 1 unit and $\sim q$ is true at 1 and recurs every 1 unit).

The exact expressive power of this language will be examined in a subsequent part 3 of this series of papers. It is connected with the language **USF** of [8].

The above seem to be the most natural options to consider. We can already see that it makes no sense any more to check how the computation rules of definition D4 of section 2 simplify for our case. Our case is so specialised that we may as well devise computation rules directly for it. This should not surprise us. It happens in mathematics all the time. The theory of abelian groups for example, is completely different from the theory of semigroups, although abelian groups are a special case of semigroups. The case of abelian groups is so special that it does not relate any more to the general case.

Let us go back to the question of how to answer a query from our newly defined simplified databases. We start with an even more simple case, assuming only persistence and assuming that the flow of time is the integers. This simple assumption will allow us to present our point of view of how to evaluate a formula at a point or at an interval. It will also ensure we are still within what is expressible in first order logic. Compare [13] for a similar system based on persistence.

Assume that the atom q is true at the maximal intervals $[x_n, y_n], x_n \leq y_n < x_{n+1}$. Then $\sim q$ is true at the intervals $[y_n + 1, x_{n+1} - 1]$, a sequence of the same form, ie $y_n + 1 \leq x_{n+1} - 1$ and $x_{n+1} - 1 < y_{n+1} + 1$.

It is easy to compute the intervals corresponding to the truth values of conjunctions, we take intersection.

If $I_j = \cup_n [x_n^j, y_n^j]$ then $I_1 \cap I_2 = \cup_n [x_n, y_n]$ and the points x_n, y_n can be effectively linearly computed. Also, if I_j is the interval set for A_j, the interval set for $U(A_1, A_2)$ can be effectively computed.

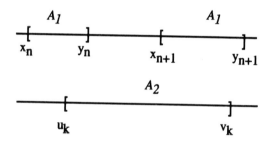

Figure 7

In the diagram, $U(A_1, A_2)$ is true at $[u_k, y_n - 1], [u_k, y_{n+1} - 1]$ which simplifies to the maximal $[u_k, y_{n+1} - 1]$.

The importance of the above is that we can regard a query formula of the full language with Until and Since as an operator on the model (database) to give a new database. If the database Δ gives for each atom or its negation the set of intervals where it is true, then a formula A operates on Δ to give the new set of intervals Δ_A thus to answer $\Delta?t : A$ the question we ask is $t \in \Delta_A$. The new notion is that the query operates on the model.

This approach was adopted by I Torsun and K Manning [16] when implementing the query language **USF**. The complexity of computation is polynomial (n^2). Note that although we have restricted the database formulas to atoms, we discovered that at no additional cost we can increase the query language to include the connectives Since and Until. It is well known that in the case of integers the expressive power of Since and Until is equivalent to quantification over time points, [11].

We shall say more about these systems in a subsequent Part 3 of this series. I hope the reader gets an idea of what is to be investigated.

To give the reader another glimpse of what is to come, note that intuitively we have several options:

1. We can assume persistence of atoms and negation of atoms. In this case we can express temporal models in first order logic. The query language can be full Since and Until logic. This option does not allow for recurrence. In practical terms this means that we cannot generate or control easily recurrent events. Note that the database does not need to contain Horn clauses as data. Clauses of the form $\Box$ (Present $\mathrm{wff}_1 \rightarrow$ Present wff_2) are redundant and can be eliminated (this has to be properly proved!).

   Clauses of the form $\Box$ (Past $\mathrm{wff}_1 \rightarrow$ Present wff_2) are not allowed as they correspond to recurrence. Temporal IQ of B Richards and Bethke is an example of such a system.

2. This option wants to have recurrence, is not interested in first order expressibility. How do we generate recurrence?

   The language **USF** (which was introduced for completely different reasons) allows one to generate the database using rules of the form $\Box$ (Past formula $\rightarrow$ Present or Future formula).

The above rules together with some initial items of data of the form $t : A$, A a literal, can generate persistent and recurrent models.

References

[1] M. Abadi and Z. Mana. Temporal logic programming. In *Proceedings of 1987 Symposium on Logic programming*, 1987.

[2] H. Barringer, M. Fisher, D. M. Gabbay, G. Gough, and R. Owens. METATEM: A framework for programming in temporal logic. In *Rex Workshop on Stepwise Refinement of Distributed Systems: Models, Formalisms, Correctness*, LNCS, Mook, Netherlands, June 1989. Springer Verlag.

[3] M. Baudinet. Temporal logic programming is complete and expressive. In *Conference record of the 16th ACM Symposium on the principles of programming languages*, 1989.

[4] F. del Cerro and M. Penttonen, editors. *Non Classical Logic Programming*. Oxford University Press, 1990.

[5] M. Fujita, S. Kono, H. Tanake, and T. Motooka. Tokio—logic programming language based on temporal logic and its compilation in Prolog. In Ehud Shapiro, editor, *Third International Conference on Logic Programming*. Springer Verlag, 1986.

[6] D. M. Gabbay. *N*-Prolog, an extension of Prolog with hypothetical implication part 2. *Journal of Logic Programming*, 2:251–283, 1985.

[7] D. M. Gabbay. Modal and temporal logic programming 1. In A Galton, editor, *Temporal Logics and their Applications*, pages 197–237. Academic Press, 1987.

[8] D. M. Gabbay. The declarative past and imperative future. In H. Barringer, editor, *Proceedings of the Colloquium on Temporal Logic and Specification*, volume 398 of *LNCS*, pages 409–448. Springer Verlag, 1989.

[9] D. M. Gabbay. LDS—labelled deductive systems. Technical report, Imperial College, 1989. To be published by Oxford University Press, 1991.

[10] D. M. Gabbay. Modal and temporal logic programming 3: Metalevel features in the object level. Technical report, Imperial College, 1990. To appear in [4].

[11] H. Kamp. *Tense Logic and the Theory of Linear Order*. PhD thesis, 1968.

[12] M. A. Orgun and W. W. Wadge. Temporal logic programming in Chronolog. Technical report, 1989.

[13] B. Richards and I. Bethke. The temporal logic IQ. In B. Richards et al., editors, *Temporal Representation and Reference*, pages 211–231. Academic Press, 1989.

[14] T. Sakuagawa. Temporal Prolog. In *Rims Conference on Software Science and Engineering*, 1987.

[15] I. Torsun and K. Manning. Execution and applications of temporal modal logic. Technical report, University of Bradford.

[16] I. Torsun and K. Manning. Logic database demonstrator. Internal Report ♯ Comp 89/11, Department of Computing, University of Bradford, 1989.

Evaluating Different Strategies for Handling Incomplete Information in a Logic Database

Qinzheng Kong   M. H. Williams

Abstract

The problem of handling incomplete information in a relational database is well understood and various researchers have investigated strategies for solving it. By contrast, the problem of incomplete information in a logic database is much more difficult and poses considerable challenges.

A formalism for incomplete information in a logic database has been put forward based on Lipski's work on relational databases, and a model has been developed which accounts for the behaviour of a logic database using such a formalism. To implement this formalism two different approaches have been investigated. These are described and their performance when applied to a given set of test examples, is compared.

1   Introduction

In many applications of databases, instances arise where the value of an attribute is not known exactly[2],[3],[4],[13]. Such situations are usually handled by using a null value as the value of the attribute concerned, provided that such a facility is available [7],[8],[10],[11],[12],[18]. However, if one has some information about an attribute value, even though the exact value is not known, then by simply using a null value, one is discarding what information one does have.

Two obvious forms of incomplete information which have been identified are sets and ranges. An extension of the relational model which caters for attribute values of these two types has been developed by Lipski [9]. These

124

ideas have been used as a basis for an extended form of QBE which handles incomplete information in the forms of sets, ranges and sets of ranges [16].

To demonstrate the problem, consider a database which is part of an office information system. Within such a database one might have the following relation which contains details about meetings scheduled.

meeting	meeting_no	time	date	group
	1	1000	15_Feb	Research_ctee
	2	1400	16_Feb	Finance_ctee

This can be represented in logic as the following set of clauses:

$$meeting(1, 1000, 15\_Feb, research\_ctee)$$
$$meeting(2, 1400, 16\_Feb, finance\_ctee).$$

Now suppose that one wants to add a meeting of the Executive Committee which is due to take place at 10am on 17th, 18th or 19th February (the exact date has not yet been finalised). Rather than represent this as

meeting	meeting_no	time	date	group
	3	1000	NULL	Exec_ctee

one might write

meeting	meeting_no	time	date	group
	3	1000	{17_Feb, 18_Feb, 19_Feb}	Exec_ctee

or represent this as the clause

$$meeting(3, 1000, \{17\_Feb, 18\_Feb, 19\_Feb\}, Exec\_ctee)$$

where $\{17\_Feb, 18\_Feb, 19\_Feb\}$ represents the fact that the date is not known exactly but is known to be one of 17th February, 18th February or 19th February.

Extending these ideas to a logic database is a more difficult task [1], [6], [17], [5]. Not only can incomplete information occur in facts but also in rules. In the latter case, it may occur as:

1. Uncertain consequence.

For example, suppose that one is planning a new rota of duties and either Miss Jones or Mrs Smith is to be assigned to take minutes for the Executive committee. This might be expressed as

$$secretary(X, \{miss\_jones, mrs\_smith\})$$
$$\leftarrow \quad meeting(X, Y, Z, exec\_ctee)$$

2. Uncertain condition

   To illustrate this, suppose that one of the secretaries responsible for taking the minutes for the Executive committee or for the Finance committee must also handle the Research committee. One might express this knowledge as a rule as follows:

$$secretary(X, Y) \quad \leftarrow \quad meeting(X, A, B, research\_ctee),$$
$$meeting(Z, C, D, \{exec\_ctee, finance\_ctee\}),$$
$$secretary(Z, Y).$$

A model has been put forward by Williams and Kong [14] to account for the behaviour of incomplete information in this form in a logic database. This is described briefly in the next section.

This paper describes two strategies which have been used to implement this model of incomplete information and compares their performance when applied to a given set of test examples.

2   Model of incomplete information

An item of incomplete information represents an uncertain value which may be used as an argument in a database fact or rule. When it appears, it represents a disjunction. For example, let x_i be a complete constant and X be a variable. The database fact

$$p(\{x_1, x_2\})$$

represents the situation where either the fact $p(x_1)$ is true or the fact $p(x_2)$ is true or both. It is equivalent to

$$p(x_1) \vee p(x_2).$$

A database rule containing incomplete information with the form:

$$p(X, \{a, b\}) \leftarrow q(X)$$

represents the knowledge that if $q(X)$ is true then either $p(X, a)$ is true or $p(X, b)$ is true. This is equivalent to a rule with a disjunction in the rule head:

$$p(X, a) \lor p(X, b) \leftarrow q(X).$$

A simple model representation of a single argument fact is given in Fig. 1. If the argument is a definite constant, e.g. x_1, the fact is represented by the model shown in Fig. 1(a). If the argument is a variable, e.g. X, then $p(X)$ is represented as a collection of ground facts, one for each value of the variable, as illustrated in Fig. 1(b). If the argument is an incomplete constant, e.g. $\{x_1, x_2\}$, then $p(\{x_1, x_2\})$ may be viewed as a set of separate models corresponding to each distinct value in the constant, as shown in Fig. 1(c).

A query is handled by negating it and adding it to the database. Thus the query

$$? - p(x_1)$$

will correspond to the addition of $\neg p(x_1)$ to the database. Likewise the query

$$? - p(X)$$

results in the addition of a set of negated facts, one for each value of the variable. The query

$$? - p(\{x_1, x_2\})$$

which asks whether either $p(x_1)$ or $p(x_2)$ is true in the database, i.e.

$$? - p(x_1) \lor p(x_2)$$

results in the two negated facts

$$\neg p(x_1)$$

$$\neg p(x_2)$$

being added to the database. This is illustrated in Fig. 2.

This approach can be used to represent rules, both with and without incomplete information. This is explained in greater detail in [14]. Using this model one can picture clearly the effects of resolution and hence the results of any query which involves both inference and incomplete information.

3 Tuple oriented evaluation strategy

One strategy for handling incomplete information is the so called tuple oriented approach. Under this approach, the system evaluates a user query and returns one answer at a time. If more than one answer is required by the user query then the system will backtrack to re-search the database to find each successive answer.

3.1   Simple tuple oriented query evaluation

This strategy is similar to the fail and back-tracking strategy used by Prolog to find more than one solution. The difference is that in order to handle incomplete information, an extended resolution mechanism is required, which unifies two literals and produces a group of resolvents in a slightly different way from standard Prolog. The approach can be briefly described as follows:

1. An extended unification mechanism is used to unify the first literal of the query with the head of a clause and a substitution θ is obtained.

2. If the query contains more than one literal, (i.e., a conjunctive query) then the substitution is applied to the remaining literals of the query to produce a group of resolvents.

3. All the resolvents must be satisfied in the database to establish the answer.

4. Once the answer is established (or disproved), backtracking is invoked to find the next solution.

To understand this approach, consider the following example. Suppose a database has the following facts:

$$has\_opportunity(\{peter, mary\}).$$
$$has\_opportunity(john).$$
$$has\_opportunity(tom).$$
$$has\_motive(\{tom, john\}).$$
$$has\_motive(mary).$$
$$has\_motive(peter).$$

and a rule:
$$is\_suspect(X) : -has\_opportunity(X), has\_motive(X).$$

If a user wants to find all suspects, i.e.,
$$? - is\_suspect(X).$$

the set of answers to this query will be:

$$\{\langle X\rangle | is\_suspect(X)\}$$

The evaluation procedure will be as follows:

1. The unification between the query $? - is\_suspect(X)$ and the rule head $is\_suspect(X)$ follows the ordinary Prolog unification mechanism and yields the substitution $\theta = \{X/X\}$. Thus the rule body $has\_opportunity(X), has\_motive(X)$ is picked up as the goal to be further evaluated.

2. An extended unification mechanism is used to unify the first literal of the new goal $has\_opportunity(X)$ with the first clause defining $has\_opportunity$ and a substitution $\theta_1 = \{\langle\{peter, mary\}/X\rangle\}$ is obtained.

3. The substitution θ_1 is applied to the remainder of the goal, which is $has\_motive(X)$. Since the term value in the substitution is an incomplete data item, it stands for several possibilities. In this example X might be either *peter* or *mary*, and consequently two resolvents $has\_motive(peter)$ and $has\_motive(mary)$ are produced.

4. To establish the answer that *peter* or *mary* is a suspect, one has to prove that both of them have motive. (If one of them has motive, it may lead to the situation that *peter* has opportunity and *mary* has motive or vice versa—in both cases the answer "one of them is a suspect" cannot be established). In this case the two goals $has\_motive(peter)$ and $has\_motive(mary)$ are both satisfied and hence $\{peter, mary\}$ is returned as a solution to the query.

5. Backtracking is invoked to find further answers.

3.2 Improved query evaluation

There is a serious problem with the above procedure. When backtracking fails, it is not necessarily the case that there are no alternative answers, but simply that no further answer can be established under this particular order of the literals in the goal. In this example, $\{tom, john\}$ is also an answer to the query, but there is no way to obtain this other than to perform the evaluation in a different order. In other words, if the rule were changed to:

$$is\_suspect(X) : -has\_motive(X), has\_opportunity(X).$$

and evaluated again, it would yield the answer $\{tom, john\}$. It is obvious that when the number of literals in the query (or the rule body) increases, the complexity of the evaluation increases exponentially.

To solve this problem, an improved query evaluation strategy is required. The main point of the improvement is that if a variable unifies with a complete constant t in the evaluation of literal p, it remains possible that the variable can be further unified with an incomplete set, S, containing t as its element, and this incomplete set might be the final substitution of the variable if each remaining element of S can be proved to be a solution of p. In this case a re-evaluation mark is used to indicate that the literal p has to be re-evaluated and succeed with each element in S to establish the answer. If there is more than one variable in literal p, this re-evaluation mark can only be made when each variable is substituted by a complete constant. The evaluation procedure can be described as follows:

1. Unify the negative and positive literals by using the extended unification rules.

2. If the substitution contains an incomplete data item as the term value, then apply it to the remainder of the query to produce a group of resolvents. If the substitution does not contain incomplete data but contains some complete data as term values, then apply it to the remaining literals of the query to get a resolvent and mark the current literal re-evaluable.

3. Prove all the resolvents to establish the answer. If the proof fails, and there is a re-evaluating mark, then try to find an incomplete proof of the resolvent, and re-evaluate the previous literals.

4. Backtrack to find more answers.

To illustrate this approach, consider the same suspect example. The derivation of the first answer *peter or mary is a suspect* is exactly the same as above. When backtracking to step 2 to find the next solution, the algorithm proceeds as follows:

2. An extended unification mechanism is used to unify the first literal of the new goal $has\_opportunity(X)$ with the second clause defining $has\_opportunity$ and a substitution $\theta_2 = \{\langle john/X\rangle\}$ is obtained.

3. The substitution θ_2 is applied to the remainder of the rule body, yielding the goal $has\_motive(john)$. Since the term value in the substitution does not contain incomplete data, it is marked for re-evaluation.

4. *has_motive(john)* cannot be proved from the data in the database, but it can be partly proved because there is a fact *has_motive*({*john*, *tom*}) which has the reading that *john* or *tom* has motive. If it can be proved that Tom also has opportunity, then the answer that *John or Tom is a suspect* can be established. Since the re-evaluating mark exists, the re-evaluation of the literal *has_motive(tom)* is carried out and succeeds, the incomplete data item {*john*, *tom*} constitutes another answer of the query.

5. Mark the clause *has_motive*({*john*, *tom*}) to indicate that the incomplete data item {*john*, *tom*} has already been generated as one answer.

6. Backtracking is invoked and step 2 and 3 are repeated as before with the substitution $\theta_3 = \{\langle tom/X \rangle\}$ for the variable X in the literal *has_opportunity(X)*. Although the literal *has_motive(tom)* can also be partly proved by matching the clause *has_motive*({*john*, *tom*}), it does not constitute another answer because the answer has already been generated.

7. Further backtracking is invoked and no more answers obtained.

By applying this approach, all answers can be obtained without change to the order of the literals in the query (or in the rule body). However, it still has many problems.

1. When the first occurrence of variable X is unified with an incomplete constant (e.g. {*peter*, *mary*}), the rest of the query will be split into groups of queries with occurrences of the variable X being replaced in turn by each element in the incomplete constant. The whole query succeeds only when each of the branches succeeds. (In our example when X in *has_opportunity(X)* unifies with {*peter*, *mary*}, both *has_motive(peter)* and *has_motive(mary)* must succeed). If the query is complicated, the formulation of the splitting operation might not be acceptable. For example, if the first literal contains n variables and each of them unifies with an incomplete data item with m_i elements, then the remaining literals of the query will be split into $m_1 \times m_2 \times \ldots \times m_n$ branches. Each branch has to succeed to commit the answer.

2. When the first occurrence of a variable X unifies with a complete constant, a re-evaluating mark is required to enable this variable to be further unified with an incomplete constant. This greatly increases the complexity of the system control.

3. The system efficiency is reduced by the repeated backtracking and re-evaluation. For example, the literal *has_motive(tom)* is evaluated twice.

4 Set oriented evaluation strategy

An alternative strategy for query evaluation is the *set oriented approach*. This approach follows the basic idea of query evaluation in relational databases. Each literal in the query is regarded as a table generated by evaluating the literal. If there is only one literal in the query, then the result table is the final answer of the query. If there is more than one literal in the query (i.e. the query is a conjunctive query), then the join of all result tables generates the final answer to the query as a whole, and the shared variables in the literals give the attributes of the join.

The basic strategy of this approach is as follows:

1. Evaluate each literal in the query and generate its result set.

2. Perform the join operation on these result sets if required (i.e. for a conjunctive query).

3. To evaluate each literal, first unify it with each fact or rule head (with the same predicate name) in the database. If a fact is unified, then return the substituted value as one result, if a rule head is unified then recompose the rule body by applying the substitution to it and recursively invoke the whole strategy to evaluate the new rule body, returning all the results.

Consider again the example given in previous section. The evaluation procedure of the query

$$? - is\_suspect(X)$$

can be briefly described as follows:

1. Unify the query with the head of the rule in the database

$$is\_suspect(X) : -has\_opportunity(X), has\_motive(X).$$

and then treat the rule body $has\_opportunity(X), has\_motive(X)$ as a new goal to be evaluated.

2. An extended unification mechanism is used to unify the first literal $has\_opportunity(X)$ with all possible clauses defining $has\_opportunity$ and all substitutions of the variable X are returned as a result set. (In this example, the result set is $\{\{peter, mary\}, john, tom\}$).

3. An extended unification mechanism is used to unify the second literal $has\_motive(X)$ with all possible clauses defining has_motive and a result set is obtained. (In this example, it is the set $\{\{john, tom\}, peter, mary\}$).

4. An extended join function is applied to these two result sets using the shared variable X, and a joined set is obtained. (The extended join function will be given in detail in a later section. In this example, the joined result is $\{\{john, tom\}, \{peter, mary\}\}$).

The *set oriented* approach is based on the following main components:

1. The unification mechanism.

2. The extended join operation.

3. The recomposition of the rule body after successful unification of the rule head.

The details of the unification mechanism are described in detail in [15]. The remander of this section is devoted to a discussion of the extended join and the rule body recomposition.

4.1 The extended join operation

In general, a query or a rule body has the following format

$$B_1(\vec{X_1}) \wedge B_2(\vec{X_2}) \wedge \cdots \wedge B_n(\vec{X_n})$$

in which $n \geq 1$. After the evaluation of each literal $B_i(\vec{X_i})$ in the rule body, a set of results is obtained. The extended join operation is performed on these results. The ordinary join operation in relational algebra can be used for this purpose if there is no incomplete constant in the results. However, if incomplete constants occur, the ordinary join needs to be extended to cope with the situation.

Let $p(X_1, \ldots, X_k, Y_1, \ldots, Y_m)$ and $q(X_1, \ldots, X_k, Z_1, \ldots, Z_n)$ be two literals in a query (or in a rule body), where X_1 through X_k are shared variables.

Let $S = \{\langle x_1, \ldots, x_k, y_1, \ldots, y_m \rangle\}$ be the result set of $p(X_1, \ldots, X_k, Y_1, \ldots, Y_m)$, $R = \{\langle x_1, \ldots, x_k, z_1, \ldots, z_n \rangle\}$ be the result set of $q(X_1, \ldots, X_k, Z_1, \ldots, Z_n)$ and $T = \{\langle x_1, \ldots, x_k, y_1, \ldots, y_m, z_1, \ldots, z_n \rangle\}$ be the result set of the join of S and R. Let $\otimes$ denote the extended join and $\oplus$ the ordinary join, and a_i and A_i denote the complete data and incomplete data respectively. The extended join between two result sets can be given as follows:

Case 1 If neither set contains incomplete data, the function performs exactly the same as the join operator in relational algebra, i.e., $S \otimes R = S \oplus R$.

$$
\begin{aligned}
T = \ & \{\langle x_1, \ldots, x_k, y_1, \ldots, y_m, z_1, \ldots, z_n \rangle | \langle x_1, \ldots, x_k, y_1, \ldots, y_m \rangle \in S \\
& \wedge \langle x_1, \ldots, x_k, z_1, \ldots, z_n \rangle \in R\}
\end{aligned}
$$

Case 2 If no variable sharing occurs between p and q, (i.e. $k = 0$), even in the presence of incomplete data, the join performs as the ordinary relational join $\oplus$. i.e., $S \otimes R = S \oplus R$.

$$
T = \{\langle y_1, \ldots, y_m, z_1, \ldots, z_n \rangle | \langle y_1, \ldots, y_m \rangle \in S \wedge \langle z_1, \ldots, z_n \rangle \in R\}
$$

Case 3 If there is a single shared variable with incomplete data as its value, i.e. both p and q contain only one argument which is a shared variable, (i.e. $k = 1$, $n = 0$ and $m = 0$), the result $T = S \otimes R$ can be given as:

$$
\begin{aligned}
& a \in S \wedge a \in R \rightarrow a \in T. \\
& A \in S \wedge \forall_{a \in A}(a \in R) \rightarrow A \in T. \\
& A \in R \wedge \forall_{a \in A}(a \in S) \rightarrow A \in T.
\end{aligned}
$$

As an example consider the join in the evaluation of $is\_suspect(X)$. The evaluation of the literal $has\_opportunity(X)$ has the result

$$
S = \{\langle peter \rangle, \langle mary \rangle, \langle \{john, tom\} \rangle\},
$$

whereas the result set of literal $has\_motive(X)$ is

$$
R = \{\langle \{john, tom\} \rangle, \langle peter \rangle, \langle mary \rangle\}
$$

Since

$$
\begin{aligned}
& \langle \{john, tom\} \rangle \in S \wedge \langle john \rangle \in R \wedge \langle tom \rangle \in R \\
& \quad \rightarrow \quad \langle \{john, tom\} \rangle \in T \\
& \langle \{peter, mary\} \rangle \in R \wedge \langle peter \rangle \in S \wedge \langle mary \rangle \in S \\
& \quad \rightarrow \quad \langle \{peter, mary\} \rangle \in T
\end{aligned}
$$

the joined result is

$$
T = \{\langle \{john, tom\} \rangle, \langle \{peter, mary\} \rangle\}.
$$

Case 4 The most general case. In this case both p and q may contain any number of arguments, some of which are shared variables, and incomplete data items may occur as the values of the shared variables. To simplify the explanation a complete data item a can be regarded as a single element set $\{a\}$. Let S be a result set of $p(X_1, \ldots, X_k, Y_1, \ldots, Y_m)$ and ES_i be an element of S, i.e., $S = \{ES_1, \ldots, ES_s\}$. If ES_i contains only complete data items, it has the standard form

$$ES_i = \langle x_1, \ldots, x_k, y_1, \ldots, y_m \rangle.$$

If ES_i contains some incomplete data items as values, then ES_i can be re-expressed as a set of alternative values each of which contains only complete data, i.e.,

$$ES_i = \{Es_{i,1}, \ldots, Es_{i,j}\}$$

and each $Es_{i,j}$ has the standard format

$$Es_{i,j} = \langle x_1, \ldots, x_k, y_1, \ldots, y_m \rangle.$$

Similarly let R be a result set of $q(X_1, \ldots, X_k, Z_1, \ldots, Z_n)$ and ER_i be an element of R, i.e., $R = \{ER_1, \ldots, ER_r\}$. If ER_i contains only complete data it has the standard form

$$ER_i = \langle x_1, \ldots, x_k, z_1, \ldots, z_n \rangle,$$

If ER_i contains some incomplete data, then re-express it as a set of alternative complete values as follows:

$$ER_i = \{Er_{i,1}, \ldots, Er_{i,l}\}$$

where each $Er_{i,j}$ has the standard format

$$Er_{i,j} = \langle x_1, \ldots, x_k, z_1, \ldots, z_n \rangle.$$

The joined result $T = S \otimes R$ can be evaluated as follows:

$$
\begin{aligned}
ES_i = {}& \langle x_1, \ldots, x_k, y_1, \ldots, y_m \rangle \in S \\
& \wedge ER_j = \langle x_1, \ldots, x_k, z_1, \ldots, z_n \rangle \in R \\
& \rightarrow ET_h = \langle x_1, \ldots, x_k, y_1, \ldots, y_m, z_1, \ldots, z_n \rangle \in T. \quad (1) \\
ES_i = {}& \{Es_{i,1}, \ldots, Es_{i,l}\} \in S \\
& \wedge \forall_{Es_{i,j} \in ES_i}(Es_{i,j} = \langle x_{j_1}, \ldots, x_{j_k}, y_{j_1}, \ldots, y_{j_m} \rangle \wedge \\
& \exists_{ER_h \in R}(ER_h = \langle x_{h_1}, \ldots, x_{h_k}, z_{h_1}, \ldots, z_{h_n} \rangle \wedge \\
& x_{j_1} = x_{h_1} \wedge \cdots \wedge x_{j_k} = x_{h_k} \\
& \rightarrow Et_g = \{\langle x_{j_1}, \ldots, x_{j_k}, y_{j_1}, \ldots, y_{j_m}, z_{h_1}, \ldots, z_{h_n} \rangle\})
\end{aligned}
$$

$$\wedge ET = \bigcup_g Et_g \wedge ET \in T. \tag{2}$$

$$
\begin{aligned}
ER_i \;=\; & \{Er_{i,1}, \ldots, Er_{i,l}\} \in R \\
& \wedge \forall_{Er_{i,j} \in ER_i}(Er_{i,j} = \langle x_{j_1}, \ldots, x_{j_k}, z_{j_1}, \ldots, z_{j_n} \rangle \wedge \\
& \exists_{ES_h \in S}(ES_h = \langle x_{h_1}, \ldots, x_{h_k}, y_{h_1}, \ldots, y_{h_m} \rangle \wedge \\
& x_{j_1} = x_{h_1} \wedge \cdots \wedge x_{j_k} = x_{h_k} \\
& \rightarrow Et_g = \{\langle x_{j_1}, \ldots, x_{j_k}, y_{h_1}, \ldots, y_{h_m}, z_{j_1}, \ldots, z_{j_n} \rangle\}) \\
& \wedge ET = \bigcup_g Et_g \wedge ET \in T. \tag{3}
\end{aligned}
$$

To illustrate the above join rules consider the following example. Suppose a database has the following data:

$$p(\{a, b\}, \{c, d\}, e)$$
$$p(a, c, f)$$

$$q(a, c, s)$$
$$q(a, d, t)$$
$$q(b, c, s)$$
$$q(b, d, r)$$

A query has the form

$$? - p(X, Y, U), q(X, Y, V).$$

The result of evaluating $p(X, Y, U)$ is

$$S = \{ES_1, ES_2\} = \{\{\langle a, c, e \rangle, \langle a, d, e \rangle, \langle b, c, e \rangle, \langle b, d, e \rangle\}, \langle a, c, f \rangle\}$$

in which ES_1 is a set of alternative values each element of which has the standard form $\langle x, y, z \rangle$, and ES_2 contains only complete data. The result of evaluating $q(X, Y, V)$ is

$$R = \{ER_1, ER_2, ER_3, ER_4\} = \{\langle a, c, s \rangle, \langle a, d, t \rangle, \langle b, c, s \rangle, \langle b, d, r \rangle\}$$

in which all ER_is contain only complete data. The joined result of $p(X, Y, U)$ and $q(X, Y, V)$ is:

$$T = \{ET_1, ET_2\} = \{\{\langle a, c, e, s \rangle, \langle a, d, e, t \rangle, \langle b, c, e, s \rangle, \langle b, d, e, r \rangle\}, \langle a, c, f, s \rangle\}$$

4.2 Recompose the rule body

Consider the following query and clauses in a database:

$$? - q(V, \{a, b\}, c)$$

$$q(X, Y, Z) : -p(X, Y), r(Y, Z)$$
$$p(1, a).$$
$$p(1, b).$$
$$p(2, s).$$
$$r(\{a, b\}, c).$$
$$r(a, c).$$
$$r(a, t).$$
$$r(s, c).$$

When the query unifies with the rule head, a substitution $\theta = \{V/X, \{a, b\}/Y, c/Z\}$ is obtained. Due to the occurrences of incomplete data, the substituted values cannot be applied directly to the rule body. The simplest strategy is to evaluate the rule body without applying the substitution. Such an evaluation is performed by evaluating $p(X, Y)$ and $r(Y, Z)$ separately, joining the results of p and r, and then performing a selection on these joined results according to the rule head substitution θ. In the above example the joined result of p and r is

$$T = \{\langle 1, \{a, b\}, c\rangle, \langle 1, a, c\rangle, \langle 1, a, t\rangle, \langle 2, s, c\rangle\}$$

and after applying the substitution, the final result should be

$$T = \{\langle 1, \{a, b\}, c\rangle, \langle 1, a, c\rangle\}$$

However, in such a strategy unnecessary intermediate results such as $< 1, a, t >$, $< 2, s, c >$ are generated which not only reduce the efficiency but also occupy unnecessary space. A new rule to recompose the rule body is introduced to handle this problem. This process can be defined as follows:

1. If a variable is substituted by a complete constant, i.e. there is an element in the substitution having the form t/X in which t is a complete constant, then replace all the occurrences of the variable X in the rule body with the complete constant t.

2. If a variable is substituted by another uninstantiated variable, i.e. there is an element in the substitution having the form Y/X in which Y is a variable, then replace all the occurrences of the variable X in the rule body with the variable Y.

3. If a variable is substituted by an incomplete constant, i.e. there is an element in the substitution having the form A/X in which A is an incomplete constant arising from a negative literal, then replace all the occurrences of the variable X in the rule body by a dummy variable X'. The linkage between the incomplete constant A and the dummy variable X' specifies the constraint that the dummy variable X' can only be unified with an uninstantiated variable or with a subset of the incomplete data A. This constraint will be referenced by further evaluation.

Consider the above example after application of the substitution θ. The recomposed rule body has the following form:

$$p(V, Y'), r(Y', c)$$

with the condition that:

$$\{T/Y'\} \rightarrow variable(T) \vee A \supseteq T \vee T \in A.$$

which means that the condition of a valid substitution

$$\{T/Y'\}$$

is:

1. T is an uninstantiated variable or

2. T is an incomplete data item which is a subset of A or

3. T is a complete data item which is an element of A.

4.3   The handling of recursive rules

A special strategy is required for handling recursive rules in the *set oriented* approach. Suppose that one of the rules defining $p(X, Y)$ is a recursive rule (direct or indirect recursion). The algorithm for evaluating the recursive rule can be described as:

1. Assign a dummy predicate name p' to the recursive rule defining p.

2. Evaluate all facts and non-recursive definitions of p and store the results under some new predicate p'.

3. Replace the occurrences of p in the body of the recursive rule by the dummy predicate p' and evaluate the new rule (since each occurrence of p has been replaced, the rule is no longer recursive).

4. If new results are obtained which are not already present in p', then add them to p' and evaluate p again. Repeat this until no new result is obtained. The accumulated results of p' are the results of p.

Consider the ancestor example. Suppose the database has the following information:

$$father(tom, peter).$$
$$father(tom, john).$$
$$father(peter, rob).$$
$$father(peter, harry).$$
$$father(harry, mike).$$

$$ancestor(X, Y) : -father(X, Y).$$
$$ancestor(X, Y) : -father(X, Z) \wedge ancestor(Z, Y).$$

If a query seeks all the ancestors in the database, the evaluation procedure proceeds as follows:

1. A dummy predicate name for *ancestor* is *ancestor'*.

2. The results generated by evaluating the non-recursive rule of ancestor are

$$ancestor'(tom, peter).$$
$$ancestor'(tom, john).$$
$$ancestor'(peter, rob).$$
$$ancestor'(peter, harry).$$
$$ancestor'(harry, mike).$$

3. The recursive rule is updated as:

$$ancestor(X, Y) : -father(X, Z) \wedge ancestor'(Z, Y).$$

and the results of evaluating this rule are:

$$ancestor'(tom, rob).$$
$$ancestor'(tom, harry).$$
$$ancestor'(peter, mike).$$

4. As the evaluation continues, the following clause is added:

$$ancestor'(tom, mike)$$

5. No further clauses are generated and the final results are:

$$ancestor(tom, peter).$$
$$ancestor(tom, john).$$
$$ancestor(tom, rob).$$
$$ancestor(tom, harry).$$
$$ancestor(tom, mike).$$
$$ancestor(peter, rob).$$
$$\overset{.}{a}ncestor(peter, harry).$$
$$ancestor(peter, mike).$$
$$ancestor(harry, mike).$$

This way of handling recursive rules does not depend on the order of the literals defining the recursive rules. For example, if the definition of ancestor is changed to

$$ancestor(X, Y) : -ancestor(X, Z), father(Z, Y).$$

the same answer will be generated. On the other hand, the tuple based approach (and even Prolog itself) cannot handle this kind of rule since it will lead to a non-terminating loop.

4.4 The optimisation

The *set oriented* approach makes the order of the literals in the query irrelevant and is suitable for most database applications since most database queries seek all answers. This approach avoids repeated backtracking and reevaluating sets of resolvents produced each time. However, it needs more space than the *tuple oriented* approach especially when the database size is very large. To alleviate this shortcoming, an optimisation can be introduced in which the evaluation of database facts is delayed until the join operation is performed. Thus, the space required to store the intermediate results generated by evaluating the facts is saved. Under the assumption that in a logic database the number of facts is much greater than the number of rules, the space cost will be reduced greatly. Consider again the "suspect" example. Before the optimisation, space is required to store:

1. The internal format of the evaluating result of *has_opportunity*(X)

   $\{peter, mary\}$

   john

   tom

2. The internal format of the evaluating result of *has_motive*(X)

   $\{john, tom\}$

   peter

   mary

3. The internal format of the joined result

   $\{peter, mary\}$
   $\{john, tom\}$

After the optimisation, the total space required is the space to store the joined intermediate result

   $\{peter, mary\}$
   $\{john, tom\}$

5   Comparison of the two approaches

Both *set oriented* and *tuple oriented* approaches have been implemented in Prolog to handle incomplete information. Some comparisons have been made by testing both systems for a set of given examples. Table 1 gives the execution times of three examples in both systems; Figure 3 shows how the execution time increases as the database size is increased; Table 2 gives the space cost of the *set oriented* system—the third column gives the space required for storing the original data and the fourth column the maximum space required during execution. Although the *set oriented* approach needs more space than the *tuple oriented* approach, it has shorter execution times and is more suitable for database applications which require all answers.

References

[1] P. Chisholm, G. Chen, D. Ferbrache, P. Thanisch, and M.H. Williams. Coping with indefinite and negative data in deductive databases:, a survey. *Data and Knowledge Engineering*, 2:259–284, 1987.

Query	Database	Set-or. system	Tuple-orien	
			one	al...
$? - p(X, Y, U), q(X, Y, V).$	94 facts of $p(X, Y, U)$	9.06	0.55	296.
	86 facts of $q(X, Y, V)$			
$? - s(X, Y, V), p(X, Y, U)$	rule $s(X, Y, V)$	17.35	0.2	547.
	$s(X, Y, V) : -$			
	$r(X, Y), q(X, Y, V)$			
	85 facts of $r(X, Y)$			
	86 facts of $q(X, Y, V)$			
	94 facts of $p(X, Y, U)$			
$? - teaching(T, D, N, H)$	62 facts of	179.63	1.93	$> 60r$
	$teaching(T, D, N, H)$			
$marks(D, S, N, M)$	5000 facts of			
	$marks(D, S, N, M)$			

Table 1: Execution times for three examples in the two systems (measured in CPU seconds)

Query	Database	Space requirements	
		original data	join
$? - p(X, Y, U), q(X, Y, V).$	94 facts of $p(X, Y, U)$	8112	4040
	86 facts of $q(X, Y, V)$		
$? - s(X, Y, V), p(X, Y, U)$	rule $s(X, Y, V)$	11480	4944
	$s(X, Y, V)) : -$		
	$r(X, Y), q(X, Y, V)$		
	85 facts of $r(X, Y)$		
	86 facts of $q(X, Y, V)$		
	94 facts of $p(X, Y, U)$		
$? - teaching(T, D, N, H)$	62 facts of	222,622	183,512
	$teaching(T, D, N, H)$		
$marks(D, S, N, M)$	5000 facts of		
	$marks(D, S, N, M)$		

Table 2: Space (in bytes) required for evaluating queries using the set oriented approach

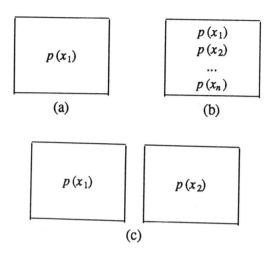

Figure 1: Model representations of (a) $p(x_1)$ (b) $p(X)$ (c) $p(\{x_1, x_2\})$

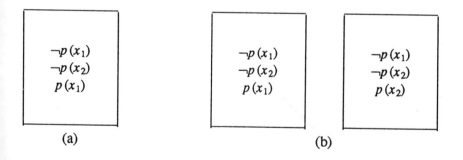

Figure 2: Model representations of query $?-p(\{x_1, x_2\})$ applied to database containing (a) $p(x_1)$ (b) $p(\{x_1, x_2\})$.

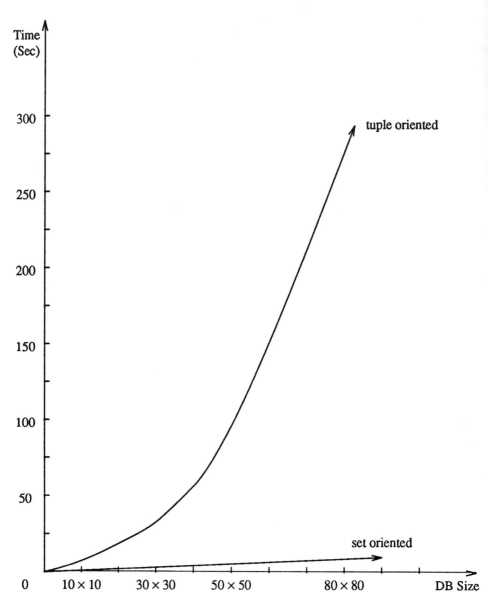

Figure 3: Execution times taken by set oriented and tuple oriented approaches for varying sizes of database

[2] E.F. Codd. Extending the database relational model to capture more meaning. *ACM Trans. on Database Systems*, 4(4):397–434, December 1979.

[3] C.J. Date. Null values in databases. In *Proc. of the Second British National Conference on Databases*, 1982.

[4] J. Grant. Null values in a relational data base. *Information Processing Letters*, 5:156–157, 1977.

[5] J. Grant and J. Minker. Answering queries in indefinite databases and the null, value problem. *Advances in Computer Research*, 3:247–267, 1986.

[6] T. Imielinski. *Query processing in deductive databases with incomplete information*, pages 268–280. October 1984.

[7] T. Imielinski and W. Lipski. On representing incomplete information in a relational databases. In *Proc. of International Conference of VLDB*, pages 388–, 1981.

[8] H.J. Levesque. The logic of incomplete knowledge base. In M.L. Brodie et al., editors, *On Conceptual Modeling*, pages 165–189. Springer, 1984.

[9] W. Lipski. Informational systems with incomplete information. In S. Michaelson and R. Milner, editors, *Proc. 3rd Int. Symp. on Automata, Languages and Programming*, pages 120–130, Edinburgh, 1976. Edinburgh University Press.

[10] R. Reiter. Towards a logical reconstruction of relational database theory. In M.L. Brodie et al., editors, *On conceptual modelling: Perspectives from artificial intelligence,, databases and programming languages*, pages 191–233. Springer, 1984.

[11] R. Reiter. A sound and sometimes complete query evaluation algorithm for, relational database with null values. *Journal of ACM*, 33(2):349–370, 1986.

[12] L. Siklossy. Efficient query evaluation in relational databases with missing values. *Information Processing Letters*, 13(4/5):160–163, 1981.

[13] Y. Vassiliou. Null values in data base management: A denotational semantics approach. *Proc. ACM-SIGMOD International Symposium on Management of Data*, pages 162–169, 1979.

[14] M.H. Williams and Q. Kong. Incomplete information in a deductive database. *Data and Knowledge Engineering*, 3:197–220, 1988.

[15] M.H. Williams, Q. Kong, and G. Chen. Handling incomplete information in a logic database. In *UK IT 88 Conference Publication*, pages 224–227, 1988.

[16] M.H. Williams and K.A. Nicholson. Implementation of incomplete information in databases. *The Computer Journal*, 1985. (to appear).

[17] A. Yahya and L.J. Henschen. Deduction in non-horn databases. *Journal of Automated Reasoning*, 1:141–160, 1985.

[18] C. Zaniolo. Database relations with null values. *Proc. ACM SIGACT-SIGMOD Symposium on principles of Database Systems*, pages 27–33, 1982.

Virtual Logic Neurons

F. Kozato   G. A. Ringwood

Abstract

For high-level thought processes, such as logical deduction, intro-
spection suggests that on time scales of minutes and spatial scales of
meters cognition is sequential and localized. For lower level thought
processes, such as perception, neurophysiology has revealed that on a
scale of milliseconds and microns cognition is parallel and distributed.
Ideograms (symbols) have proved to be indispensible forms of representation for the slow, high-level cognitive processes but have been
painfully discovered to be inappropriate for the fast, lower level tasks
of speech and vision. As real neural networks already successfully implement speech and vision recognition systems it seems more than
likely that artificial ones should be able to do the same. Despite
the inability of computer symbolic systems to adequately cope with
the problem of perception they are much more powerful at symbolic
processing than humans are. The combination of artificial neural networks and symbolic processing holds the promise of being better than
the sum of the parts. As a first step towards investigating this thesis
a simulation of neural networks in a Concurrent Logic Language is
presented. A Concurrent Logic Language is chosen, firstly, because
it is a logic language, so is able to represent knowledge expressed
symbolically and, secondly, it has a computational model which is
essentially the same as that found in neural networks. Thus, the
language itself provides a natural bridge between symbolic logic and
neural networks. For the sake of definiteness, a pyramidal network
of PLNs was chosen for simulation and it was taught to recognise the
parity of binary vectors.

1   Introduction

It has to be admitted that logic programming is no longer the height of
computing fashon it once was. There has been a second, or is it third, wave
of disenchantment with symbolic processing in general, because of the fail-

ure of the symbolic AI community to deliver on some of its more extravagant promises. After initial euphoria, another generation of researchers in this area have reluctantly become aware of what the real limitations are. Symbolic systems are quite good at the higher thought processes such as logical inference but are particularly weak at tasks of perception, such as speech and vision. The problem is the combinatorial search explosion [4]; many competing hypotheses need to be screened and filtered. Human-level performance and robustness in perception requires enormous amounts of processing power.

As organic brains already implement speech and vision recognition systems, many researchers in the 1940's and 50's concluded that neuromorphic networks should be able to do the same. Interest in neural nets languished in the shadow of the success of sequential von Neumann computers. The revival of neural computing in the late 80's can be put down to a number of factors not the least of which is the current fashion for parallel machines. Both the literature and the number of professional society meetings focusing on artificial neural systems are growing at an amazing rate. Driving this second outbreak of neural fever is, to some extent, military funding. DARPA announced a $390 million fund for research into neural computing; artificial neurons for some inexplicable reason appeal to the military intellect.

Organic brains and computers have about the same number of processing elements, 10^{10}, so it might seem that the power advantage of organic brains might be due to the speed of its electrochemical processing elements, neurons. This is not the case; neurons are significantly slower than logic gates, the corresponding elementary processing agents in electronic computers. Neurons fire in milliseconds whereas off-the-shelf solid-state technology can switch state in microseconds. If raw processing power is calculated as the product of the number of processing elements and the response rate then the computer has an apparent power advantage of a thousandfold. However, this advantage is not realized because only a small fraction of logic gates actually change state simultaneously. It is one thing to have the capacity for parallel processing, it is another to be able to make use of it. It can only be the way in which the power potential of parallelism is exploited in organic brains that gives it greater effective power than conventional computers.

Conscious thought, examined on time-scales of seconds or minutes has sequential characteristics. Current psychological thinking on perception is that we continuously relate fragmentary stimuli to knowledge familiar from various experiences and we unconsciously test and reiterate our perceptions at different levels of abstraction. In other words, what we believe we perceive, is in fact only a mental reconstruction of fragments of sensory data. This is not too far removed from the philosophies of Husserl and Heidegger.

Linguists have speculated that higher levels of thought are only possible because of the adoption of phonograms and ideograms. The superiority of ideograms over phonograms has proved itself in mathematics, science and computing. Uncritical surrender to neural fever threatens the transparency and maintainability of computer software latterly realized to be so important. An alternative to surrender is compromise, the two approaches of AI should form two parts of the solution to producing Artificial Intelligence. Symbolic processing corresponds to the higher conscious levels of human thought processes and the connectionist approach to the lower levels. If thought processes are organised in hierarchical layers of abstraction then interfaces between symbolic AI and artificial neural networks are legitimate areas of research. The use of semiconductor logic gates as the processing elements of artificial neural systems holds the promise that the combination of neuromorphic networks and symbolic processing may be better than the sum of the parts.

As a first step towards investigating the interface between knowledge expressed in logic and knowledge possessed by neural systems this paper describes the simulation of neural networks in a Concurrent Logic Language, CLL. A CLL is, as will be demonstrated, a suitable initial vehicle for this investigation because in itself it bridges the layer: knowledge is represented by a term algebra; each computational step is a deduction and the computational model of neural networks is a more rudimentary form of that found in CLLs.

2   Biological and Artificial Neural Networks

Neurons are the fundamental constituents of organic brains. A neuron is a nerve cell which consists of a nucleus, dendrites, axon and synapses as depicted in Figure 1. The synapses form the connection between the axon of one cell and the dendrite of another. In essence, the dendrites are receptors and the axon and synapses emitters of bursts of electrochemical pulses generated by the cells. Whether or not a neuron decides to 'fire', produce a pulse, depends on the combination of the present state of the neuron and the pulses received from its immediate neighbours. (For more precise discussion on the physiology of nerve cells the reader is referred to [3]).

Neurons in organic brains are autonomous computational units and each

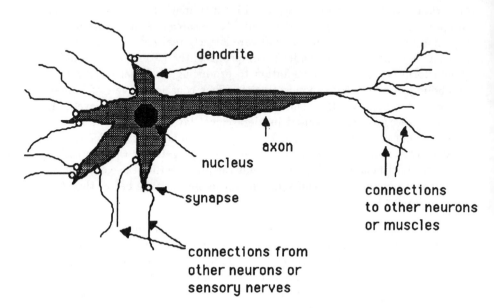

Figure 1: A Simplified Organic Neuron

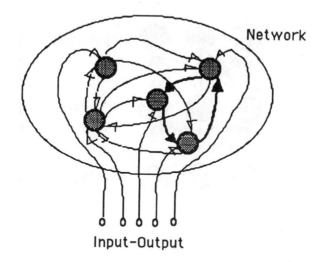

Network

Input-Output

Figure 2: The 'Feed-all' Network

may be directly connected with up to several thousand other neurons forming a network. It can only be the autonomy of neurons, viewed as processing
elements and the complexity of their interconnection wherein lies the ability
to explore simultaneously many competing hypotheses. The way neurons
interconnect and fire allows the possibility of chain reactions in much the
same way as chain reactions occur in atomic explosions. This analogy reveals the way in which explosive computational parallelism can be achieved
by neural systems.

Artificial neural nets can be characterised by the net topology, node characteristics and the training or learning rules. Though in what follows the three
components are treated separately for pedagogical purposes they should not
be considered as independent.

Neuron connectivity can be represented as a directed graph with neurons
at the vertices with directed edges the synaptic connections. In general
there can be cycles, closed loops, so that feedback is possible as depicted
in Figure 2. An oft quoted artificial neural system adopting this type of
topology is the Hopfield net [7].

If there is no feedback the network forms a DAG (directyed acyclic graph)
and is stratified, as in Figure 3. This form of topology is suitable for
associative memories and a well known example is NETtalk [18] a network

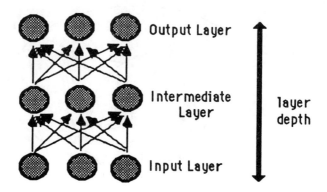

Figure 3: The Feed-forward Network

which can be taught to articulate text in relatively short periods of time. External stimuli feed into a bottom layer of neurons and the output is taken from the top layer. There can be many layers of hidden neurons in between. There may be different numbers of nodes in each layer and such networks can be used to classify input patterns, the number of output nodes reflecting the number of classes. It is in the DAG topology where the potential for a chain reactive explosive parallelism can most readily be anticipated.

3 Simulation of a Neural Network

For the sake of definiteness, the topology chosed for simulation is a binary tree. As will be illustrated, such a neural network can be taught to determine the parity of input bit vectors. The language of simulation FGDC (Flat Guarded Definite Clauses) [11, 12], is a Concurrent Logic Language, CLL, which is descended from FCP (Weizmann Institute, Israel), FGHC (ICOT, Japan) and Parlog (Imperial College, UK) but is used here as representative of the class. For a state-of-the-art review of concurrent logic languages the reader is referred to [13]. The syntax is similar to but sufficiently different from Prolog to need some explanation.

A CLL clause consists of a guard and a body.

$$< clause >::=< guard >< - < body > .$$

The body is a conjunction of atoms with shared variables as in Prolog. The calls in the body of a clause are not viewed as hierarchical procedure calls as in Prolog but as a set of communicating concurrent processes. Each goal in a query reduces independently of its conjuncts, there is no sequencing as in Prolog. Process synchronisation in FGDC is achieved by the guard condition.

$$< guard >::=< head >< - < constraint >$$

The $< head >$ is the atom expected from Prolog but the constraint is a conjunction of system primitives which only test the input bindings. Constraints are of the form of equations, inequations, comparison, and type tests which produce no output. The operation of FGDC is very unlike Prolog; clause invocation in FGDC is not determined by unifiability. Rather, the goal must pattern match the head of a clause (no goal instantiations) and the goal arguments must satisfy the constraints. That is, the deduction step is guarded and this is because there is no backtracking; invocation of the body goals is irrevocable. (For the procedurally minded the implication symbol between the body and guard can be compared with the Prolog cut).

This will hopefully become clearer with an example. A binary tree network or pyramid with three layers can be brought into existence by the FGDC goal:

```
<- pyramid(3,0,I).
```

where the **pyramid** relation is defined by:

```
/* pyramid(NumberOfLayers,OutputStream,ListOfInputStreams */
pyramid(1,0,I) <- true <-
        I = [I1,I2], neuron(0,I1,I2).
pyramid(N,0,I) <- N > 1 <-
        neuron(0,01,02),
        N1 is N-1,
        pyramid(N1,01,I1),
        pyramid(N1,02,I2),
        concatenate(I1,I2,I).

/* concatenate(List1,List2,JoinedList) */
concatenate([],List,JoinedList) <- true <-
        JoinedList = List.
concatenate([Item|List1],List2,JoinedList) <- true <-
        JoinedList = [Item|List],
        concatenate(List1,List2,List).
```

The primitive **true** is the trivial constraint and is used to indicate the mandatory presence of a guard for each clause. The directed nature of the relations in FGDC, as opposed to Prolog, is indicated by the equality primitives in the body of the clauses for concatenate. This is the only mechanism by which local bindings can be broadcast to the higher scope.

A graphical trace of a parallel reduction of this goal [14] is shown in Fig 4: active(reducible) processes are shaded. Unlike Prolog, which is a transformational language, FGDC is a reactive programming language [6]. Transformational systems begin with the input of data, transform the input, output the result and terminate. This is just how an unintelligent machine would behave. On the other hand, reactive programs continuously interact with the environment. Their reason for being is not the output they produce on termination but, rather, their interaction with the environment; sometimes reactive programs are effectively perpetual (they do not terminate). An intelligent machine would acquire knowledge continuously during its lifetime, infer from it and output inferences as external situations demanded. Systems programs such as environments with multiple windowing systems, operating systems and event-driven real-time systems are more conventional forms of reactive programs. Reactive systems consist of conceptually parallel processes that communicate with each other and cooperatively respond to events that occur indeterminately in real time. CLL processes can be perpetual. The resolvent at the end of the trace in Figure 4 is to be understood as a logical consequence of the initial goal [11]; it is not the intention of the program to produce a refutation of the initial <- pyramid goal. In the final frame of Figure 4, the neuron processes of the net are suspended waiting for input.

4   Simulation of a single Neuron

The form of neuron in the pyramid is as yet unspecified. There are essentially two types of artificial neurons: the Pitts-McCulloch model [9], which is reasonably biologically accurate and RAM-like models, which are more motivated by computer hardware. The RAM-like models are, of course, ideally suited to digital input and because of local affiliations, one such, the PLN, Probabilistic Logic Neuron [1] was chosen for this simulation. However, the simulation that follows can easily be adapted for the Pitts McCulloch type neurons.

The PLN is essentially a programmable, probabilistic, logic gate. Initially, the gate type is unspecified (Fig 5). The 'unknown' indicates that an input pattern corresponds to an undetermined response. In this situation the PLN produces a 1 or 0 output with equal probability. This stochastic

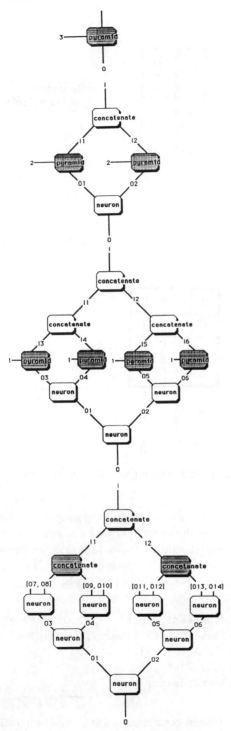

Figure 4: Subsequent Reductions of the Initial Three Layer Goal

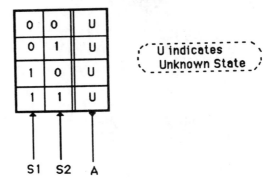

Figure 5: Initial State of the PLN

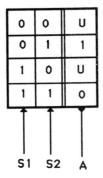

Figure 6: Some partially learnt state

nature endows the PLN with indeterminate properties similar to those of organic neurons [17]. As the neural network undergoes training, which will be described later, undetermined truth table entries become learnt with respect to approved responses to controlled input (Fig 6). The response behaviour is captured by the FGDC process `pln`.

```
/* pln(State,InputStream1,InputStream2,Output) */
pln(State,[r(S1)|Rest1],[r(S2)|Rest2],Output) <- true <-
        Output = [r(A)|Rest3],
        gate((S1,S2),State,A),
pln(State,Rest1,Rest2,Rest3).
```

The `pln` process is defined recursively. Thus, while operationally a call to pln is ephemeral, recursion imitates a long-lived process which can, as will be seen later, change state. The functor r on the input and output indicate that the response mode (as opposed to the training mode, see later) is current.

The reponse consists of truth table lookup. If the table value has been learnt, this value is returned. If the table value is 'unknown' the indeterminacy in the clause choice is used to generate an indeterminate response.

```
/* gate(InputPair,LookUpTable,Output) */
gate((0,0),table(learnt(T),U,V,W),A) <- true <- A=T.
gate((0,0),table(unknown,U,V,W),A) <- true <- A=0.
gate((0,0),table(unknown,U,V,W),A) <- true <- A=1.
gate((0,1),table(T,learnt(U),V,W),A) <- true <- A=U.
gate((0,1),table(T,unknown,V,W),A) <- true <- A=0.
gate((0,1),table(T,unknown,V,W),A) <- true <- A=1.
gate((1,0),table(T,U,learnt(V),W),A) <- true <- A=V.
gate((1,0),table(T,U,unknown,W),A) <- true <- A=0.
gate((1,0),table(T,U,unknown,W),A) <- true <- A=1.
gate((1,1),table(T,U,V,learnt(W)),A) <- true <- A=W.
gate((1,1),table(T,U,V,unknown),A) <- true <- A=0.
gate((1,1),table(T,U,V,unknown),A) <- true <- A=1.
```

(In a real implementation of the language FGDC the choice of clause from the candidates which can reduce a goal cannot be guaranteed to be fair. The present program is only used to illustrate the similarities between the operational behaviour of neural nets and the language. The real simulation uses a pseudo-random number generator to produce the indeterminate response.)

A trace of how inputs propagate in parallel through a PLN pyramid network is shown in Figure 7. (The word *propagate* doesn't really convey the correct sense of urgency associated with explosively parallel computation).

5   Simulation of the Training Phase

In artificial neural networks there is no conventional stored database; no carefully worked out application specific rules. The only principle that guides the machine is that it incorporates some notion of *right* and *wrong* and is constructed so as to strive for correctness. In this way the network can be self-learning; each input produces an output; correct outputs are

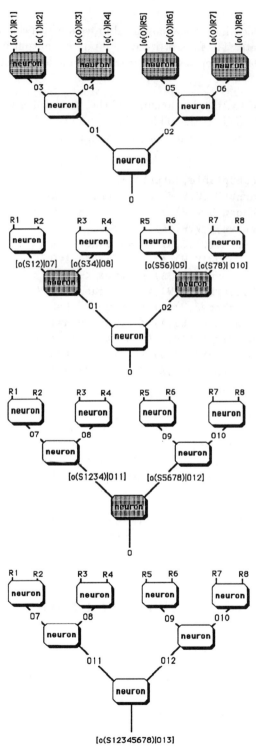

Figure 7: Trace of virtual neurons firing in response to input

reinforcing, incorrect outputs cause internal reconfiguration. By adjusting its internal state the network strives to achieve favourable responses. At first the response is by blind trial and error; later on, as the learning process continues, it becomes a mixture of trial, error and experience. Eventually the machine behaves as if it 'knew' exactly what it was the instructor (she cannot really be called a programmer) was trying to tell it. By the time the neural machine has learned something, the instructor does not know at the conceptual level what is going on inside the machine—it is generally far too complex for that.

Training of the PLN neuron can be effected by a second clause for **pln**: the functor **t** on the input and output are used to indicate that the training mode is current.

```
/* pln(State,InputStream1,InputStream2,OutputStream) */
pln(OldTable,[t(S1,R1)|Rest1],[t(S2,R2)|Rest2],O) <- true <-
        O=[t(A,R)|Rest],
        gate((S1,S2),OldTable,S),
        training((A,R),((S1,R1),(S2,R2)),OldTable,NewTable),
        pln(NewTable,Rest1,Rest2,Rest).
```

Here, the recursive **pln** clause simulates a long lived process which changes state according to the **training** relation. Output response pairs **(S1,R1)**, **(S2,R2)** and **(A,R)** are used to direct the responses to the preferred outputs back to the nodes responsible. This technique, familiar to logic programmers as partial instantiation, has been renamed *back-communication* by adherents to CLLs. In essence, it is very similar to the technique of *back-propagation* used in the training of multi-layered neural nets. The **training** process records the output and amends the look up table as dictated by the response for the recursively reincarnated **pln**. The response is propagated backwards through the net. In this clause, it can be seen how recursion imitates long-lived processes which change state.

It then remains to specify the training algorithm. The one chosen for the simulation is exemplary [10]:

Step 1 Choose an input pattern from some training set and apply it to the input nodes.

Step 2 Allow values to propagate through all neurons in the network. (Each PLN responds according to the state of its truth table).

Step 3 If the values on the output connections are the ones expected, then the output of each neuron becomes established (learnt).

Step 4 Otherwise, return to Step 2 and try again (because the output of each neuron is stochastic the output will generally be different) until a correct output is generated or

Step 5 A 'sufficient' number of errors have been made indicating the probability of ever succeeding is effectively zero. In this case all nodes return to their initial indeterminate state.

Step 6 Repeat Steps 1 to 5 until 'consistent' success indicates all patterns have been learnt.

```
/* training(OutputResponsePair,OldLookUpTable,
   InputResponsePair,NewLookUpTable) */
training((A,confirmed),table(T,U,V,W),((0,R1),(0,R2)),NewTable)
    <- true <-
    NewTable=table(learnt(A),U,V,W), R1=confirmed, R2=confirmed.
training((A,incorrect),table(T,U,V,W),((0,R1),(0,R2)),NewTable)
    <- true <-
    NewTable=table(unknown,U,V,W), R1=incorrect, R2=incorrect.
training((A,confirmed),table(T,U,V,W),((0,R1),(1,R2)),NewTable)
    <- true <-
    NewTable=table(T,learnt(A),V,W), R1=confirmed, R2=confirmed.
training((A,incorrect),table(T,U,V,W),((0,R1),(1,R2)),NewTable)
    <- true <-
    NewTable=table(T,unknown,V,W), R1=incorrect, R2=incorrect.
training((A,confirmed),table(T,U,V,W),((1,R1),(0,R2)),NewTable)
    <- true <-
    NewTable=table(T,U,learnt(A),W), R1=confirmed, R2=confirmed.
training((A,incorrect),table(T,U,V,W),((0,R1),(0,R2)),NewTable)
    <- true <-
    NewTable=table(T,U,unknown,W), R1=incorrect, R2=incorrect.
training((A,confirmed),table(T,U,V,W),((1,R1),(1,R2)),NewTable)
    <- true <-
    NewTable=table(T,U,V,learnt(A)), R1=confirmed, R2=confirmed.
training((A,incorrect),table(T,U,V,W),((1,R1),(1,R2)),NewTable)
    <- true <-
    NewTable=table(T,U,V,unknown), R1=incorrect, R2=incorrect.
```

Any other training scenario can be modelled in a similar way. The infamous back-propagation training method of neural nets can, as suggested above, be easily modelled by back-communication in FGDC.

6 Conclusion

The form of parallelism exhibited by organic neural nets is of a very different nature to that which is now achieved by multiprocessor machines with relatively small numbers of processors. With a small number of processors the best speedup that can be obtained is linear, but it usually smaller because either the computational problem cannot be decomposed into equal sized portions or when it can, there is conflict over shared resources. In principle the computational model of neural nets indicates that search can be performed in a time proportional to the length of the longest branch of the search tree, regardless of how many nodes the search tree contains overall. For short bushy trees, as in deductive databases, the speedup could be staggering.

The above FGDC program (but using a pseudo-random number generator in place of indeterminate clause choice) has been succesfully taught to recognise the parity of input bit vectors [8]. Clearly this means that each PLN has learnt to behave as an exclusive-or gate. The simulation was carried out on a uniprocessor machine in Parlog [5] with the parallelism simulated by coroutining. In the simulation neurons are emulated by processes, hence the name virtual neurons. The implementation is quite slow, not the least because of the overload of process switching, and the simulation as is would not be a practical realization of neural nets. However, organic neural networks illustrate how incredibly fast processing can be achieved by relatively slow processing elements. This can only be due to the way in which parallelism is organised into small equal sized portions with single producers and multiple consumers. This produces a process communication topology without any synchronisation problems. The feed-forward network topology is amenable to the explosive computational parallelism of which organic brains are capable. With this topology of processes in FGDC there is no binding conflict problem [2]. If for slow processing elements you read "slow virtual processing elements" (i.e. processes), as the number of processors is increased there will be less demand for process switching and the simulation of neurons by software processes could be a viable proposition.

The simulation presented chose to implement a pyramid network of PLN neurons but the choice was just for the sake of definiteness; the techniques used appear to be capable of simulating any topology, any type of artificial neuron, and any training rules. There are some interesting features of the *virtual* neurons allowed by the simulation in CLL. Because the language, FGDC, allows dynamic process creation it also allows dynamic virtual neuron creation. Thus, in a learning situation new neurons can be created as necessary. Because the language lends itself to partial evaluation the training sessions could be viewed in this light. At the end of a training session a virtual neural net will have acquired some knowledge. As partial evaluation, this is a new programme which has been specialized for the training data. Once a particular neural net has acquired some knowledge it can be saved as a partially evaluated goal. Such goals can be composed to give more complex nets with accumulated knowledge.

Concurrent Logic Languages present a style of programming which corresponds to a large extent with the connectionist one. Relations (processes) fire or not depending on their internal state and on data received from other processes via shared variables [11]. While shared variables do give a potential synchronisation problem when there are multiple producers, a style of programming can be adopted, such as the feed-forward network, where there are only single producers for shared variables [13]. Any number of consumers is possible. The indeterminacy of the clause chosen to reduce a goal process imitates the indeterminacy of output of both organic and artificial neurons.

References

[1] I. Aleksander. Logical connectionist system. In R. Eckmiller and C. H. von der Malsburg, editors, *Neural Computer*, pages 189–197. Springer Verlag, 1988.

[2] A. Burt and G. A. Ringwood. The binding conflict problem in concurrent logic languages. *IJPP*. Submitted 1988, still being referred.

[3] F. H. Crick and C. Asanuma. Certain aspects of the anatomy and physiology of the cerebral cortex. In Rumelhart and McClelland [16], pages 333–371.

[4] S. E. Fahlman. *NETL: a System for Representing and Using Real-World Knowledge*. MIT Press, 1979.

[5] I. T. Foster, A. Burt, and G. A. Ringwood. An abstract machine for the implementation of Parlog on uniprocessors. *New Generation Computing*, 1987.

[6] A. Harel and A. Pnueli. On the development of reactive systems. In K. R. Apt, editor, *Logics and Models of Concurrent Systems*. Springer Verlag, 1985.

[7] J. J. Hopfield. Neural networks and physical systems with emergent collective computational abilities. *Proc. Natl. Acad. Sci. USA*, 79:2554–8, 1982.

[8] F. Kozato. Modelling neural networks in Parlog. Master's thesis, Imperial College, London, 1988.

[9] M. W. McCulloch and W. Pitts. A logical calculus of the ideas immanent in nervous activity. *Bulletin of Mathematical Biophysics*, 5:115–88, 1943.

[10] C. Myers and I. Aleksander. Learning algorithms for probabilistic neural nets. *Neural Networks*. Submitted 1988.

[11] G. A. Ringwood. Pattern-directed, markovian, linear, guarded definite clause resolution. Submitted to Journal of Logic Programming but rejected after 21 months, 1987.

[12] G. A. Ringwood. Parlog86 and the dining logicians. *CACM*, 31:10–25, 1988.

[13] G. A. Ringwood. A comparative exploration of concurrent logic languages. *Knowledge Engineering Review*, 4:305–332, 1989.

[14] G. A. Ringwood. Predicates and pixels. *New Generation Computing*, 7:59–80, 1989.

[15] D. E. Rumelhart, G. Hinton, and R. J. Williams. Learning internal representations by error propagation. In Rumelhart and McClelland [16], pages 318–362.

[16] D. E. Rumelhart and J. L. McClelland, editors. *Parallel Distributed Processing*. MIT Press, 1986.

[17] T. J. Sejnowski. Skelton filters in the brain. In G. E. Hinton and J. A. Anderson, editors, *Parallel Models of Associative Memory*, pages 49–82. Lawrence Erlbaum Associates, 1981.

[18] T. J. Sejnowski and C. R. Rosenberg. NETtalk: a parallel network that learns to read aloud. Technical Report 13, John Hopkins University, Cognitive Neuropsychology Laboratory, 1985.

Implementing Logic Languages By Graph Rewriting

Peter McBrien

Abstract

This paper outlines the techniques used in the implementation of the Pure Logic Language (work partly funded by Alvey IKBS 084). A simple graph rewrite machine suitable for executing logic languages is described, and the set of rewrites needed to execute a subset of the Pure Logic Language presented. The rewrite machine is not intended to be a proposal for a new abstract machine architecture, but is provided as an abstraction of the techniques used in the Pure Logic Language implementation. The interpreter was written in 'C', and implements the rewrite rules directly as functions, passing the graphs as parameters. The architecture is capable of executing a form of pure Prolog, and the rewrite rules needed are sketched out. The implementation was designed for a sequential von Neumann architecture, and the issues concerning parallel execution are not addressed.

1   Introduction

The Alvey Pure Logic Language project set out to investigate the application of mathematical logic to the specification and computation of information systems. The results of the project were several prototype languages, the Pure Logic Language (PLL) being the result of work conducted at ICL's System Strategy Centre in Bracknell.

This paper describes the computational model of the PLL, using an abstract rewrite machine language to describe the transformation process applied to logic formulae. Other abstract rewrite machines which serve as the basis of declarative languages already exist, a notable example being Dactl [3], which supports a wide range of functional and logic languages. The implementation of a language on a Dactl machine involves writing a compiler to

164

translate the language into Dactl rules. The abstract machine presented here is intended to act as an interpreter for the PLL language, and thus has a more procedural air. The rules differ, *inter alia*, from Dactl rules in the following respects:

1. The logical variable is supported by providing built-in functions to record the binding of variables in such a way that the variables may be returned to their original condition by calling a single function.

2. Global variables are supplied to provide convenient ways of executing some of the algorithms used.

3. No consideration is given to the possibility of execution on a parallel machine. The order by which rewrite rules are searched to match an expression is fixed.

4. The rewrite language was designed solely to describe the implementation of the PLL, and at this stage of development cannot be regarded as sufficiently general to support a range of logic programming languages. However a Prolog-like language could be implemented with the system described, and the way this might be achieved is discussed.

At the outset of the Alvey project, the PLL was intended to be principally a database query language, where the problems would be expressed in classical first-order predicate calculus. By the end of the project, the query language had many of the features of a logic programming language. Some features of the PLL which differentiate it from Prolog are:

1. A step by step reduction process is applied to formulae, and if at any step the system cannot proceed, then the partially reduced formula is returned. For example $\exists x.x = 2 \land y < x$ would give $y < 2$ as the result.

2. A corollary of the above is that negation by failure is not used, since the evaluation of an expression can never 'fail' (but may give false as the result of a computation). If the predicate q is undefined, then the PLL query $q(x)$ will return $q(x)$, and the query $\neg q(x)$ returns $\neg q(x)$. In a pure Prolog language the results of these queries would be *no* and *yes* respectively, whilst a practical interpreter would warn that the predicate q is undefined and contains a free variable.

3. The order of terms in a conjunction is in general not critical, a term may be skipped over if it cannot be completely reduced to variable bindings, and returned to later after other terms have been evaluated.

For example $x = y*2 \wedge y = z*2 \wedge z = 2$ would give $z = 2 \wedge y = 4 \wedge x = 8$ as the result.

The basis of the PLL is the transformation of logic formulae to equivalent formulae which are in some sense 'more concrete' than the originals. No detailed description of the language is presented in this paper, but an overview of the language can be found in [1], and a guide to using the language with some example programs is available [6]. The syntax used for the PLL in these references is that which would be typed by a user at the computer keyboard, but this paper uses the conventional symbols for mathematical logic so as to make for easy reading by those unfamiliar with the PLL. Particular syntactical features are that variable names may start with small letters as well as capitals, and string literals are enclosed in double quotation marks. The list construction operator is '::', the empty list is '[]', and structures of the form $[x\ y\ z]$ can be regarded as syntactic sugaring for $x :: y :: z :: []$.

The following section describes the operation of the rewrite rule system, and the built-in functions provided. Section 2 describes the rules needed to implement the PLL, and section 3 shows how an implementation of Prolog could be approached. Section 4 gives benchmark figures comparing the PLL with a commercial Prolog interpreter for a couple of trivial problems. The benchmark programs are listed in the section to enable the reader to compare a Prolog and PLL program that carry out the same task.

2 A Graph Rewrite Machine For Logic Languages

2.1 The Representation of Logic Expressions as Graphs

First order predicate logic expressions, formed with the usual connectives ($\vee, \wedge, \neg$ etc), are stored as graphs, with the name of each node being the connective or predicate name, and the 'descendants' of the node being the arguments to the functor in question. Constants are stored as nodes with a name to indicate the data type and the constant value held in the node. Fig 1 shows as an example of how the PLL expression $x = y \wedge y = 2*z \wedge z = 1$ is stored as a graph. The first field in each node is the node name, the other fields storing either data or pointers to other nodes.

Variables are stored as one specific type of constant, with the label VAR. All occurrences of the same variable point to the same node, and it is the address that a variable node is held at in memory which distinguishes it from other variables. An advantage of this technique for the storage of variables is that binding a variable merely requires that the node be overwritten with the value that the variable takes. Then wherever that variable appeared in the graph its value would be in its place.

2.2 Rewrite Rules

The rewrite rules are like those of term rewriting systems [5] with some changes to assist in this particular application. The rules take the following form:

$$< head > \quad \xrightarrow{R} \quad < tail >$$
$$: \quad < condition >$$
$$: \quad < condition > ...$$

- The *head* must be one of a set of functions, the names of which must be exclusive from any valid function name in the language being implemented. In this paper they are denoted by being in bold type (e.g. $\mathbf{R}(x)$), whilst the name of PLL functions are written using italics (e.g. $R(x)$). The functions which are used in rewrite rules are to some extent markers which cause their parameters to be matched against rules with the same function name in the head. Taking this view, these marking functions can then be called *activation* functions, and adding such a function to a rewrite expression is termed *activating* the expression. When a rule head matches a part of an expression, them the part matched is termed the reduction expression or *redex*.

- The optional *condition* statements are constructed from assignment operations, arithmetic expressions and relational tests. All the relational tests must be true if the rule is to be used, otherwise all bindings made during the execution of the condition statement are undone. The conditions are only checked after the head has matched a redex, and may be used to find values of variables in either the head or tail using an assignment operator ':='. No formal semantics or syntax of the condition statement language is presented here, but the meaning in examples should be clear.

- The *tail* is the expression to replace the redex in the expression graph. Any duplicated variables in the tail will cause the actual subgraph they match against to be copied. This is counter to normal practice in graph rewrite systems such as Dactl, but proves to be the more useful convention for the implementation of logic languages.

The rewrite rules must be left-linear (i.e. contain no duplicated variables in the head), but may contain variables in the tail which do not appear in the head. When the rule is used, these free variables in the tail will cause new variables to be created. This is needed for the creation of quantified variables at run time.

When nested activations exist in an expression it is the leftmost innermost activation for which rewriting is first attempted. Thus the expression $\mathbf{R}(\mathbf{R}(\phi) \wedge \mathbf{R}(\psi))$ would first lead to a search for a rule head matching $\mathbf{R}(\phi)$ rewriting to ϕ', then $\mathbf{R}(\psi)$ to give ψ', and finally for $\mathbf{R}(\phi' \wedge \psi')$.

As a shorthand for placing type checking predicates in the condition statements, the variables in a head may be typed by placing a colon and then the type name immediately after the variable name. For instance the rule head $\mathbf{R}(f(x))$ my be restricted to only apply when x matches a number by writing $\mathbf{R}(f(x:number))$. The list of types available are given in the following table.

Datatype Name	Description
number	any integer or floating point value
string	any string constant
list	a list construction node i.e. ::
data	any of the above
variable	any VAR node
function	any function e.g. $f(x, y)$

To evaluate an expression graph a variant of the Markov algorithm for pattern matching rules is used [7]. Starting with the leftmost innermost activation and the first rewrite rule, the rules are checked sequentially to find a head which matches the expression. The conditions for that rewrite rule are then evaluated. If the conditions do not succeed, then the search continues for another rewrite rule head that matches. If the conditions were found to be all true, then the redex in the expression graph is replaced by the tail of the rewrite rule, after having made appropriate variable substitutions. The search for a new redex then recommences with the *first* rewrite rule.

This process is repeated until no further rewrites apply, i.e. one complete pass through the set of rewrite rules is made without finding a match, for each activation in the expression. The expression is then in *normal form* and is returned to the user as the result of the computation.

Examples

- *Rule System*:
$$\mathbf{R}(\neg(\phi \wedge \psi)) \quad \xrightarrow{R} \quad \mathbf{R}(\neg\phi \vee \neg\psi)$$

  Example of Execution: This would match the expression $\mathbf{R}(\neg(a = 1 \wedge b = 2))$, making $\phi = (a = 1)$ and $\psi = (b = 2)$, and replacing it with $\mathbf{R}(\neg a = 1 \vee \neg b = 2)$.

  (Note that the use of Greek script for variable names in the examples is made only to stress that any graph may be matched by an unrestricted variable in a rule head. Latin script is used for a variable that is restricted by one of the condition statements or by type checking in the rule head.)

- *Rule System*:
$$\mathbf{R}(n_1 : number = n_2 : number) \quad \xrightarrow{R} \quad \top$$
$$: \quad n_1 = n_2$$
$$\mathbf{R}(n_1 : number = n_2 : number) \quad \xrightarrow{R} \quad \bot$$

  Example of Execution: The head of the first rewrite would match $\mathbf{R}(2 = 3)$, making $n_1 = 2$ and $n_2 = 3$, but the condition would fail. Hence the search would continue with the second rewrite rule, which matches the expression and rewrites it to $\bot$. (The symbol $\top$ represents logical truth, and $\bot$ falsity.)

2.3 Variable Binding

All occurrences of a certain variable will point to the same node, initially set to VAR. To bind the variable the node is overwritten with the new value. Thus when bound to a value, all occurrences of the variable in the graph are replaced by the value it is bound to. In practice the constant node overwriting the variable node may be larger in size and thus not fit in the space. This may be overcome by either making variable nodes large enough to hold any type of constant node (the method used in the PLL implementation) or by having an indirection to the constant node held at a different location in store.

Obtaining the value that variables have been bound to during rewriting of expressions requires that a record be kept of the location of each variable we are interested in. If the location for a variable still contains VAR after rewriting, then no value for the variable has been found. Otherwise the node will be the value of the variable.

Unfortunately this scheme does not deal with the evaluation of logical disjunctions, where we wish to obtain possibly different values for the variables after rewriting the two arguments of the disjunction. An efficient technique used in Prolog is backtracking [4], which would proceed in rewriting the formula $\phi \vee \psi$ as follows:

1. Rewrite ϕ.

2. Note any variable bindings made during step 1.

3. Reset the variables bound during step 1 to their previous values.

4. Rewrite ψ.

5. Note any variable bindings made during step 4.

To facilitate the execution of this algorithm three built-in functions and a global stack to record variable bindings being made are provided. The functions are defined below using a slight corruption of the rewrite rule language.

- **Bind**

  The **Bind** function copies a value node (anything which a variable may be bound to in the target language) on top of the variable node, and notes the address of the variable node on the *variable_stack* (the & operator finds the address that the node is held at in memory).

$$\textbf{Bind}(var, value) \quad \xrightarrow{\ R\ } \quad \top$$
$$: \quad variable\_stack[top\_stack] := \&var,$$
$$: \quad top\_stack := top\_stack + 1,$$
$$: \quad var := value.$$

- **Free**

  The **Free** function returns a structure showing the values of variables bound since *top_stack* was last at a given value. All such variables are all reset to VAR and an expression of the form $variable_1 = value_1 \wedge variable_2 = value_2 \wedge ....$ is returned. If there are no such variables then $\top$ is returned. (The $*$ symbol is the indirection operator, storing the value of the assignment at the address pointed to by the $*$'s operand).

$$\textbf{Free}(stack\_pos) \quad \xrightarrow{R} \quad \top$$
$$: \quad stack\_pos = top\_stack.$$
$$\textbf{Free}(stack\_pos) \quad \xrightarrow{R} \quad var = value$$
$$: \quad stack\_pos = top\_stack + 1$$
$$: \quad top\_stack := top\_stack - 1,$$
$$: \quad \&var := variable\_stack[stack\_pos],$$
$$: \quad value := var,$$
$$: \quad var := \text{VAR}$$
$$\textbf{Free}(stack\_pos) \quad \xrightarrow{R} \quad var = value \; \& \; \textbf{Free}(stack\_pos)$$
$$: \quad top\_stack := top\_stack - 1,$$
$$: \quad \&var := variable\_stack[stack\_pos],$$
$$: \quad value := var,$$
$$: \quad var := \text{VAR}$$

The $\&var := variable\_stack[stack\_pos]$ condition causes the address of var to be that held in $variable\_stack[stack\_pos]$. In effect we cause an old node to be used as the location to hold the contents of var. Then $value := var$ causes the data held in var to be copied into $value$, and $var := $ VAR resets the variable to be free again.

- **Level**

  The **Level** function returns the next free position in the variable stack. By recording this value at a given point in the computation, the system knows which variables have been bound since that point, and so can retrace the variable bindings made.

$$Level \quad \xrightarrow{R} \quad top\_stack$$

An example of how the variable binding process works is given in Figures 2, 3 and 4. In Figure 2 the initial condition of the stack is shown before the expression $x = 1 \wedge y = 2 * x$ is evaluated. Figure 3 shows the state after the two variables have been bound, where the variable stack contains entries which point to the variable nodes just bound, and the nodes contain the value the variable has been bound to. Figure 4 gives the graph produced by a call to **Free** with the value of **Level** before execution of the expression. The original variable nodes are reset to VAR, and the values copied into new nodes.

3   Rewrite Rules To Execute The PLL

The following subsections give the rewrite rules necessary to implement the core operators of the PLL. For clarity the rewrites are grouped by the PLL operator they implement. The order of rewrites within the group is significant since in many cases the patterns matched by the various members of a group overlap. This was done to take advantage of the sequential nature that the pattern matching process would take on conventional von Neumann architecture computers. To assist with evaluation on parallel machines, it would be possible to make all the rules presented here mutually exclusive by the addition of extra constraints in the condition statements of rules.

Execution of a PLL formula should be started by applying the **PLL** activation, the rewrites for which are described in the subsection dealing with disjunction.

3.1   Equality

$$\mathbf{R}(\text{VAR} = d{:}data) \xrightarrow{\ R\ } \mathbf{Bind}(\text{VAR}, d)$$

$$\mathbf{R}(d{:}data = \text{VAR}) \xrightarrow{\ R\ } \mathbf{Bind}(\text{VAR}, d)$$

$$\mathbf{R}(n_1{:}number = n_2{:}number) \xrightarrow{\ R\ } \top$$
$$: \quad n_1 = n_2$$

$$\mathbf{R}(s_1{:}string = s_2{:}string) \xrightarrow{\ R\ } \top$$
$$: \quad s_1 = s_2$$

$$\mathbf{R}(\phi_1 :: \psi_1 = \phi_2 :: \psi_2) \xrightarrow{\ R\ } \mathbf{R}(\phi_1 = \phi_2 \wedge \psi_1 = \psi_2)$$

$$\mathbf{R}(d_1{:}data = d_2{:}data) \xrightarrow{\ R\ } \bot$$

$$\mathbf{R}(\phi = \psi + \theta) \xrightarrow{\ R\ } \mathbf{A}(\mathbf{R}(\psi + \theta), \mathbf{R}(\phi))$$

$$\mathbf{R}(\phi + \psi = \theta) \xrightarrow{\ R\ } \mathbf{A}(\mathbf{R}(\phi + \psi), \mathbf{R}(\theta))$$

$$\mathbf{R}(\phi = \psi - \theta) \xrightarrow{\ R\ } \mathbf{A}(\mathbf{R}(\psi - \theta), \mathbf{R}(\phi))$$

$$\mathbf{R}(\phi - \psi = \theta) \xrightarrow{\ R\ } \mathbf{A}(\mathbf{R}(\phi - \psi), \mathbf{R}(\theta))$$

The first two rewrites cause a variable being equated with a data value to be rewritten to a binding operation of the variable to the value. The next four check for data structures, the last rewrite of this group giving $\perp$ if none of the three rewrites equating like data types has succeeded. The rest of the rewrites use the **A** set of rewrites to deal with arithmetic operators (just those for addition and subtraction are shown above, those for other operators would take a similar form, with just the symbol for the operator changed). The semantics of an **A** set rewrite are to try and rewrite the first argument to have the value of the second argument.

3.2 Arithmetic Operators

The rewrites to execute the addition operator of the PLL are given here, the rewrites to deal with subtraction, division and multiplication take a similar form with just the obvious changes to the symbol used, and the condition statements in R_2, R_4 and R_5 altered. Note that the arithmetic operators in the condition statements have their usual meaning, and are distinct from any symbols in the object language being implemented. The subscripts applied to the rewrite symbol are merely to allow for numbering of rewrite rules in this text, and have no effect on the operation of the rewrite rule system.

$$\mathbf{R}(\phi + \psi) \quad \xrightarrow{R_1} \quad \mathbf{A}(\mathbf{R}(\phi) + \mathbf{R}(\psi))$$
$$\mathbf{A}(n_1\text{:}number + n_2\text{:}number) \quad \xrightarrow{R_2} \quad n_3$$
$$: \quad n_3 := n_1 + n_2$$
$$\mathbf{A}(\phi + \psi) \quad \xrightarrow{R_3} \quad \phi + \psi$$
$$\mathbf{A}(n_1\text{:}number + \phi, n_2\text{:}number) \quad \xrightarrow{R_4} \quad \mathbf{R}(\phi = n_3)$$
$$: \quad n_3 := n_2 - n_1$$
$$\mathbf{A}(\phi + n_1\text{:}number, n_2\text{:}number) \quad \xrightarrow{R_5} \quad \mathbf{R}(\phi = n_3)$$
$$: \quad n_3 := n_2 - n_1$$
$$\mathbf{A}(n\text{:}number, \text{VAR}) \quad \xrightarrow{R_6} \quad \mathbf{Bind}(\text{VAR}, n)$$
$$\mathbf{A}(n\text{:}number, \phi) \quad \xrightarrow{R_7} \quad \mathbf{A}(\phi, n)$$
$$\mathbf{A}(\phi + \psi, \theta) \quad \xrightarrow{R_8} \quad \theta = \phi + \psi$$

The first three rewrites reduce an addition on two numbers to their sum, but otherwise leaves the expression unchanged. The rewrites R_4 and R_5 deal with an expression of the form $\phi + \psi = \theta$, where θ and either ϕ or ψ are numbers, rearranging the formula so that both numbers are on the same side of the equality. Note that these rewrites would never be reached if both ϕ and ψ were numbers. Rewrite R_7 allows for the situation where a number is being evaluated to take the value of a formula, to be reversed, and the rewrites rechecked. R_8 returns the expression to its original form if none of the other **A** rules apply (the PLL leaves expressions it can not reduce to comprise solely of variable bindings, in the partially reduced form).

The arithmetic rules of the PLL allow the value of a variable to be found in any equality made of arithmetic operators, numbers and variables, provided that it is the only free variable in the expression, and occurs only once.

Addition Example

The example shows the rewrites applied to the expression $3 + 4 = 5 + x$, the rule being applied at each step being given to the left in brackets. The result of the evaluation is $\top$ with the side effect of binding the variable x to 2.

$$\mathbf{R}(3 + 4 = 5 + x)$$

$$[\text{use } \mathbf{R}(\phi = \psi + \theta) \xrightarrow{R} \mathbf{A}(\mathbf{R}(\psi + \theta), \mathbf{R}(\phi))]$$
$$\xrightarrow{R} \mathbf{A}(\mathbf{R}(3 + 4), 5 + x)$$
$$[\text{use } R_1 \text{ and } R_2] \qquad \mathbf{R}(3 + 4) \xrightarrow{R} 7$$
$$\xrightarrow{R} \mathbf{A}(7, 5 + x)$$
$$[\text{use } R_7] \qquad \xrightarrow{R} \mathbf{A}(5 + x, 7)$$
$$[\text{use } R_4] \qquad \xrightarrow{R} \mathbf{R}(x = 2)$$
$$[\text{use } \mathbf{R}(\text{VAR} = d{:}data) \xrightarrow{R} \mathbf{Bind}(\text{VAR}, d)]$$
$$\xrightarrow{R} \mathbf{Bind}(x, 2)$$
$$\xrightarrow{R} \top$$

3.3 Negation

$$\mathbf{R}(\neg\top) \xrightarrow{R} \bot$$
$$\mathbf{R}(\neg\bot) \xrightarrow{R} \top$$
$$\mathbf{R}(\neg\neg\phi) \xrightarrow{R} \mathbf{R}(\phi)$$
$$\mathbf{R}(\neg(\phi \wedge \psi)) \xrightarrow{R} \mathbf{R}(\neg\phi \vee \neg\psi)$$
$$\mathbf{R}(\neg(\phi \vee \psi)) \xrightarrow{R} \mathbf{R}(\neg\phi \wedge \neg\psi)$$
$$\mathbf{R}(\neg(\phi \rightarrow \psi)) \xrightarrow{R} \mathbf{R}(\phi \wedge \neg\psi)$$
$$\mathbf{R}(\neg\forall x{:}variable.\phi) \xrightarrow{R} \mathbf{R}(\exists x.\neg\phi)$$

$$\mathbf{R}(\neg\phi) \xrightarrow{\quad R \quad} \mathbf{R}(\neg\phi')$$

$$: \quad Old\_Inside\_Not := Inside\_Not$$
$$: \quad Inside\_Not := \top,$$
$$: \quad \phi' := \mathbf{R}(\phi),$$
$$: \quad Inside\_Not := Old\_Inside\_Not,$$
$$: \quad \phi' \neq \phi$$

Except for the last rewrite above, the rules for negation are all simple theorems such as De Morgan's laws. The last rule applies the $\mathbf{R}$ rules to the expression ϕ inside the negation, giving ϕ'. If any apply then some change will have occurred in the formulae (i.e. $\phi' \neq \phi$), and it is worth while retrying the rewrite rules on $\neg\phi'$. The purpose of the global variable *Inside_Not* is to assist with the evaluation of existential quantifiers, and is explained in the section dealing the rewrites for them.

3.4 Conjunction

The technique used to evaluate a conjunction $\phi \wedge \psi$ is to apply the $\mathbf{R}$ rewrite set to ϕ and ψ alternately, applying it at least once to both formulae, and continuing there after until the application of the rewrite rules fails to bind any variables. This strategy succeeds since the only possible information shared between ϕ and ψ would be in any common variables that the two formulae contain. If applying the $\mathbf{R}$ set to (say) ϕ fails to bind any variable (indicated by the value of the **Level** function not changing) then there could not be a change in ψ, and so the application of the rewrites could not produce a different result from that when they were last applied.

$$\mathbf{R}(\phi \wedge \psi) \xrightarrow{\quad R_1 \quad} \mathbf{Conj}(\mathbf{R}(\phi) \wedge \psi, \text{``}right\text{''}, -1)$$
$$\mathbf{Conj}(\top \wedge \psi, \_, \_) \xrightarrow{\quad R_2 \quad} \mathbf{R}(\psi)$$
$$\mathbf{Conj}(\bot \wedge \psi, \_, \_) \xrightarrow{\quad R_3 \quad} \bot$$
$$\mathbf{Conj}(\phi \wedge \top, \_, \_) \xrightarrow{\quad R_4 \quad} \mathbf{R}(\phi)$$
$$\mathbf{Conj}(\phi \wedge \bot, \_, \_) \xrightarrow{\quad R_5 \quad} \bot$$
$$\mathbf{Conj}(\phi \wedge \psi, \text{``}left\text{''}, c) \xrightarrow{\quad R_6 \quad} \mathbf{Conj}(\mathbf{R}(\phi) \wedge \psi, \text{``}right\text{''}, c')$$
$$: \quad \textbf{Level} > c,$$
$$: \quad c' := \textbf{Level}$$
$$\mathbf{Conj}(\phi \wedge \psi, \text{``}right\text{''}, c) \xrightarrow{\quad R_7 \quad} \mathbf{Conj}(\phi \wedge \mathbf{R}(\psi), \text{``}left\text{''}, c')$$

$$\begin{array}{rcl}
 & : & \textbf{Level} > c, \\
 & : & c' := \textbf{Level} \\
\textbf{Conj}(\phi \wedge \psi, \_, \_) & \xrightarrow{R_8} & \phi \wedge \psi
\end{array}$$

The first rewrite listed above starts this process, which will be executed by the **Conj** rewrites. These have three parameters, the first is the conjunction to be reduced, the second says if the left or right term of the conjunction should be reduced next, and the third parameter gives the number of variables that were bound before the rewriting of the previous term. The -1 value for variables bound in the first rewrite ensures that ψ has the rewrites applied at least once (i.e. R_7 matches at least once). Rewrites R_6 and R_7 will match alternately, by changing the value of the second parameter between "*left*" and "*right*" provided that the value of **Level** is higher than the value recorded at the start of the previous rewrite. Rules R_2, R_3, R_4 and R_5 remove the conjunction if either ϕ or ψ becomes $\bot$ or $\top$. The final **Conj** rewrite leaves the conjunction in its reduced state if none of the other rules apply.

Conjunction Example

$$\begin{array}{lcl}
 & & \mathbf{R}(a = b * 2 \wedge b = 2) \\
[\text{use } R_1] & \xrightarrow{R} & \textbf{Conj}(\mathbf{R}(a = b * 2) \wedge b = 2, \text{``}right\text{''}, -1) \\
[\text{use } \mathbf{R}(\phi = \psi * \theta) & \xrightarrow{R} & \mathbf{A}(\mathbf{R}(\psi + \theta), \mathbf{R}(\phi)) \text{ etc}] \\
 & & \mathbf{R}(a = b * 2) \xrightarrow{R} a = b * 2 \\
[\text{result of rewriting subterm}] & & \\
 & \xrightarrow{R} & \textbf{Conj}(a = b * 2 \wedge b = 2, \text{``}right\text{''}, -1) \\
[\text{use } R_7] & \xrightarrow{R} & \textbf{Conj}(a = b * 2 \wedge \mathbf{R}(b = 2), \text{``}left\text{''}, 0) \\
[\text{use } \mathbf{R}(\text{VAR}=d\text{:data}) & \xrightarrow{R} & \textbf{Bind}(\text{VAR,d})] \\
 & & \mathbf{R}(b = 2) \xrightarrow{R} \top \\
[\text{result of rewriting subterm}] & & \\
 & \xrightarrow{R} & \textbf{Conj}(a = 2 * 2 \wedge \top, \text{``}left\text{''}, 0) \\
[\text{use } R_4] & \xrightarrow{R} & \mathbf{R}(a = 2 * 2) \\
[\text{use } \mathbf{R}(\phi = \psi * \theta) & \xrightarrow{R} & \mathbf{A}(\mathbf{R}(\psi + \theta), \mathbf{R}(\phi)) \text{ etc}] \\
 & \xrightarrow{R} & \top
\end{array}$$

3.5 Quantifiers

$$\begin{array}{lcl}
\mathbf{R}(\forall x.\phi) & \xrightarrow{R} & \mathbf{R}(\neg \exists x. \neg \phi) \\
\mathbf{R}(\exists x.\phi) & \xrightarrow{R} & \mathbf{R}(\phi)
\end{array}$$

$$\begin{array}{rcl}
& : & Inside\_Not = \bot \text{ OR } x \neq \text{VAR} \\
\mathbf{R}(\exists x.\phi) & \xrightarrow{\;R\;} & \mathbf{R}(\exists x.\phi') \\
& : & \phi' := \mathbf{R}(\phi), \\
& : & \phi' \neq \phi \\
\mathbf{R}(\exists x.(\phi \vee \psi)) & \xrightarrow{\;R\;} & \mathbf{R}((\exists x.\phi) \vee (\exists y.\psi')) \\
& : & \psi' := \mathbf{Subs}(x, y, \psi)
\end{array}$$

An existential quantifier can be ignored if it does not appear inside a negation. The effect is like the variables are skolemized [2] (i.e. turned into constant symbols which we are not interested in the value of). No action needs to be taken in order to achieve this, except that the **Free** function should ignore these variables in creating the conjunction of equalities. We cannot drop the quantifier inside the scope of a negation since $\neg\exists x.\phi \not\equiv \exists x.\neg\phi$. If the quantifier cannot be dropped, then an attempt is made to rewrite what is inside the quantifier, and if the expression changes then the rewrites are reapplied to the new expression. The final rewrite pushes existential quantifiers inside disjunctions, but since in doing this we create new quantified variables, the variables in either ϕ or ψ must be renamed to make them distinct from each other. The set of rewrites for the **Subs**(x, y, ϕ) functions replace all occurrences of variable x in formula ϕ by variable y. It is placed last since the operation of renaming variables is relatively slow and so is to be avoided.

Quantification of several variables can be regarded as syntactic sugaring for nested quantification of single variables i.e. $\exists ab... \equiv \exists a.\exists b...$

The issue of distinguishing quantified and free variables with the same name is fudged here, in that it is assumed that the input handler will do renaming of variables for us. For instance the PLL expression $x = 1 \wedge \exists x.x = 2$ will be translated to $a = 1 \wedge \exists b.b = 2$ before execution, and the renaming process reversed before supplying the answer to the user ($x = 1$ in this case).

3.6   User Defined Rules

The PLL allows for at most one rule for any function name, and restricts the rules to be left-linear. Thus we may replace a PLL rule of the form $f(a, b, ...) \xrightarrow{\;R\;} \phi$ with the rewrite rule $\mathbf{R}(f(a, b, ...)) \xrightarrow{\;R\;} \mathbf{R}(\phi)$, and no condition statements added.

Guarded PLL rules specify a set of variables which must be bound before the rule is used. Once the head of a guarded rule is satisfied, the tail is executed in isolation to produce its normal form. This greatly improves the computational efficiency since it localizes the rewrites to apply to a part of the expression which the user has defined (by using the guard) as solvable without reference to the rest of the expression.

Guarded rules of the form:

$$f(a, b, c, ...) \; guard \; (a, b) \vee (a, c) \vee ... \; \xrightarrow{R} \; \mathbf{R}(\phi)$$

may be replaced by a set of rules with conditions that variables must be bound to a ground value:

$$\mathbf{R}(f(a{:}data, b{:}data, c, ...)) \quad \xrightarrow{R} \quad \mathbf{R}(\phi)$$
$$\mathbf{R}(f(a{:}data, b, c{:}data, ...)) \quad \xrightarrow{R} \quad \mathbf{R}(\phi)$$

3.7   Disjunction

A possible strategy for execution of PLL expressions would be to rewrite a formula to disjunctive normal form (DNF) and execute each of the disjunctions. However this would be inefficient, and instead of changing a formulae directly into DNF a more stepwise method is used similar to that used by Prolog. A formula of the form $(\phi \vee \psi) \wedge (\theta \vee \eta)$ will be rewritten to $(\phi \wedge (\theta \vee \eta)) \vee (\psi \wedge (\theta \vee \eta))$, and hence the rewrites need only be applied once to the formulae ϕ and ψ.

$$
\begin{aligned}
\mathbf{PLL}(\phi) \quad &\xrightarrow{R} \quad \mathbf{Exec}(\phi) \\
: \quad & or\_delay := \top \\
: \quad & inside\_not := \bot \\
\mathbf{R}(\phi \vee \psi) \quad &\xrightarrow{R} \quad \mathbf{Insert}(\phi \vee \psi, or\_delay) \\
\mathbf{Insert}(\phi, \top) \quad &\xrightarrow{R} \quad or\_delay := \phi \\
\mathbf{Insert}(\phi, \psi \vee \theta) \quad &\xrightarrow{R} \quad or\_delay := (\psi \wedge \phi) \vee (\theta \wedge \phi) \\
\mathbf{Exec}(\phi) \quad &\xrightarrow{R} \quad \mathbf{S}(\mathbf{Exec\_Delay}(\mathbf{R}(\phi), or\_delay) \wedge \mathbf{Free}(l)) \\
: \quad & l = \mathbf{Level} \\
\mathbf{Exec\_Delay}(\phi, \top) \quad &\xrightarrow{R} \quad \phi \\
\mathbf{Exec\_Delay}(\phi, \psi \vee \theta) \quad & \\
&\xrightarrow{R} \quad \mathbf{S}(\mathbf{Exec}(\phi \wedge \psi) \vee \mathbf{Exec}(\phi \wedge \psi))
\end{aligned}
$$

$$: \quad or\_delay := \top$$

To achieve this method of execution, disjunctions are put into a global variable *or_delay* when they are found inside an **R** activation. At the start of execution of a PLL formula *or_delay* is set to $\top$. Then when a disjunction is found in the rewritting process, and no previous disjunction has been found (i.e. *or_delay* $= \top$) then *or_delay* is bound to the disjunction formula, otherwise the disjunction just found is added to each term of the disjunction already held in *or_delay*.

The **Exec** rewrite applies the **R** set to a formula, and then uses **Exec_Delay** to recombine any residual formulae with any disjunctions held in *or_delay*. Then **Exec** is applied to each term of the disjunction.

$$
\begin{array}{rcl}
\mathbf{S}(\top \vee \phi) & \xrightarrow{R} & \top \\
\mathbf{S}(\bot \vee \phi) & \xrightarrow{R} & \phi \\
\mathbf{S}(\phi \vee \top) & \xrightarrow{R} & \top \\
\mathbf{S}(\phi \vee \bot) & \xrightarrow{R} & \phi \\
\mathbf{S}(\phi \vee \psi) & \xrightarrow{R} & \phi \vee \psi \\
\mathbf{S}(\top \wedge \phi) & \xrightarrow{R} & \top \\
\mathbf{S}(\bot \wedge \phi) & \xrightarrow{R} & \phi \\
\mathbf{S}(\phi \wedge \top) & \xrightarrow{R} & \top \\
\mathbf{S}(\phi \wedge \bot) & \xrightarrow{R} & \phi \\
\mathbf{S}(\phi \wedge \psi) & \xrightarrow{R} & \phi \wedge \psi \\
\end{array}
$$

The **S** set of rewrites simplify conjunctions and disjunctions by looking for either $\top$ or $\bot$ as one of the terms of the connective. No attempt is made to rewrite the terms, and they are used to tidy up a formula before returning it as an answer to a query.

Disjunction Example

$$\textbf{PLL}((y = x + 2 \lor y = x * 2) \land x = 6)$$
$$\xrightarrow{\ R\ } \textbf{Exec}((y = x + 2 \lor y = x * 2) \land x = 6)$$
$$\xrightarrow{\ R\ } \textbf{S}(\textbf{Exec\_Delay}(\textbf{R}((y = x + 2 \lor y = x * 2) \land x = 6), \mathit{or\_delay})$$
$$\land \textbf{Free}(0))$$

[now rewrite **R**, then **Exec_Delay**, and finally **Free**]
$$\textbf{R}((y = x + 2 \lor y = x * 2) \land x = 6)$$
$$\xrightarrow{\ R_*\ } \top$$

[with x bound to 6 and $\mathit{or\_delay} = (y = 6 + 2 \lor y = 6 * 2)$]
$$\textbf{Exec\_Delay}(\top, y = 6 + 2 \lor y = 6 * 2)$$
$$\xrightarrow{\ R\ } \textbf{S}(\textbf{Exec}(\top \land y = 6 + 2) \lor \textbf{Exec}(\top \land y = 6 * 2)))$$
$$\textbf{Exec}(\top \land y = 6 + 2)$$
$$\xrightarrow{\ R_*\ } y = 8$$
$$\textbf{Exec}(\top \land y = 6 * 2)$$
$$\xrightarrow{\ R_*\ } y = 12$$
$$\xrightarrow{\ R\ } \textbf{S}(y = 8 \lor y = 12)$$
$$\xrightarrow{\ R\ } y = 8 \lor y = 12$$
$$\textbf{Free}(0)$$
$$\xrightarrow{\ R\ } x = 6$$
$$\xrightarrow{\ R\ } \textbf{S}((y = 8 \lor y = 12) \land x = 6)$$
$$\xrightarrow{\ R\ } (y = 8 \lor y = 12) \land x = 6$$

The example shows the rewrites used in evaluating the query $(y = x+2 \lor y = x * 2) \land x = 6$, beginning with the initial **PLL** activation applied to all queries, and ending with the result supplied to the user. The $*$ subscript applied to the rewrite symbol indicates where a chain of several rewrites has been omitted.

3.8   The Last Rewrite

The PLL returns expressions it cannot compute (or partially compute) unchanged (or partially evaluated). For instance given $\neg(v = w \lor x = y)$ the answer returned would be $(\neg v = w) \land (\neg x = y)$. To return partially evaluated formulae we need a final rewrite which, after none of the other rules has matched, will strip off the activation function **R**.

$$\textbf{R}(\phi) \quad \xrightarrow{\ R\ } \quad \phi$$

4 Rewrite rules for Prolog

At the time of writing, no attempt has been made to construct an implementation of Prolog based on the rewrite rule system described in this paper. What is given here must be taken as merely a flavour of the approach that could be taken. Since Prolog is to a large extent a more imperative form of the PLL, much of the work in constructing a Prolog interpreter is in making the rewrite rules execute a simpler search pattern over conjunctions, and in catering for multiple definitions of the same rule. A description of how the implementation of Prolog is usually approached can be found in [4].

The areas which would require the most substantial changes from the approach taken for the PLL are listed below.

- **Negation by Failure**

  For Prolog negation is much easier to compute than for the PLL. We need only rewrite the formula inside the negation, and if it rewrites to $\top$ then the result of the negation is $\bot$, otherwise the result is $\top$.

$$\mathbf{R}(\neg\phi) \xrightarrow{R} \bot$$
$$: \quad \top = \mathbf{R}(\phi)$$
$$\mathbf{R}(\neg\phi) \xrightarrow{R} \top$$

- **Conjunctions**

  For conjunctions we must enforce left to right evaluation, stopping if one of the terms rewrites to $\bot$.

$$\mathbf{R}(\phi \wedge \psi) \xrightarrow{R} \mathbf{Conj}(\mathbf{R}(\phi) \wedge \psi)$$
$$\mathbf{Conj}(\top \wedge \psi) \xrightarrow{R} \mathbf{R}(\psi)$$
$$\mathbf{Conj}(\bot \wedge \psi) \xrightarrow{R} \bot$$
$$\mathbf{Conj}((\phi \vee \psi) \wedge \theta) \xrightarrow{R} \mathbf{R}((\phi \wedge \theta) \vee (\phi \wedge \theta))$$

- **Disjunctions**

  What is presented here is a simplistic approach to returning alternative answers during Prolog execution. The approach taken is to print the bindings of the variables (that were free in the query), at the bottom of each branch of the search tree. To have a full Prolog implementation we would need to return from the bottom of each branch an expression, which when rewritten would follow the next branch of the search tree.

Since disjunctions are the backtrack points during execution, we need to note the state of variable bindings before rewriting either term of the disjunction. If the term of a disjunction rewrites to true, we have found a solution, so all free variables in the query should have their bindings printed. The disjunction rewrites to ⊥ to ensure only the bottom of the search tree has variables printed, since disjunctions (i.e. backtrack points) further up the search tree will not print the variable values if the expression they evaluate rewrites to ⊥.

$$\mathbf{R}(\phi \vee \psi) \quad \xrightarrow{R} \quad \bot$$
$$: \qquad l := \mathbf{Level}$$
$$: \qquad \phi' := \mathbf{R}(\phi)$$
$$: \qquad \text{IF } \phi' = \top \text{ DO print variables}$$
$$: \qquad \mathbf{Free } \, l$$
$$: \qquad \psi' := \mathbf{R}(\psi)$$
$$: \qquad \text{IF } \psi' = \top \text{ DO print variables}$$
$$: \qquad \mathbf{Free } \, l$$

- **Rules**

  The PLL's restriction that all rules have at most one occurrence makes the rewrite process much simpler than if we allow for multiple definitions. To allow for Prolog's multiple instances of rules we must return a disjunction which when rewritten will generate all instances of the rule.

  To achieve this, rules with the same functor and arity are numbered sequentially, and stored in a similar way to the PLL rules. However since unification cannot be done by the pattern matching on rewrite rule heads, it must be done by explicit equalities at the start of the rule. For example the Prolog rules $prev(0,0)$. and $prev(X,Y) :- Y \text{ is } X - 1$. would be stored as:

$$\mathbf{R}(prev(X,Y),1) \quad \xrightarrow{R} \quad \mathbf{R}(X = 0 \wedge Y = 0)$$
$$\mathbf{R}(prev(X,Y),2) \quad \xrightarrow{R} \quad \mathbf{R}(Y \text{ is } X - 1)$$

  To rewrite a predicate, we now return the first instance of the rules for that predicate in a disjunction with an expression which when rewritten will generate the next instance. If no more instances exist then it will return $\perp$.

$$\mathbf{R}(f\mathord{:}function) \xrightarrow{\ R\ } Produce(f, 1)$$

$$\mathbf{R}(Produce(f, n)) \xrightarrow{\ R\ } \mathbf{R}(\mathbf{R}(f, n) \vee Produce(f, next))$$
$$: \qquad next := n + 1$$
$$\mathbf{R}(Produce(f, n)) \xrightarrow{\ R\ } \perp$$

- **The Last Rewrite**

  If Prolog can not evaluate an expression, then the computation fails, and result is $\perp$. This differs from the PLL's computational model that the expression in its reduced form as is returned. Hence the last rewrite, which only applies when all other rules do not match, should be changed to give $\perp$.

$$\mathbf{R}(\phi) \xrightarrow{\ R\ } \perp$$

5   Benchmarks

Since the implementation of the PLL decribed here is the only one in existence, there can be no direct comparisons made with another version. Instead two simple programs, *reverse* and *permute*, are compared with Quintus Prolog programs which carry out the same task. The figures given in the table are average execution times on a SUN 3/75 for reversing a list of 40 integers, and finding all permutations of a list of six integers.

	Quintus Prolog Time (s)	PLL Time (s)	Ratio of Times
reverse 40 element list	0.8	4.0	5.0
permute 6 element list	1.8	7.8	4.3

The programs in the two languages are listed here for comparison by the reader.

- **Prolog**

  Reverse

  % reverse(x,y) will reverse the order of the elements in x to give y
  reverse([],[]).
  reverse([X|Y],Z) :- reverse(Y,Y1),append(Y1,[X],Z).

  % append(a,b,c) will concatenate the lists a and b to form the list
  c
  append([],X,X).
  append([X|XT],Y,[X|ZT]):-append(XT,Y,ZT).

  Permute

  % insert(a,b,c) will insert element a anywhere in list b to give list c
  insert(X,Y,[X|Y]).
  insert(X,[H|Y1],[H|Y2]) :- insert(X,Y1,Y2).

  % permute(x,y) will permute the elemens of list x to give list y
  permute([],[]).
  permute([X|Y],Z):-permute(Y,Y1),insert(X,Y1,Z).

- **PLL**

  Reverse

  $$append(x,y,z) \; guard \; (x,y) \vee (z) \quad \xrightarrow{R} \quad \begin{aligned} &x = [] \wedge y = z \\ &\vee \exists xh \; xt \; zt. \\ &\quad x = xh :: xt \\ &\quad \wedge append(xt,y,zt) \\ &\quad \wedge z = xh :: zt \end{aligned}$$

  $$reverse(x,y) \quad \xrightarrow{R} \quad \begin{aligned} &(x = [] \wedge y = []) \\ &\vee \exists xh \; xt \; xtr. \\ &\quad x = xh :: xt \\ &\quad \wedge reverse(xt,xtr) \\ &\quad \wedge append(xtr,[xh],y) \end{aligned}$$

  Permute

$$permute(x, y) \xrightarrow{\quad R \quad} \begin{aligned} &x = [] \wedge y = [] \\ &\vee \exists xh \; xt \; xt2. \\ &\quad x = xh :: xt \\ &\quad \wedge permute(xt, xt2) \\ &\quad \wedge insert(xh, xt2, y) \end{aligned}$$

$$insert(xh, xt, y) \; guard \; (xh, xt) \vee (y) \xrightarrow{\quad R \quad} \begin{aligned} &y = xh :: xt \\ &\vee \exists xth \; xtt \; yt. \\ &\quad xt = xth :: xtt \\ &\quad \wedge insert(xh, xtt, yt) \\ &\quad \wedge y = xth :: yt \end{aligned}$$

6 Conclusions

The Benchmark figures shown that the PLL is about five times as slow as Prolog for equivalent problems. However the PLL allows for programs to be expressed in a more declarative style, and the execution strategy is more sophisticated. Hence we would expect some difference in the execution times, and can conclude that using graph rewriting as the implementation technique has caused only a small decrease in preformance of the system. This must be balanced with the great gain in having a much more flexible environment in which to specify the execution algorithms of a language. The way that the PLL rules for conjunctions can be replaced by rules to force left to right evaluation for Prolog illustrates this point.

The success of the first PLL interpreter has led ICL to fund work at its Future Systems Division to produce a commercial version of the language, and for it to be used as part of the *Visilog* Eureka project.

The ability to express the computational model of a logic language as rewrite rules allows the implementation to follow closely the evolution of the semantics of the language. To this end, a system is being developed at Imperial College to allow the programmer to use rewrite rules as the implementation language, rather than translate then into 'C' functions as was the approach taken with the PLL.

Acknowledgements

I would like to thank Ed Babb and David Cooper of the ICL Future Systems (formerly System Strategy Centre), Bracknell, for their efforts in using the PLL interpreter when it was in development, and their suggestions for improvements. I am also grateful to Dov Gabbay, Richard Owens and Chris Hankin of Imperial College for their comments and suggestions during the preparation of this paper.

References

[1] E. Babb. Pure logic language with constraints and classical negation. In Tony Dodd, Richard Owens, and Steve Torrance, editors, *Expanding the Horizons*, Oxford, 1990. Intellect Ltd.

[2] D. Gabbay and F. Guenthner. *Handbook of Philosophical Logic*, volume 1. D.Reidel Publishing Company, 1983.

[3] J.R.W. Glauert et al. Final specification of Dactl. Internal Report SYS-C88-11, University of East Anglia, 1988.

[4] C.J. Hogger. *Introduction to Logic Programming*. Academic Press, 1984.

[5] J. Klop. Term rewriting systems. In S. Abramsky, D. Gabbay, and T. Maibaum, editors, *Handbook of Logic in Theoretical Computer Science*, volume 1. OUP, 1990.

[6] P.J. Mcbrien. PLL user's guide. Internal report, ICL System Strategy Centre, Bracknell, Berks, 1988.

[7] J.P. Trembley and P.G. Sorenson. *An Introduction to Data Structures with Applications*. McGraw-Hill, 1976.

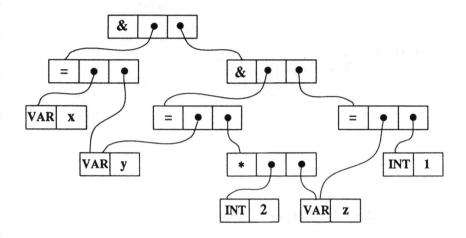

Figure 1: Example of the graphical representation of a PLL expression

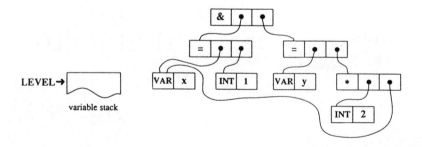

Figure 2: State of variable stack and expression graph before rewriting

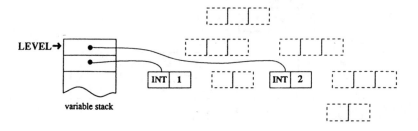

Figure 3: State of stack and graph after rewriting

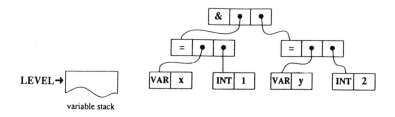

Figure 4: Graph produced by use of **Free** function

Kelpie: a Concurrent Logic Programming System for Knowledge Based Applications

Hamish Taylor

Abstract

A software architecture that interfaces a concurrent logic programming system to a Prolog database machine is described. The concurrent logic programming system connects a guarded clause inference engine with a definite clause inference engine to support concurrent execution of mutually invoking guarded and definite clause programs. An interface to a Prolog database machine allows the concurrent logic programming system to invoke its clause retrieval facilities via the definite clause inference engine. The result is a concurrent system able to handle both systems programming tasks on the guarded clause inference engine and exhaustive search on the definite clause inference engine that can support sizable concurrent knowledge based applications in logic.

1 Introduction

Alvey Project IKBS 90 *Parlog on Parallel Architectures* has been concerned with the development of the concurrent logic programming language Parlog on parallel architectures. An implementation of Parlog on a multi-processor machine has been developed, a development environment for Parlog programs has been produced and an architecture suitable for linking a Parlog system to a Prolog database machine has been designed and prototyped. At Imperial College the project has been concerned with

- Parlog to DACTL compiler for Alice

- Parlog development environment and other Parlog applications

At Heriot-Watt University the project concerns

- Parlog system interfaced to a Prolog Database Machine

The Parlog to DACTL compiler is a project that has implemented the flat subset of Parlog without the control meta-call on the ALICE machine [17]. Parlog is compiled to an intermediate target language which in turn is compiled to the ALICE machine's run-time code. Associated with this work has been work on the Parlog Programming System, a software development environment for Parlog [7].

The *Parlog for Knowledge Bases* part of the project at Heriot-Watt University is concerned with establishing the suitability of Parlog for use with sizable knowledge based applications. It comprises three main activities.

- development of a Parlog system
- deductive engine extension to Parlog system
- Parlog system interface to a Prolog database machine

A parallel architecture for such a Parlog system might be realised in one of two ways. Either by

| concurrency | multi-tasking of Parlog's resolution |
| multi-processing | simultaneous co-processing of Parlog's resolution |

Concurrency achieved by dynamically synchronised multi-tasking with optimisations like activity biased scheduling does not speed up processing, but it enables the multiple threads of Parlog's execution state to be processed at the same time in a responsive fashion. This is important in enabling Parlog to program the management of asynchronously interacting parts of systems and in dealing with multiple interfaces to a knowledge based system without there being undue delays in processing each interface. Multi-processing would offer real execution speed ups by enabling Parlog's concurrently executable tasks to be processed in an overlapped rather than in a context switching fashion. It would best exploit processing opportunities for Parlog but is only made possible by having access to suitable hardware. Because no such multi-processor hardware was available at Heriot-Watt University to use with the project, it was decided to attempt only a concurrent implementation of Parlog on a single processor.

Two alternative ways of achieving a single processor implementation presented themselves. Either the Parlog system could be based upon Imperial

College's Sequential Parlog Machine or SPM [13] or an independent Parlog system could be developed. The advantages of a development based on SPM were

- economies of time and effort in using a working system

- established user base for an add-on package

- risk of unviable outcome to an independent system avoided

The advantages of developing an independent system were

- better primitive provision and development environment possible

- total source control without compatibility worries

- no restriction on development and innovation

SPM deviated significantly from Prolog's model in its provision of a software development environment and in its provision of primitives. The result was significantly less transparency in following the detail of execution and rather less amenable provision of primitives. The Parlog Programming System has recently ameliorated some of these problems, but SPM still lags behind typical implementations of Prolog in its transparency and primitive functionality. SPM's compilation overheads are also rather high, which makes for poor turnaround in iterative program development. Furthermore, complete control over source code was needed and that couldn't be achieved with a system like SPM that was continually evolving in answer to quite different development concerns at a distant site. For these reasons and because it was thought to be interesting to attempt something rather different, an independent development of an architecture for executing Parlog was initiated. A full-blooded implementation of this independent development has not been attempted yet. Current development work has so far only produced a working interpreter prototype of the architecture.

Parlog systems employ committed choice resolution over guarded Horn clauses to perform an incomplete search for solutions. In order that a complete search over pure Horn clauses can be performed, a Parlog system needs to employ a different inference strategy than its own. For this reason the independent Parlog system being developed at Heriot-Watt University is being coupled with an extra deductive engine to perform these complete searches in a manner to be described later. It is also being interfaced to a Prolog database machine, enabling the Parlog system to use the special facilities of the Prolog database machine to handle deduction over large knowledge spaces.

2   The Prolog Database Machine

The context of the *Parlog for Knowledge Bases* work is defined by an associated Alvey research project IKBS 37 at Heriot-Watt University that has constructed a *high-speed multi-user Prolog Database Machine* [20]. Its objective has been to construct an integrated Prolog system capable of handling very large sets of clauses. The Prolog system stores some clauses in main memory and large numbers of clauses on disc, and special hardware and software is used to accelerate retrieval by head unification of goal matching clauses stored on disc. The system is able to handle resolution over a million clauses of the same relation name and arity. Multiple logic programming systems are allowed concurrent access to these clauses. Apart from access constraints caused by concurrent use of the same set of clauses, access to all clauses is transparent to a connected Prolog system.

Several applications have been developed for the Prolog Database Machine and these form the basis of related Alvey projects.

Logic Database	IKBS 85
Expert Systems Interface	IKBS 85
Parlog Demonstrator Applications	IKBS 90

A logic database system written in Prolog uses the extended clause handling facilities of the Prolog Database Machine to manage deduction over significant amounts of knowledge [32]. An expert systems interface in turn uses the facilities of the logic database to handle access to large sets of expert system rules [23]. Finally demonstrator programs using the Parlog interface will show how multi-user logic database management systems can be programmed in Parlog and perform concurrent retrievals through the Parlog system's deductive engine extension and its interface to the Prolog Database Machine.

The two main clause retrieval components of the knowledge base part of the Prolog Database Machine are

Clause Retrieval Server	software server for fetching clauses for client systems
Clause Retrieval Hardware	hardware filter for fetching clause unifiers from disc

By separating the functionality of clause retrieval from a logic programming system and embedding it in a quasi-autonomous server, it becomes possible to provide a standardised interface to it, that can be used to handle clause retrieval for several different clients. The two main clients are

Prolog-X+	Prolog client
Kelpie	concurrent logic programming client

Prolog-X is an abstract machine based implementation of Prolog [10]. Prolog-X is compiled to an abstract machine code which is emulated in software. It was chosen for development as the Prolog Database Machine's target Prolog because of the project's collaboration with ICL. Kelpie is the name for the concurrent logic programming system being discussed here that is being developed for use with the Prolog Database Machine.

Once the retrieval functionality was separated off into an independent server, it became possible to configure the Clause Retrieval Server [20] to support

- concurrent access by multiple clients

- distributed operation

- knowledge base sharing

- persistent clause storage

- transaction based access arbitration

One server could support clause retrieval requests from several different clients concurrently using request scheduling with a single thread of control. Furthermore there was no requirement for the Clause Retrieval Server to reside on the same machine as its clients. Access across a Local Area Network could be provided almost as easily. Delocalisation made it worthwhile to allow the Clause Retrieval Server to split up its retrieval responsibilities into a number of servers connected across the network, each able to handle retrieval requests by clients and by other servers. Thus retrieval requests that were not able to be handled directly on one server could be passed on to the relevant server for that relation elsewhere. Because the server stored clauses on disc and organised full access to them, the Prolog clauses held under its charge need not be reconsulted every Prolog session. Once these clauses had been put under the clause retrieval server's charge, they could be accessed only by making visible relevant relations. By giving clauses to a clause retrieval server in this way, client Prolog systems are able to function as persistent Prolog systems. Multiple clients interrogating a single server might want common access to a single set of clauses. This created no difficulty where only retrievals were concerned, but where clients wanted to update shared sets of clauses, it became important to support locking and access arbitration to maintain consistency in clients' views of shared sets of clauses. Thus the clause retrieval server was given full control over concurrency and clause update management using a locking scheme.

Each clause retrieval server is able to manage a software search for clause satisfiers of a goal over clauses stored on disc. A variety of indexing methods are employed to accelerate this. However, the main use of clause retrieval servers is to serve as a software means of invoking specialised clause retrieval hardware for accelerating clause retrieval from disc. ICL's Content Addressable File Store is one possible hardware engine for performing this task. A more specialised device is the CLARE engine [33]. The main features of the CLARE clause retrieval hardware are

- VME bus based co-processor searching on-the-fly

- two stage filter—superimposed codeword indexing & partial test unification

A backend co-processor performs its search on-the-fly as clause data streams off disc. Two filters are employed for recognising clauses whose heads unify with a call. Either filter can be used independently or both can be employed in the given order. The first filter employs superimposed codeword plus mask bits matching [22]. A superimposed codeword is associated with each clause and matched codewords cause their corresponding clause to be retrieved directly from disc. The second filter performs tests directly on clause data to see whether unification between the goal and a clause head is possible. Both filters yield false positives but neither filter yields false negatives. These false positives are eliminated by the clause retrieval server before it passes retrievals back to its client. The filters are designed for use with a VME bus. Each fills a standard VME board.

A configuration of client logic programming systems, clause retrieval servers and hardware might look like Figure 1. Multiple clients, several Prolog-X+s and a Kelpie system, are using a network of clause retrieval servers linked to several pieces of hardware. The whole forms a distributed multi-user knowledge base machine.

3   Forms of Resolution

The Kelpie system implements the execution of Parlog (and GHC) by means of a high level logic programming language to and from which Parlog and

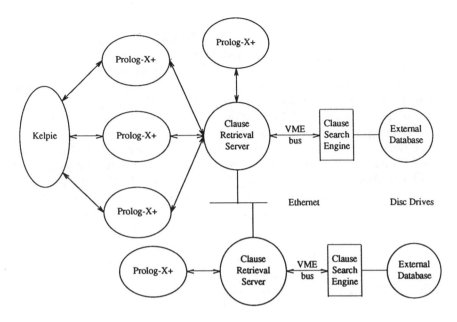

Figure 1: Possible configuration

GHC is translated ([28] chapter 4). The simple nature of the translation enables the emulator of the implementation language to execute GHC and Parlog transparently. The details of the design of this emulator have been dealt with extensively elsewhere ([28] chapter 5). This still leaves the question as to how the deductive engine extension to the Parlog system is to be achieved. Understanding how this question is resolved requires stepping back and looking at the overall issues of concurrency and resolution strategies in relation to logic programming. Resolution affords two main kinds of opportunities for concurrent or parallel execution

or-parallelism	computing alternative solutions in parallel
and-parallelism	computing different parts of one solution in parallel

Except for common ancestor binding environments or-parallel computations are always independent whereas and-parallel computations can be either

independent	no shared variables
dependent	shared variables
stream	dependent and-parallelism with dataflow constraints

Concurrent logic programming languages support both independent and dependent and-parallelism and allow general dataflow constraints to synchronise dynamically dependent and-parallelism. To achieve this effect efficiently, these languages limit or-parallelism to parallel evaluations of alternative guards. The result is the powerful programming technique of stream and-parallelism that is indispensable for supporting general systems programming. Canonical implementations of Prolog support neither or-parallel nor and-parallel execution. However, they are able to support co-routining, independent and-parallelism achieved by multi-tasking, and they can delay evaluation of goals in an asynchronous and data-driven fashion. Recent logic programming schemes have extended the capabilities of Prolog to support general or-parallel execution [30], [5], [31]. Other schemes combine independent and-parallelism with backtracking using tests at runtime to determine whether conjoined literals are independent of each other or not. These tests are based upon data flow graphs constructed at compile time, that are used to determine which literals can be solved in parallel [12] and which goals need to be redone when backtracking upon goal failure [19],[11]. Yet further schemes [15] aim at formulating execution models other than the And-Or process model in the hope of revealing as much scope as possible for both or-parallel and and-parallel execution of logic programs.

As well as exhibiting various opportunities for concurrent execution, resolution strategies adopted by logic programming implementations exhibit different kinds of non-determinism [16]. Such non-determinism can be distinguished as being either

> don't know   not known which alternative clause to pick
> to resolve goal with
> don't care   not cared which clause to pick to resolve goal with

Prolog mostly exhibits *don't know* non-determinism using backtracking to recover from resolutions that fail to succeed in reducing a goal. Concurrent logic programming languages like GHC and Parlog mostly exhibit *don't care* non-determinism by committing a goal to being reduced to the body of a clause once that choice is initially made. Prolog is also able to exhibit *don't care* non-determinism using the cut, which prunes considerations of further alternatives. Concurrent logic programming languages with deep guards are also able to exhibit a limited amount of *don't know* non-determinism. Deep guard searches can be used to determine which clause to select to reduce a goal, but these evaluations must be careful not to instantiate the goal without being used in its reduction.

The two kinds of non-determinism shape or-parallel opportunities for execution. Where the non-determinism is *don't know* then the alternative clauses can be resolved within or-parallel in the search for a single goal satisfier. Or where the roots of the *don't know* non-determinism lie in the fact that more than one solution is wanted, this can also be realised in an or-parallel fashion. Where the non-determinism is *don't care*, then alternative clauses need not be considered at all and or-parallel execution of the choice is not wanted.

However, concurrent logic programming or CLP languages limit their ability to use *don't know* non-determinism by making committed bindings and committed clause choices. These committed bindings and committed clause choices limit the ability to search for other satisfiers of a goal, and by doing so limit the possibility for a complete search. This in turn limits the useful of concurrent logic programming languages for programming knowledge based systems, because solutions to queries over knowledge bases must be based upon a complete search and are often required to produce every solution. Committed clause choices are likely to preclude a complete search for solutions and definitely preclude being able to produce multiple solutions.

Stream and-parallelism is necessary for programming concurrent systems and resolution exhibiting don't know non-determinism is necessary for supporting exhaustive search in knowledge based applications. Thus both are necessary for supporting concurrent knowledge based systems. The problem is how to square their conflicting requirements. Proposals for combining don't know non-determinism with stream and-parallelism are

- compile away exhaustive search in CLP language [29] [27]

- interpret exhaustive search in CLP language [24] [8]

- compile away stream and-parallelism in Prolog [21]

- devise integrated language [14],[4]

- couple CLP and Prolog resolution engines [9]

Each approach has advantages and limitations. The consideration of their relative merits is beyond the scope of this paper. For a general discussion of these approaches see [3] and [28] chapter 2. The last approach has been adopted by the *Parlog for Knowledge Bases* project.

4 Parlog and Prolog United

One obvious way of being able to profit from efficient implementations of both don't know non-determinism and stream and-parallelism would be to couple a CLP resolution engine to a Prolog resolution engine. Clark and Gregory first advocated this approach in detail in terms of coupling a Prolog system with a Parlog system in their paper Parlog and Prolog United [9]. They explore a number of different options for supporting such coupling. In particular they mention six types of interface. Three interfaces enable a Parlog computation to call a Prolog computation

- eager all solutions predicate $set(List, Term?, Conj?)$

- lazy multiple solutions predicate $subset(List?, Term?, Conj?)$

- single solutions predicate $prolog\_call(Conj?)$

The constructors $set/3$ and $subset/3$ are eager and lazy multiple solutions constructors like Prolog's $findall/3$. They deliver solutions incrementally on the List argument. The third interface $prolog\_call/1$ appears as a Parlog goal to the Parlog system which can execute concurrently with other Parlog goals. It can have its variables bound either by other Parlog goals executing concurrently with it or by the Prolog computation it represents at any time during its execution. These new bindings are visible during the Prolog computation to both it and its calling environment. They may not be rescinded by the Prolog computation once made. Since the multiple solutions constructors can be supported fairly easily using $prolog\_call/1$, the real functionality in question is represented by $prolog\_call/1$ alone. Three interfaces are proposed for enabling a Prolog computation to call a Parlog computation

- deterministic conjunction $prolog\text{-}conj :: parlog\text{-}conj$

- eager non-deterministic conjunction $prolog\text{-}conj <> parlog\text{-}conj$

- lazy non-deterministic conjunction $prolog\text{-}conj << parlog\text{-}conj$

Each of the three interfaces represents co-routing conjunctions. The first spawns the Parlog conjunction immediately on execution and then continues executing the Prolog conjunction. The Prolog conjunction may engage in backtracking so long as no bindings passed to the Parlog conjunction are undone. The whole meta-conjunction succeeds when both conjuncts succeed. When the Prolog conjunct is *true*, the Prolog system is just synchronously invoking a Parlog computation. The second and third interfaces allow failures in the Prolog conjunction to fail and undo bindings to variables shared with the Parlog conjunction. The result is to cause rollback in the Parlog computation to the point at which the uncommitted binding that was undone was made. If the Parlog computation itself fails, failure of the goal that caused the most recent uncommitted binding in the Prolog conjunction is supposed to be initiated. The difference between the second and the third interface is that the second interface $<>$ /2 allows the Prolog conjunction to carry on making uncommitted bindings to variables shared with the Parlog computation eagerly, while the third interface $<<$ /2 makes deterministic bindings to shared variables eagerly yet suspends upon making an uncommitted binding (i.e. one it could undo on backtracking) and only proceeds if and when the Parlog conjunction deadlocks.

The motivation behind Clark and Gregory's proposals is to explore the range of possible ways of coupling Parlog and Prolog systems together with a view to stimulating further research into the design, implementation and use of hybrid don't know and don't care non-deterministic logic programming systems. The two non-deterministic interfaces $<>$ /2 and $<<$ /2 represent the really radical departure in Clark and Gregory's paper, because they entail extending Parlog to allow bindings in a Parlog computation to be undone and the Parlog computation rolled back, and Clark and Gregory devote much of their attention in their paper to the non-deterministic operators. However, the motivation for the research being pursued here is not to explore the full range of possible interfaces between Prolog and CLP computations but to support a general type of application requiring concurrency—knowledge based systems. This kind of application is mostly concerned with interfaces from Parlog-like computations to Prolog-like computations. However, interfaces that enable Prolog computations to invoke CLP computations are also useful to allow knowledge based applications in Prolog to deal with concurrent interfaces.

Clark and Gregory argue for a shared memory approach to storing variables shared between Prolog and Parlog computations. Coupled Parlog and Prolog computations are allowed to bind variables in each others heaps. A different approach would be to make each Prolog and CLP computation maintain a completely separate binding environment and to copy bindings across the interfaces both ways. This would make variable management simpler, make garbage collection easier, make parallel multi-processing more efficient, and would allow more modular development of coupled systems with a lower degree of intervention into the implementation of the component resolution engines. Thus a non-shared memory approach has been adopted by the *Parlog for Knowledge Bases* project.

5   Coupled Resolution Engines

CLP and Prolog resolution engines couplings should be flexible and efficient, while preserving as much concurrency as possible to enable several CLP and Prolog evaluations to invoke each other and execute at the same time. However, CLP computations cannot support backtracking and Prolog computations cannot support stream and-parallelism without making major extensions to their canonical execution models that would seriously undermine their efficiency. As efficiency is crucial and as our approach takes as its starting point the idea of forming a hybrid of Prolog and CLP styles of resolution engine, neither of these extensions will be countenanced. Bindings made to variables in a Prolog computation that are shared with a CLP computation will always be committed once they are communicated.

Furthermore, Prolog relation literals in a Prolog computation will always be resolved away sequentially unless they are computed asynchronously in a $freeze/2$ like fashion. In this way conceptual simplicity and the merits of the existing forms of implementation of each kind of resolution engine can be preserved. Clark and Gregory's two non-deterministic interfaces from Prolog to Parlog $<> /2$ and $<< /2$ envisage backtracking in a CLP implementation. The state information that must be preserved in a CLP computation to enable this will often be large and not very tractable to manage for each *backtrack point* that must be preserved in the Parlog computation. The approach will require extensive re-design of the CLP engine to support backtracking, and any advantage of a hybrid approach like this over an integrated language approach like Andorra Prolog [14] or Parallel NU-Prolog [21] would be likely to vanish. Accordingly, interfaces like these will not be used.

The various needs for coupled resolution require a variety of coupling interfaces. These interfaces will operate under the basic assumption that the environments of the two resolution engines are completely separate, except when invoked, as explained below, so as to share code areas and symbol tables. All communication across interfaces will be by full unification with variable restoration on failure and involve copying terms across where a variable has been bound. If the unification fails, the invoked computation will fail with normal goal failure consequences for the invoking environment. The following two interfaces to a CLP computation from a Prolog computation are to be supported. Calls using these interfaces are never resatisfiable.

call to CLP relation

- communication at boundaries

- input argument suspension on invocation possible
- synchronous

call to *clp(Goal)*

- communication transiently both ways (with a restriction)
- input argument suspension on invocation of Goals possible
- asynchronous

Goals in a Prolog computation that are not defined by Prolog clauses invoke the CLP resolution engine. The invocation is synchronous, and values are passed at the boundaries of invocation without any concurrency between the calling computation and the computation that is called. Input matching suspension on invocation may take place. This interface is similar to that proposed by Clark and Gregory's deterministic operator

$$true :: relation(Arg1, ..., ArgN)$$

where the first conjunction is *true* and *relation/N* is a CLP relation.

In the second type of interface the *clp/1* goal in the Prolog computation coroutines with the goals after it in the body of its clause. Argument values are passed transiently during invocation subject to the following restriction on shared variables

No Complex Term CLP Bindings	CLP execution may not bind variables shared with a Prolog computation to complex terms during execution

A CLP computation is only allowed to bind shared variables to simple terms when executing on behalf of a *clp/1* call. The interface is responsible for detecting the attempt to communicate to a Prolog computation the binding of a shared variable to a complex term. This restriction has to be made because such bindings cannot be safely made at the top of the heap at the time of communication. In the event of a *clp/1* call failing, the Prolog computation backtracks and attempt to resatisfy the parent of the *clp/1* goal. The parent goal of the spawned call to the committed choice resolution engine is not able to exit until the *clp/1* call has succeeded or failed. This type of invocation performs a role similar to Clark and Gregory's deterministic :: fork primitive but in a more natural fashion. The following two interfaces to a Prolog computation from a CLP computation are to be supported.

call to Prolog relation

- asynchronous
- communication at boundaries
- executes concurrently with CLP resolution engine
- no suspension on invocation

call to *prolog(Goals)*

- asynchronous
- communication transiently both ways (with a restriction)
- executes concurrently with CLP resolution engine
- input argument suspension if *Goals* unbound

Goals in a CLP computation, that are not defined by a guarded clause relation, invoke the Prolog resolution engine. The invocation is synchronous, and values are passed at the boundaries of invocation without any concurrency between the calling computation and the computation that is called. No suspension on invocation takes place. Calls in a CLP computation to *prolog*/1 invoke the Prolog resolution engine asynchronously in a fully concurrent fashion. Input and output bindings are communicated transiently. *prolog*/1 is rather similar to Clark and Gregory's proposed interface *prolog_call*/1, although the implementation approach is quite different. Because *prolog*/1 subsumes the functionality of *set*/3 as Clark and Gregory have shown, and as reasonably functional restricted versions of *subset*/3 can be realised by *prolog*/1, multiple solutions interfaces like *set*/3 and *subset*/3 do not need to be directly supported.

To allow flexible private access to and sharing of Prolog databases by the CLP resolution engine the following principle is adopted

One Database per Meta-call   each separate CLP meta-call environment is associated with a separate persistent Prolog database state.

This database state is created by the first call to a Prolog computation from within that meta-call's environment. Subsequent to that, each call to a Prolog computation within that meta-call environment accesses the same database state, and once created that Prolog database state persists for as long as the CLP meta-call environment persists. Invocations of Prolog computations within different CLP meta-calls are always to different Prolog database states.

6 Implementation Issues

A multi-user knowledge based system can be supported on this sort of coupled CLP-Prolog system using one Unix process (or several tightly interacting Unix-like processes sharing memory on a multi-processor) to execute the CLP language and one or a few Unix processes per user to execute sequential Prologs. The Unix operating system sustains overall concurrency among the multiple sequential Prologs and the sole CLP engine. The CLP resolution engine is used to process the closely interacting and communicating tasks of the knowledge based system as CLP computations with fine granularity concurrency, leaving the remaining knowledge processing tasks requiring don't know non-determinism to be processed with low degrees of interaction and large granularity concurrency by one or a few separate sequential Prologs per user. The whole system is programmed by a CLP program executing on the CLP engine and separate Prolog programs executing in each Prolog process. Multiple Prolog processes executing at the same time on a single processor share code segments, and thus only one copy of the Prolog engine code is kept resident in that processor's fast memory at a time.

In order to sustain concurrent execution of multiple Prologs on a more closely coupled basis as required by the *One database per Meta-call* rule, the Prologs are also able to share common memory areas. This is realised under Sun Unix OS 4.0 using lightweight processes sharing the memory of a single Unix process. A conventional Prolog engine adapted to run as a multi-threaded Prolog engine divides up shared memory up so that these separate Prolog computation threads have their own non-virtual local, global and trail stacks and share only the code area and symbol tables using monitors to handle the critical code of updates to these areas. The lightweight process scheduler switches the engine between threads on a resource sliced basis.

The CLP resolution engine uses an and-parallel guarded clause adaptation of the And-Or tree execution model [26]. Three kinds of process are used. Primitive processes represent system predicates, literal processes represent goals before they are reduced, and clause processes represent clauses being examined to assess the reducibility of a goal. Processes are linked to their parent, to their siblings and to their children, and they are either in the state of being executed, being executable or are suspended. Suspended processes are either suspended upon their children, suspended upon one or more variables, suspended upon an input stream or are suspended upon a Prolog computation. Processing is done on a *bounded depth first* basis and concurrency is achieved by resource quotas of execution cycles allowed with children inheriting their parent's quota less one. An activity bias operates in favour of recently awoken processes of being executed early ([28] chapter 5).

The Prolog resolution engine is based upon Prolog-X, a conventional Prolog engine based upon Clocksin's Zip abstract machine for Prolog [10]. Execution can be suspended on the primitive $data/1$, synchronously upon an input stream or upon a CLP computation. Processing is done upon a purely depth first basis and concurrency between lightweight Prolog processes is achieved by attaching resource quotas to reductions performed, and context switching after quotas are consumed. Prolog-X also supports two special features needed for implementing the interfaces defined above.

- delayed goal execution
- escape exception handling

In the updated version of Prolog-X used on the Prolog Database Machine [20] goals may be delayed using $freeze/2$ [6]. At whatever point their variable is bound, they become re-attached to the computation. If they fail, they initiate backtracking at that point only. Prolog-X also features escape exception handling somewhat like that featured in Ada and ML. Named exceptional choice points can be defined that are invisible to normal backtracking. When an exception of that name is raised by the system or the user, the system backtracks directly to the most recent exceptional choice point of that exception name ([28] chapter 6). The implementation of the interfaces between Prolog and CLP Computations using these extensions will be the subject of a future paper.

7   Conclusion

A concurrent logic programming system consisting of two connected resolution engines has been described. It is being prototyped in C to run on a single processor workstation under Unix. The rationale for and a defence of the design of the system have been given and its general characteristics have been specified. The overall system looks as in Figure 2. The CLP resolution engine is connected with a Prolog resolution engine and interfaced through it to a Prolog Database Machine. One way of demonstrating the capabilities of both parts of the connected system and its Prolog database machine interface would be to have a logic database management system with a number of interfaces on separate terminals running on the CLP resolution engine. Retrievals over the knowledge base would invoke the Prolog resolution engine concurrently which in turn would be able to exercise the

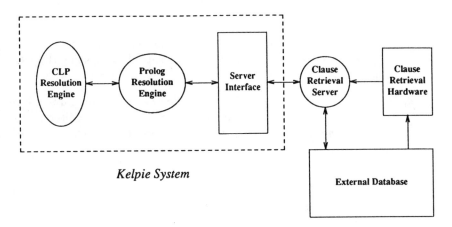

Figure 2: Overall system

facilities of the Prolog database machine. In this way the combined system would realise a concurrent logic programming system for sizable knowledge based applications by combining the systems programming virtues of the CLP engine with the complete knowledge base search capabilities of the Prolog engine.

Acknowledgements

The author wishes to acknowledge the contributions of David Ferbrache, Paul Massey, Howard Williams and Kam Fai Wong, who worked on the Prolog Database Machine project, the financial support of the SERC under the Alvey initiative, help from members of Imperial College's Parlog group, the support of his wife and colleagues at Heriot-Watt University and his project's industrial collaborator ICL.

References

[1] *Proceedings of the Int. Conf. on 5th Generation Computer Systems,* Tokyo, 1984.

[2] *Proceedings of the Symposium on Logic Programming*, San Francisco, August 1987.

[3] R. Bahgat. Towards an integrated don't know stream and-parallel logic language. Research Report DOC 88/1, Dept. of Computing, Imperial College, London, February 1988.

[4] R. Bahgat and S. Gregory. Pandora: Non-deterministic parallel logic programming. In Giorgio Levi and Maurizio Martelli, editors, *Logic Programming: Proceedings of the Sixth International Conference*. MIT Press, 1989.

[5] R. Butler, E. Lusk, R. Olson, W. McCune, and R.A. Overbeek. ANL-WAM: a parallel implementation of the Warren Abstract Machine. Technical report, Mathematics and Computer Science Division, Argonne National Lab., August 1986.

[6] M. Carlsson. Freeze, indexing and other implementation issues in the WAM. In Lassez [18].

[7] K.L. Clark and I.T. Foster. A declarative environment for concurrent logic programming. In Hartmunt Ehrig, editor, *Proceedings of the International Joint Conference on Theory and Practice of Software Development, Pisa*, number 250 in Lecture Notes in Computer Science. Springer Verlag, 1987.

[8] K.L. Clark and S. Gregory. Notes on the implementation of Parlog. *Journal of Logic Programming*, 2(1), July 1985.

[9] K.L. Clark and S. Gregory. Parlog and Prolog united. In Lassez [18], pages 927–961.

[10] W.F. Clocksin. The design and simulation of a sequential Prolog machine. *New Generation Computing*, pages 101–120, 1985.

[11] J.S. Conery. Implementing backward execution in non-deterministic AND-parallel systems. In Lassez [18], pages 633–653.

[12] D. DeGroot. Restricted AND-parallelism. In *Proceedings of the Int. Conf. on 5th Generation Computer Systems* [1], pages 471–478.

[13] S. Gregory, I.T. Foster, A. Burt, and G.A. Ringwood. An abstract machine for the implementation of Parlog on uniprocessors. *New Generation Computing*, 6(4):389–420, 1989.

[14] S. Haridi and P. Brand. Andorra Prolog: an integration of Prolog and committed choice languages. In *Proceedings of the Int. Conf. on 5th Generation Computer Systems* [1].

[15] L.V. Kale. The REDUCE-OR process model for parallel evaluation of logic programs. In Lassez [18], pages 616–632.

[16] R. Kowalski. *Logic for Problem Solving.* Elsevier/North-Holland, New York, 1979.

[17] M. Lam and S. Gregory. Parlog and ALICE: A marriage of convenience. In Lassez [18].

[18] Jean-Louis Lassez, editor. *Logic Programming.* MIT Press, 1987.

[19] Y. Lin, W. Kumar, and C. Leung. An intelligent backtracking algorithm for parallel execution of logic programs. In Shapiro [25], pages 55–68.

[20] P. Massey, D. Ferbrache, and M. H. Williams. Adapting Prolog for knowledge based applications. Technical report, Dept. of Computer Science, Heriot-Watt University, Edinburgh, May 1989.

[21] L. Naish. Parallelizing NU-prolog. In Robert A. Kowalski and Kenneth A. Bowen, editors, *Logic Programming: Proceedings of the Fifth International Conference and Symposium*, pages 1546–1564. MIT Press, 1988.

[22] K. Ramamohanarao and J. Shepherd. A superimposed codeword indexing scheme for very large prolog databases. Technical Report 85/17, Dept. of Computer Science, University of Melbourne, 1985.

[23] S. Salvini. An expert systems interface to a logic database. Technical report, Dept. of Computer Science, Heriot-Watt University, Edinburgh, April 1989.

[24] E. Shapiro. An Or-parallel execution algorithm for Prolog and its FCP implementation. In Lassez [18], pages 311–337.

[25] Ehud Shapiro, editor. *Third International Conference on Logic Programming.* Springer Verlag, 1986.

[26] A. Takeuchi and K. Furukawa. Parallel logic programming languages. In Shapiro [25], pages 242–254.

[27] H. Tamaki. Stream-based compilation of ground I/O Prolog into committed choice choice languages. In Lassez [18], pages 376–393.

[28] H. Taylor. *Coupled Resolution Engines for Programming Knowledge Based Systems in Logic.* PhD thesis, Heriot-Watt University, December 1989.

[29] K. Ueda. *Guarded Horn Clauses*. PhD thesis, Tokyo University, March 1986.

[30] D.H.D. Warren. The SRI model for Or-parallel execution of Prolog—abstract design and implementation issues. In *Proceedings of the Symposium on Logic Programming* [2], pages 92–102.

[31] H. Westphal, P. Robert, J. Chassin, and J-C. Syre. The PEPSys model: combining backtracking, and- and or-parallelism. In *Proceedings of the Symposium on Logic Programming* [2], pages 436–448.

[32] M.H. Williams, G. Chen, D.J. Ferbrache, P.A. Massey, S. Salvini, H. Taylor, and K.F. Wong. Prolog and deductive databases. *Knowledge Based Systems*, pages 188–192, June 1988.

[33] K.F. Wong and M.H. Williams. Design considerations for a Prolog database engine. In *Proceedings of the 3rd Int. Conf. on Data and Knowledge Bases*, Jerusalem, June 1988.